DAY HIKING
Oregon
Coast

N

1
2 3 ASTORIA
6 4
5

8 7 SEASIDE
9
10 11 CANNON BEACH

12 13 MANZANITA
14 15
16

NORTH COAST

17 18
19 20
21 TILLAMOOK
22 25
23
24

27 26
28
29
30 NORTH-CENTRAL COAST
32 31 35
33 36
34 LINCOLN CITY
38 37
39
40 DEPOE BAY

41 42 43
44 45 46 47 NEWPORT
48 WALDPORT

49
50 51 52
53 54 55 56 CENTRAL COAST
57 58 59
60 61 62
63 64
65
66 67 68 FLORENCE

70 71 72
74 75 76 73
80 69
81 77 78 79
82 REEDSPORT
83
84 SOUTH-CENTRAL COAST
85 NORTH BEND
88 89 90 COOS BAY
91 86 87
92
93 BANDON
94
95 96 97
98
99
100 101
102 103
104 SOUTH COAST

GOLD BEACH
105
107 108 109 106
110 111 112 113
114 115 116 117 119 BROOKINGS
118 120

O R E G O N

DAY HIKING

Oregon
Coast

Bonnie Henderson

THE MOUNTAINEERS BOOKS

THE MOUNTAINEERS BOOKS
is the nonprofit publishing arm of The Mountaineers Club, an organization founded in 1906 and dedicated to the exploration, preservation, and enjoyment of outdoor and wilderness areas.

1001 SW Klickitat Way, Suite 201, Seattle, WA 98134

© 2007 by Bonnie Henderson

First edition: First printing 2007, second printing 2009.

Manufactured in the United States of America

Copy Editor: Carol Poole
Cover and Book Design: The Mountaineers Books
Layout: Mayumi Thompson
Illustrations: Barbara B. Gleason
Cartographer: Mayumi Thompson
All photos by the author except pages 33, 34, 49, 50, and 54 (Randall Henderson) and pages 99, 169, and 227 (Michael Thompson)
Page 1 photo: *Whalen Island*
Page 2 photo: *Berry Creek Trail, Baker Beach*
Page 4 photo: *Indian Beach*
Cover photograph: © Darrell Gulin/Corbis

Library of Congress Cataloging-in-Publication Data
Henderson, Bonnie.
  Day hiking : Oregon coast / by Bonnie Henderson. — 1st ed.
    p. cm.
  Includes bibliographical references and index.
  ISBN-13: 978-1-59485-026-4
  ISBN-10: 1-59485-026-7
  1. Hiking—Oregon—Guidebooks. 2. Oregon—Guidebooks. I. Title.
GV199.42.O7H47 2007
796.5109795—dc22

                                2006039218

 Printed on recycled paper

"To stand at the edge of the sea, to sense the ebb and flow of the tides, to feel the breath of a mist moving over a great salt marsh, to watch the flight of shorebirds that have swept up and down the surflines of the continents for untold thousands of years, to see the running of the old eels and the young shad to the sea, is to have knowledge of things that are as nearly eternal as any earthly life can be."

Under the Sea-Wind by Rachel Carson
Copyright © 1941 by Rachel L. Carson
Reprinted by permission

Contents

NATURE NOTES

LEGEND

—🛡101🛡—	U.S. Highway
—⬡42—	State Highway
————	Secondary Road
=======	Gravel Road
- - - - - - -	Hiking Route
▬ ▬ ▪▪ ▬	State Boundary
▬ ▬ ▪ ▬ ▪	Park Boundary
▨	Town
Ⓣ	Trailhead
▲	Mountain Summit
⬭	Sand
∼	River/Stream
⠠⠁⠄	Marsh
⬛	Boat Launch
▪	Building
⊓	Picnic Area
⧌	Campground
⬆	Restroom
⬎	Viewpoint
ⵗ	Lighthouse
⬥	Forest
] [	Bridge
▬	Viewing Platform

A Quick Guide to the Hikes

Use this guide to quickly hone in on a hike you'll like. The hikes are grouped by their single most outstanding feature, with a summary of additional information. To pick a hike:

- Glance over the categories to find the one you want.
- Narrow your choices to those close to where you are or where you're going (N means North Coast, NC means North Central Coast, etc.)
- Look over the features and other information (OCT indicates Oregon Coast Trail link).

Note that mileage for some hikes is one-way and some is round-trip; refer to the full description for these and other details and driving directions. Enjoy your outing!

BEACH WALKS OR HIKES FEATURING BEACH WALKS

1. Clatsop Spit; N; 2.8; moderate; wildlife, ship traffic, adjacent to campground
2. Peter Iredale; N; 4; easy; shipwreck, adjacent to campground
10. Chapman Beach; N; 1.5; easy; creek, close to town
11. Haystack Rock; N; 1.5; easy; wildlife, tide pools, dory-launching, close to town
12. Hug Point, southbound; N; 1.75; easy; onshore rocks
12. Hug Point, northbound; N; 1.3; easy; pocket beaches, waterfall, historic road
18. Cape Meares, High Tide Trail loop; NC; 2.1; easy; ancient forest
20. Oceanside Beach; NC; 3; easy; wildlife, close to town
27. Tierra del Mar to Sand Lake; NC; 4; easy; close to homes
30. Porter Point; NC; 1; easy; wildlife, solitude
31. Proposal Rock, southbound; NC; 1.4; easy; onshore rocks, close to homes
31. Proposal Rock, northbound; NC; 8; strenuous; onshore rocks, close to homes
36. Roads End; NC; 2.5; easy; tide pools
39. Fishing Rock; NC; 4; moderate; onshore rocks, close to homes
43. Yaquina Head to Yaquina Bay; C; 3.5; easy; two lighthouses, outstanding shoreline vistas, wildlife
48. Ona Beach to Seal Rock; C; 1.75; moderate; tide pools, wildlife, adjacent to campground
63. Baker Beach; C; 0.8; easy; dunes
67. Sutton Beach; C; 2.5; moderate; creek crossing, adjacent to campground
68. Siuslaw North Jetty; C; 1.25; easy; wildlife, close to town
85. North Spit; SC; 4.2; moderate; wildlife, shipwreck site
91. Seven Devils–Whisky Run Beach; S; 1.75; easy; solitude, OCT
99. Cape Blanco South Shore; S; 2–2.26; easy; adjacent to campground
99. Cape Blanco South Shore to Port Orford; S; 5.8; strenuous; river, adjacent to campground; OCT
101. Battle Rock; S; to 5; easy to moderate; historical site, close to town
104. Otter Point; S; 1–2.6; moderate; solitude, OCT
105. Buena Vista Beach; S; 6.5; moderate to strenuous; solitude
107. Crook Point; S; 2.5; easy; wildlife, solitude

114. Whaleshead Beach–House Rock Viewpoint; S; 3; moderate; outstanding shoreline vistas, forest, OCT
117. Harris Beach; S; 1; easy; onshore rocks, tide pools, adjacent to campground
120. McVay Beach; S; 3; easy; river, onshore rocks, colorful stones, tide pools, OCT

HIKES TO HIDDEN OR POCKET BEACHES

9. Crescent Beach; N; 2.4; moderate; forest
14. Short Sand Beach; N; 1; easy; forest, creeks, surfers, primitive camping
60. Hobbit Beach; C; 0.5; easy; forest, adjacent to campground
90. Cape Arago Coves; SC; 0.4 each; easy; wildlife, tide pools, adjacent to campground
110. Secret Beach; S; 0.4; easy; onshore rocks, forest
111. Natural Bridges Cove–North Island Viewpoint (China Creek Beach); S; 2.6; moderate; outstanding shoreline vistas, forest, OCT
118. Chetco Point; S; 0.5; easy; outstanding shoreline vistas, close to town

HIKES ALONG BAY SPITS

16. Nehalem Spit; N; 4.2–5; moderate; ocean beach, bay, dunes, river, wildlife, adjacent to campground.
17. Bayocean Spit; NC; 7.3–8; moderate; ocean beach, bay, forest, wildlife, primitive camping, OCT
21. Netarts Spit; NC; 10; strenuous; ocean beach, bay, wildlife, adjacent to campground.
29. Nestucca Spit; NC; 4; moderate; ocean beach, bay, dunes, wildlife, adjacent to campground
38. Salishan Spit; NC; 7; moderate; ocean beach, wildlife, close to homes
92. Coquille Lighthouse; S; 3–3.5; easy to moderate; ocean beach, river, lighthouse, adjacent to campground

WALKS ALONG RIVERS, ESTUARIES, AND WETLANDS

4. Netul River Trail; N; 1; easy; wildlife, historic site
5. Cullaby Lake; N; 1.3; easy; ancient forest, lakeshore, wildlife
26. Whalen Island; NC; 1.5; easy; estuary, forest, beach, adjacent to campground
44. Yaquina Estuary; C; 0.5; easy; wildlife, access to two interpretive centers
69. Siuslaw South Jetty Dune; SC; 1; easy; wetlands, dunes, wildlife
70. Waxmyrtle Trail; SC; 2.5; moderate; estuary, forest, beach, wildlife, adjacent to campground
71. Lagoon Trail; SC; 1; easy; wetlands, forest, wildlife, adjacent to campground
84. Bluebill Lake; SC; 1.25; easy; wetlands, extensive boardwalk, adjacent to campground
86. South Slough, interpretive center to Sloughside; SC; 3; moderate; estuary, forest, wildlife, marsh viewing platform, insectivorous plants
86. South Slough, creek to Sloughside; SC; 2.5; moderate; estuary, creek, forest, wildlife, marsh viewing platform
86. South Slough, Big Cedar Trail; SC; 0.5; easy; estuary, forest, wildlife, marsh viewing platform
87. Wasson–Winchester Creeks; SC; 1.75; easy; wetlands, creeks, forest, old farmstead

HIKES WITH SPOUTING HORNS AND PUNCHBOWLS

40. Beverly Beach–Devils Punchbowl; NC; 3; moderate; tide pools, ocean vistas, beach walking, adjacent to campground ,OCT

49. Yachats 804 Trail; C; 1.9; easy; wildlife, pocket beaches, broad beach, close to town, OCT

53. Restless Waters Trail; C; 0.4; easy; beach, adjacent to campground

54. Captain Cook Trail; C; 0.6; easy; beach, tide pools, adjacent to campground

HIKES ACROSS SAND DUNES

45. South Jetty Trail; C; 1; easy; wildlife, adjacent to campground

46. Cooper Ridge Nature Trail; C; 1.5; easy; forest, adjacent to campground

63. Baker Beach—Lily Lake loop; C; 1; easy; beach, forest

72. Chief Tsiltcoos Trail; SC; 1.25; easy; dune forest, adjacent to campground

74. Taylor Dunes; SC; 2; moderate; forest, wildlife, adjacent to campground

75. Carter Dunes; SC; 1.5; moderate; forest, beach, solitude, adjacent to campground

76. Oregon Dunes Overlook; SC; 2-5; moderate to strenuous; forest, creek, beach

77. Tahkenitch Creek; SC; 1.5–4; easy to moderate; forest, creek, beach, wildlife

83. John Dellenback Trail; SC; 5; strenuous; extensive open dunes, beach, adjacent to campground

HIKES TO OR ALONG LAKES

3. Coffenbury Lake; N; 2.2; easy; swimming, fishing, wildlife, adjacent to campground

73. Siltcoos Lake; SC; 5; moderate; forest, primitive camping

79. Threemile Lake Trail—North Access; SC; 6–6.75; moderate to strenuous; ancient forest, dunes, beach, adjacent to campground, primitive camping

80. Threemile Lake Trail—South Access; SC; 1.5; easy; ancient forest, solitude, primitive camping

81. Lake Marie; SC; 1; easy; swimming, lighthouse, adjacent to campground

82. Eel Lake; SC; 3; easy; forest, wildlife, adjacent to campground

95. Floras Lake Beach; S; 0.8–2; easy; dunes, beach, solitude, adjacent to campground

HIKES OVER HEADLANDS

7. Tillamook Head; N; 5.8; strenuous; outstanding shoreline vistas, forest; historic site, primitive camping, OCT

7. Clatsop Loop; N; 2.7; moderate; historic site, primitive camping

13. Cape Falcon, northbound; N; 5; moderate; outstanding shoreline vistas, ancient forest, wildlife, OCT

15. Neahkahnie Mountain, from south; N; 3; strenuous; outstanding shoreline vistas, ancient forest, wildflowers, OCT

15. Neahkahnie Mountain, loop; N; 8; strenuous; outstanding shoreline vistas, ancient forest, wildflowers, OCT

15. Neahkahnie Mountain, from north; N; 9; strenuous; outstanding shoreline vistas, ancient forest, wildflowers, OCT

18. Cape Meares summit; NC; 1.7–2; moderate; outstanding shoreline vistas, ancient forest, beach, OCT

23. Cape Lookout Campground Link; NC; 2.5; moderate; adjacent to campground, OCT

24. Cape Lookout Beach; NC; 4–5.75; moderate; ancient forest, ocean views, beach, adjacent to campground, OCT
35. Cascade Head Traverse; NC; 6; strenuous; ancient forest, OCT
50. Cape Perpetua—Kittel-Amanda Trail; C; 2.2; moderate; ocean vistas, OCT
51. Cape Perpetua—St. Perpetua Trail; C; 3; moderate; outstanding shoreline vistas, forest, adjacent to campground, OCT
62. Heceta Head Lighthouse, south access; C; 1; moderate; outstanding shoreline vistas, lighthouse, forest, wildlife, OCT
62. Heceta Head Lighthouse, north access; C; 3; moderate to strenuous; lighthouse, forest, beach, wildlife, OCT
89. Cape Arago Pack Trail; SC; 2.25; moderate; forest, ocean vistas, historical site, wildlife, adjacent to campground
97. Airport–Floras Lake Trail; S; 3; moderate; solitude, OCT
100. Port Orford Heads; S; 0.6–1.2; easy; outstanding shoreline vistas, wildflowers, historical site
103. Humbug Mountain; S; 5–6; strenuous; lush forest, outstanding shoreline vistas, wildflowers, adjacent to campground
106. Cape Sebastian; S; 5; strenuous; ancient forest, outstanding shoreline vistas, beach, OCT

HIKES THROUGH FOREST OR CREEK VALLEYS

4. Fort to Sea Trail; N; 6.5; strenuous; creeks, lakes, dunes, wildlife, historic site
6. Gearhart Ridge Path; N; 0.7; easy; neighborhood charm
13. Cape Falcon, southbound; N; 8.5; strenuous; wildlife, OCT
18. Cape Meares, Big Spruce; NC; 0.4; easy; ancient forest, landmark tree
19. Cape Meares Lighthouse; NC; 0.5; easy; ancient forest, lighthouse
19. Cape Meares Lighthouse, Octopus Tree; NC; 0.25–0.75; easy; ancient forest, landmark tree, OCT
25. Munson Creek Falls; NC; 0.5; easy; ancient forest, waterfall
37. Drift Creek Falls; NC; 3.2–3.5; moderate; suspension footbridge, waterfall
47. Mike Miller Educational Trail; C; 1; easy; pond, nature trail
52. Giant Spruce Trail; C; 2; easy; ancient forest, creek, landmark tree, adjacent to campground
55. Cooks Ridge; C; 3.7; moderate to strenuous; ancient forest, ocean views, adjacent to campground
55. Cooks Ridge—Discovery Loop; C; 2; moderate; ancient forest, ocean views, adjacent to campground
56. Cape Coast Trail; C; 1.3; easy; adjacent to campground, OCT
57. Gwynn Creek; C; 6; moderate to strenuous; ancient forest, creeks, adjacent to campground
58. Cummins Creek; C; 9; strenuous; ancient forest, adjacent to campground
59. Cummins Ridge; C; 6.2; moderate; ancient forest, wilderness
61. China Creek; C; 1.6–2.4; easy; meadow, creeks, optional beach walking, adjacent to campground
64. Cape Mountain—Summit; C; 2.2; moderate; ocean view, solitude, adjacent to campground

64. Cape Mountain—Nelson Ridge; C; 6.75; strenuous; creek, solitude, adjacent to campground

65. Enchanted Valley; C; 0.8; easy; creek, wildlife

66. Sutton Trail; C; 5; moderate; dunes, creeks, adjacent to campground

78. Tahkenitch Dunes; SC; 3.5; moderate; dunes, adjacent to campground

94. New River; S; 2.1 or 2.5; easy to moderate; dunes, wildlife, solitude

102. Humbug Mountain Coast Trail; S; 1.2–2.6; moderate; adjacent to campground, OCT

119. Redwood Nature Trail; S; 1–2.5; easy to moderate; redwood forest, creek, river, adjacent to campground

HIKES WITH OUTSTANDING SHORELINE VISTAS

8. Indian Beach–Ecola Point; N; 3; easy; forest, OCT

22. Cape Lookout; NC; 5; moderate; forest, wildlife, adjacent to campground.

28. Cape Kiwanda to Tierra del Mar; NC; 4; moderate; beach, dune, tide pools, dory-launching

32. Cascade Head—North Access; NC; 2; easy; ancient forest, wildflowers, wildlife

33. Cascade Head—South Access; NC; 4.6–6; moderate to strenuous; ancient forest, wildflowers, wildlife

34. Harts Cove; NC; 5.8; moderate to strenuous; ancient forest, wildlife, primitive camping

41. Salal Hill; C; 0.6; moderate; wildlife, lighthouse

42. Communications Hill; C; 0.8; moderate; wildlife, lighthouse

88. Cape Arago Shoreline; SC; 3.5; moderate; forest, formal gardens, hidden beach, wildlife, adjacent to campground

93. Coquille Point; S; 1.25; easy; onshore rocks, beach, wildlife

96. Blacklock Point; S; 3.5–4; moderate; forest, waterfall, beach, solitude, OCT

98. Cape Blanco North Shore; S; 0.5–3.5; easy to moderate; onshore rocks, lighthouse, wildflowers, river, historical site, adjacent to campground, OCT

108. Arch Rock Point–Spruce Island Viewpoint; S; 0.3; easy; forest, OCT

109. Spruce Island Viewpoint–Natural Bridges Cove; S; 1.75–2; moderate; forest, hidden beach, OCT

112. Thomas Creek–Whaleshead Beach; S; 2.5; moderate; dunes, forest, beach, OCT

113. Indian Sands; S; 0.4; easy; forest, wildlife

115. House Rock Viewpoint–Cape Ferrelo; S; 1.5; moderate; hidden beach, OCT

116. Cape Ferrelo–Lone Ranch Beach; S; 1; easy; beach, tide pools, OCT

117. Harris Beach; S; 0.4; easy; wildlife, adjacent to campground

Acknowledgments

Many thanks to my entire family for their encouragement and enthusiasm as I worked on this and previous editions of the book, especially Charlie for hiking companionship and encouragement. Special thanks to Randall for his scouting and photography assistance on the north coast. Thanks also to the many friends who encouraged me, accompanied me on hikes, hiked *and* posed for photos (Jack!), and even provided a quiet retreat for writing, including Donna and Mike. Thanks to Barbara Gleason for her wonderful natural history illustrations and to Carol Poole for her thoughtful editing. And thank you to the many people with Oregon State Parks, the U.S. Forest Service, and other agencies who shared maps, information, and their own time to ensure the book's accuracy.

Preface

Change is a constant on the Oregon coast. Winter storms erode some trails and cover others with landslides. People repair and extend trails and create new trails, including—new to this edition—Fort to Sea and Netul River Trails (Hike 4) and trails at Cullaby Lake (Hike 5) on the north coast, Whalen Island (Hike 26) on the north-central coast, trails around Lily Lake (Hike 63) on the central coast, and the beginnings of a trail that may eventually circle Eel Lake (Hike 82) on the south-central coast.

New landmarks sometimes appear and, with them, trailheads such as one for the North Spit hike, site (at press time) of the wreck of the *New Carissa* (Hike 85). The hike descriptions in this edition have been updated where necessary, as have natural history sidebars and introductory text. All state and federal managing agencies now have Web sites with good information; those sites are included in this edition. To get (or give) trail updates, visit *www.dayhikingoregoncoast.com.*

Oregon's Hikeable Coastline

Why hike at the Oregon coast? If you like to hike, the proper question is, why not? The Oregon coast's combination of accessibility and remoteness, its combination of walkable sandy beaches and hikeable forested headlands, is unique in the United States. It's incredibly varied. Tidepools, secluded beaches, old-growth forests, shifting sand dunes: All are part of the Oregon coast hiking experience. And it's accessible. From Portland and other population centers in western Oregon, the beach isn't more than an hour or so by car. It rarely snows at the coast in winter, so its trails are hikeable year-round. Even in the stormy winter months there are always opportunities to sneak in a beach walk during a sun break or, with rain gear, a hike in the coastal forest during a drizzle.

The Oregon coast you glimpse from your car window traveling down US Highway 101, with its outlet malls and sea-view motels and golf courses, is just one Oregon coast. But there's another Oregon coast, a timeless realm of primeval forests and undulating sand dunes, secret beaches and towering headlands, elk and eagles, hermit crabs scuttling across tide-filled rock pools, seafoam-scudded beaches. The Oregon coast has not been spared development, and more is coming. Fortunately, there remain long and short stretches of wildness where the ocean's roar drowns all other sounds, where the views haven't changed much in thousands of years. This Oregon coast is the subject of this book.

Past generations of Oregonians were wise enough to preserve large stretches of beachfront land and adjacent forest for public use, and to secure beach access at frequent intervals along the 326-mile coastline. There had long been a tradition, established by the first coastal Indians and continued by white settlers arriving 9000 years later, of using the beaches as the primary north–south highway. Oregon's landmark 1967 Beach Bill formalized that tradition, granting the public access to all of the state's beaches, not just to the high-tide line but all the way to the vegetation line. Construction of US 101 in the 1930s had actually moved most purposeful travel off the beach, allowing it to become a place to contemplate and play, to stretch muscles and imagination, a place where curiosity about wild things is piqued and sometimes satisfied, and creativity can run free.

The beach isn't the only feature of the Oregon coast that's still wild, however, thanks in part to vigorous efforts to preserve adjacent shore and forest lands and to develop trails and other recreational facilities. There are trails over headlands and along estuaries, some leading to hidden beaches or deep into old-growth Sitka spruce forests; exceptional tide pools protected as marine gardens; secluded lake fingers and estuaries ideal for canoeing; interpretive centers ranging from the elegantly simple South Slough Estuarine Research Reserve interpretive center to the dazzling Oregon Coast Aquarium. Linking it all is a border-to-border coastal hiking trail, unique in the country.

This book is a comprehensive guide to hikes and beach walks on Oregon's shoreline and adjacent public lands. Its scope is the entire coastline—the beaches as well as the headlands and low mountains in the western foothills of the Coast Range—accessible via US 101. (For more hiking suggestions just inland, see The Mountaineers' 50 Hikes in Oregon's Coast Range and Siskiyous.)

Bear in mind that the trails on the Oregon

Opposite: Stairs lead down to the beach at Yaquina Head.

coast are, generally speaking, not wilderness trails. Some feel quite remote and aren't particularly well traveled, granting hikers a good degree of solitude; some beaches may not be visited by humans for days or weeks at a time. Others are popular, even crowded on summer weekends. But part of what's so appealing about the Oregon coast is its variety. It's quite easy in summer to find a popular beach abuzz with vacation energy: kites flying, beach fires burning, children building sand castles. It's really just as easy, if you know where to go, to find a very remote beach, where there are few if any other people with whom to share miles of open sand or an orange-and-rose sunset. This book is designed to help you choose the kind of coastal experience you want.

This book gives specific, accurate information that will help you get where you want to go on the Oregon coast and offers just enough description to help you evaluate possible destinations. But there's plenty about the Oregon coast that can't be adequately described in a book: the groan of a centuries-old Sitka spruce in a windstorm high up some cape, the feel of the sun on bare arms tucked into a hollow in the dunes, the clear sustained notes of a winter wren singing in the airy understory of an old-growth forest, the thrill of discovering a twenty-four-rayed sea star on the underside of a rock during a minus tide. There's a lot out there to discover. May this book be a catalyst for your own discoveries.

THE OREGON BEACH BILL

In California, in Washington—in most coastal states—it's perfectly legal to own and fence off stretches of ocean beach from public access. In Oregon, however, all 262 miles of beaches and 64 miles of headlands are open to the public, thanks to a remarkable piece of legislation signed by a remarkable governor, Tom McCall, in 1967. But the story of Oregon's Beach Bill really begins at the turn of the century with another visionary Oregon governor, Oswald West.

Elected in 1911, Governor West was an early and forceful advocate of preservation of open lands. He convinced the state legislature to designate all Oregon beaches a public highway, since there was, in fact, no other route along the coast. "I pointed out that thus we would come into miles and miles of highway without cost to the taxpayer," he later told a reporter. "The legislature and the public took the bait—hook, line and sinker."

West's legislation protected beaches only up to the high-tide line, however. As real estate interests began focusing more attention on the coast in the 1960s, clearly more action was needed to establish public ownership of the entire dry-sand beach. After several citizens complained to the state in July 1966 about being denied access to a portion of the beach in front of Cannon Beach's Surfsand Motel, a state parks committee began examining the issue. Seven months later the committee approved the Beach Bill and presented it to the legislature; within five months it was passed and was signed into law by Governor McCall. It still stands, despite appeals all the way to the Oregon Supreme Court.

Lewis and Clark River from Netul River Trail

HOW TO USE THIS BOOK

In this book, hikes, beach walks, and other recreational opportunities on the Oregon coast are divided into five sections, determined by natural geographic boundaries. The north coast extends from the Columbia River to Tillamook Bay; the north-central coast continues south to Yaquina Head; the central coast runs to the Siuslaw River; the south-central coast stretches to Cape Arago; and the south coast ends at the Winchuck River just north of the California border. Each section begins with a general description of some of that area's most outstanding natural features, followed by a list of interpretive centers with a natural history focus and suggestions for wildlife-watching, tidepooling, off-road cycling, and camping, as well as tips for travelers and the author's top picks for hikes in that section.

Following each section's introduction are descriptions of individual hikes and beach walks, listed north to south. Each section ends with a description of the Oregon Coast Trail's route through that section.

Hike descriptions. Icons at the top of each hike description let you know if this hike is kid-friendly (they all are, but keep reading the description to determine whether they might be right for your particular kids' tastes and abilities). A dog-friendly icon means dogs are allowed, though leashes may be required (dogs must be on leash or under your control in all state parks). Hikes on beaches—and, hence, with the possibility of beachcombing—and those of historical interest have special icons too. I've given each hike a rating from 1 to 5—a purely subjective assessment. Those rated 5 tend to be longer hikes with lots of variety and interest, with great shoreline views or through magnificent forest, but even those rated 1 (usually simple beach walks with no significant landmarks) are plenty enjoyable. Difficulty ratings are based on both distance (if it's a long way to reach the main destination or complete the loop) and elevation change. In this book, a difficulty rating of 1 star means flat or nearly so, and short (not more than about 1 mile round trip); a rating of 5 stars signifies a hike at least 3 miles long with a significant elevation gain. Finally, under *Terrain*, you'll get an idea of just how much climbing—if any—is involved on this hike. *Flat* is reserved for beach walks or very flat trails; *rolling* refers to trails with only moderate elevation changes. For hikes with any significant ascents or descents, the elevation change is given in feet.

Kid-friendly

Dog-friendly

Beachcombing

Historical

Maps. Nearly every hike description is accompanied by a map showing road access, trailhead locations, and the trail route. Some maps show more than one hike. The few hikes without a map are very short and self-explanatory. If you're planning to hike well-maintained trails (like most of the trails in this book) in daylight and don't plan to do any cross-country exploration, the maps in this book should suffice for a day hike. For anything more extensive, a topographical map and compass are recommended. For the north-central, central, and south-central coast, a Siuslaw National Forest map showing all roads and public campground locations, and most trailheads along the shore and in the Coast Range, is helpful; likewise, a Siskiyou National Forest map is useful for the south coast. The Oregon Dunes National Recreation Area has an even more detailed map available for the south-central coast, from Florence to Coos Bay.

WHEN TO GO

July through October are the warmest, driest months on the Oregon coast; November through January are the rainiest. Tides are generally lower in summer, making it easier (and safer) to round certain headlands, and river levels are lower too, allowing hikers to wade many stream mouths that might stop them in winter. But part of the coast's charm for hikers is its year-round appeal. Among my favorite hiking memories are a December trek across hard-frozen dunes under a dazzling blue sky, a long barefoot walk along potholed Tahkenitch Creek Trail on a mild January day, and a brisk walk with a good friend up Gwynn Creek in a steady November drizzle.

WHAT TO TAKE

For coastal trail hikes or long beach walks, carry the same gear you would on any day hiking or backpacking trip, with a few modifications. You don't need to worry about snow or even extreme cold temperatures, but good rain gear is wise in every season. Though potable water is available at many sites along the way, backpackers should carry a water filter and/or purifying tablets in case they get caught short.

Hope for sun, and carry sunscreen. You might want to wear lightweight, waterproof hiking boots on some trails; otherwise, sneakers suffice. Beach fires are nice, but backpackers should carry a lightweight stove for cooking. Mosquitoes are not a big problem in most places most of the year, but you might carry some repellent. A tide table is a must. Naturally you'll want a sleeping bag, pad, and tent for overnighting.

Otherwise, the following list of Ten Essentials developed for day hikers by The Mountaineers should serve you well (though a map and compass and fire starter are hardly necessary on beach walks or on the less-remote trails in this book).

THE TEN ESSENTIALS: A SYSTEMS APPROACH
1. Navigation
2. Sun protection
3. Insulation (extra clothing)
4. Illumination
5. First-aid supplies
6. Fire
7. Repair kit and tools
8. Nutrition (extra food)
9. Hydration (extra water)
10. Emergency shelter

CAMPING AT THE COAST
In addition to the many motels, condominiums, and B & Bs along the coast, there are hundreds of campgrounds, both public and private. With few restrictions on tent camping, backpackers have plenty of options as well.

State parks. Among the public campgrounds, the seventeen run by the Oregon state parks department are among the most comfortable, with hot and cold water, showers, and facilities for motor homes. Most also have several yurts—round, canvas-covered structures minimally furnished, with heat and light (but no attached indoor cooking or bathroom facilities). Nine campgrounds are open year-round; the remaining eight are open from mid-April through September. Oswald West State Park on the north coast offers primitive hike-in camping (and provides wheelbarrows to help visitors transport their gear); all the rest have drive-in sites with full hookups available, as well as simple tent sites for those arriving by foot or bike. Reservations are available at nine coastal state park campgrounds in summer. Since they tend to fill up

nearly every summer weekend, it's wise to make reservations (800/452-5687).

Forest Service campgrounds. The twenty national forest campgrounds on the coast are relatively primitive; most have no hot water or hookups. Most, including those in the Oregon Dunes National Recreation Area, are on the central coast. They're cheaper than state park campgrounds, and usually they don't fill up as fast. Note that Sandbeach Campground, southwest of Tillamook, and campgrounds located near dune buggy staging areas in the Oregon dunes tend to be dominated by noisy off-road vehicles (ORVs). About a dozen Forest Service campgrounds on the coast currently take reservations through ReserveAmerica (*www.reserveamerica.com* or 877/444-6777); most are on the south-central coast, plus Sutton and Cape Perpetua (central) and Sandbeach. If campgrounds at the coast are full, if it's foggy, or simply for a change of pace, pick up a forest map and head east to campgrounds in the Coast Range.

County parks. County park campgrounds range from very spartan to full-service; Windy Cove at Winchester Bay even has cable TV hookup. Fees vary. Only one, Barview in Tillamook County, currently accepts reservations (503/322-3522).

Privately owned. There are dozens of privately owned campgrounds on the coast, most of them easy to find from US 101. Though they cater primarily to RVs, tent campers might give them a try as well; some have delightful view sites, or at least wind-fenced niches for tent campers, with hot showers, no less. Fees run about the same as those at state parks.

Backpacking. Beach camping is permitted in Oregon, with a few restrictions. No overnight camping whatsoever (RV, tent, or backpack thrown on the sand) is allowed from the south jetty of the Columbia River south to the Necanicum River (between Seaside and Gearhart). Camping is also prohibited on Oregon

COASTAL WEATHER

Forecast for the Oregon coast? A mild, cloudy, wet winter with periods of storms, followed by a generally cool, dry, and clear summer with afternoon sea breezes and occasional periods of cold fog.

Temperatures are mild year-round. Average highs in the north are sixty-five degrees Fahrenheit in summer and fifty degrees in winter; average lows are fifty degrees in summer and thirty-five degrees in winter. In the south it's two or three degrees warmer year-round. At Brookings near the southern border, however, a quirk of geography causes temperatures to sometimes exceed eighty degrees when it's barely sixty degrees everywhere else.

Rarely does it snow on the coast; most precipitation falls as rain, from heavy mist to showers to nonstop deluges. Oregon's rainiest spots are in the Coast Range, where even ten miles inland annual precipitation can reach 200 inches in spots. Back on the coast, 80 to 100 inches a year is normal for the north, 60 inches for the Bandon–Coos Bay area, and about 80 inches from Port Orford south. Doused with 100 inches of rain a year, promontories such as Neahkahnie Mountain and Cascade Head are among the wettest spots. But seventy percent of that rain falls from November through March; only ten percent falls from June through September.

Wind is pretty constant, tempering summer's heat; only occasionally do extended calm periods occur. In summer the wind is persistent from the northwest or north, blowing strongest at midday. In winter, the diurnal pattern disappears and winds are influenced by migrating storm systems. Prior to the arrival of a winter storm, winds are southerly and often quite strong; after a storm passes, west or northwest winds predominate. Hurricane-force winds of seventy-five miles per hour aren't unusual before a major storm.

beaches adjacent to a developed state park, and coastal towns often have municipal laws forbidding camping on the beach adjacent to city limits. Camping right on the beach can be damp and windy; it's often preferable to camp where you can put up your tent back in the dunes or a forest clearing. There are flat clearings with informal fire pits along many of the forest paths that are part of the Oregon Coast Trail, such as at Cape Falcon (Hike 13), and there are snug three-sided shelters (and vault toilet) along the trail atop Tillamook Head (Hike 7). Access to potable water can be a problem, especially on headlands; stock up before you reach camp. Primitive camping (no fee) is allowed on national forest land provided you're at least 200 feet from any human-made structure (such as a road or restroom). Hang food out of reach of animals—four feet from a tree trunk and ten feet off the ground. Nearly all the seventeen Oregon state parks that are right along the beach also have what are called hiker/biker camps. Fees are small—about one-third of what car campers pay. For that you get a tent site, a hot shower, and access to plenty of clean drinking water. Hiker/biker sites are available only to those arriving on foot or bike.

BEACH SAFETY

Weather, waves, tides, and the landforms they create produce particular hazards for those exploring in the coastal environment. Take precautions to avoid getting into trouble with the following potential dangers.

Sneaker, or rogue, waves. In summer, waves tend to roll onto the beach with fairly predictable force and rhythm. In winter, particularly during or just after a storm, unusually large waves periodically hit the beach, knocking down anyone in their paths. Every winter on the Oregon coast at least one or two deaths are attributed to such sneaker waves. If you're knocked down near where a creek is emptying into the ocean, it's even more difficult to drag yourself out of the surf. The rule of thumb: Don't turn your back to the ocean, and be particularly careful during winter beach visits.

Logs. Winter storms carry fallen logs down coastal rivers to the sea, where they may wash in the surf until they're stranded on the sand. Such moving, and even stationary, logs are dangerous. Children playing on logs high on the beach have been crushed after a sneaker wave lifted and rolled the log. Stay away from any logs at or near the water's edge.

Cliffs and jetties. Not only does free climbing on steep cliff faces pose obvious, inherent risks, but much of the rock at the shore is crumbly sandstone, which only increases the danger of falling. Some popular trails follow right along the tops of steep seaside cliffs—safe only if you stick to the trail. Informal spur trails leading from marked trails down to hidden beaches or coves are only to be taken at your own risk. Walk out onto a jetty only with great caution. It may look (and be) safe at low tide, but when the tide rises, large waves may wash onto the jetty, particularly during storms.

Rip currents (undertows). If the Pacific Ocean along Oregon weren't an uninviting forty-seven to fifty-two degrees Fahrenheit, even more swimmers would be caught by rip currents along the coast. The danger is two-fold: A swimmer fighting a rip current may be unable to swim to shore and may drown, or may perish from hypothermia simply from excessive exposure to the cold water. If you do get caught in a current that's pulling you away from the shore, don't try to swim against it directly. It's best to work at staying afloat in a horizontal position, and remaining calm. Swim or drift parallel to the shore until you get out of the current; then attempt to swim into shore at a different spot.

Tide dangers. Algae can make rocks in tide-pool areas extremely slippery. Even if the rock is dry, you'll still slip if your shoes' soles are wet. Wear boots or athletic shoes with a gripping sole and begin exploring cautiously, noting which kinds of rocks are slipperiest. Watch the time and the water level as well, to make sure you don't get stranded on a rock by an incoming tide. Likewise, watch the time and your tide table if you're rounding a headland, so that you don't get stranded between an incoming tide and a sheer cliff face.

Falling trees. Stay off headland trails during winter storms.

Tsunami. Blue-and-white "tsunami hazard zone" signs are popping up at the coast these days, in response to research indicating that the Oregon coast is due for a big earthquake and its likely aftermath, huge sea waves. If such waves come, they'll be moving fast; by the time you see them, it will be too late to react. So if you're at the coast and an earthquake knocks you down, immediately head inland and up from sea level.

Cars. Oregon's tradition of allowing cars on the beach isn't quite so distasteful if you remember that it's this tradition upon which the Oregon Supreme Court based its ruling that all of the state's beaches are public up to the vegetation line. Since the early '60s, when a sunny day would draw some 3000 cars to

Oregon Dunes Overlook Trail

Cannon Beach alone, citizens have successfully sought restrictions on beach driving. Today 89.3 miles of Oregon's 262 miles of sandy beach are technically open to cars year-round, and nearly half those miles are on (southernmost) Curry County beaches that aren't actually accessible to cars anyway. Of more concern is the continuous 14-mile stretch between Fort Stevens State Park (just south of the Columbia River) and Gearhart—the "last bastion of beach driving in Oregon," as one state official characterizes it. In most other places, driving is permitted only from October through April, or only for pickups launching dory boats. Beach driving has been eliminated completely in Lincoln County.

Given these restrictions, cars aren't an issue on most of the state's beaches. Where cars are still allowed, treat the beach like a country road and keep an eye peeled while you're walking.

BEACH ETIQUETTE

Beach fires. Fires on the beach are allowed in Oregon. The only restrictions: Beach fires are not permitted within twenty-five feet of a wooden seawall, and they may not be built in the middle of a large pile of driftwood, which might burn long after your hot dog has been roasted and you've gone home. Using individual pieces of driftwood collected on the beach is acceptable, however. Keep any fires small; use only dead and down wood. Don't build fires near dune grass or other vegetation. And when you're ready to leave, douse your fire with water or wet sand to keep it from burning indefinitely.

Drinking water and sanitation. State park campgrounds and waysides and Forest Service campgrounds are the most reliable sources of potable water for hikers. Water from coastal creeks, rivers, and lakes should be safe as long as you filter it, thoroughly boil it, or otherwise treat it to remove impurities.

Use developed toilet facilities whenever possible, since you'll be walking through or close to developed areas, for the most part. Otherwise, be careful to bury wastes in dirt (not sand) a good distance from the trail or at least 200 feet from water sources. Don't bury toilet paper—pack it out.

Offshore rocks. Nearly all of Oregon's more than 1400 offshore rocks, reefs, and islands are protected as wildlife refuges. That puts them off-limits to humans in order to maintain undisturbed breeding habitat for seabirds and marine mammals.

Many bird species are extremely sensitive to disturbance; seabirds will flee the nest at a visitor's approach, accidentally knocking their eggs or nestlings into the sea or leaving them vulnerable to the elements and to predators. For cliff-burrowing birds such as puffins, auklets, and storm petrels, disturbance of mainland nesting sites by humans and predation by mammals on shore make protection of nesting habitat on offshore islands even more important. All watercraft are required to remain at least 500 feet away from refuge rocks and islands. Some rocks are easily accessible on foot, especially at low tide (Haystack at Cannon Beach, for example). Tempting as it may be, don't climb. Because disturbance by humans easily upsets nesting birds, no trespassing is allowed on federally protected rocks. Anyone caught walking or climbing in a protected area may be fined.

RESPECTFUL TIDEPOOLING

Most of Oregon's coastline consists of sandy beaches, but within and between those beaches are dozens of places where, twice a day, an ebbing tide reveals pools created by bedrock or boulders filled with a particular variety of plants and animals adapted to the rhythm of the tides. Tidepooling can be a treasure hunt as you search for familiar and unfamiliar creatures clinging to rocks or darting across pools.

Unfortunately, many of Oregon's tide pools

FIRST PEOPLES OF THE OREGON COAST

People have been living along the Oregon coast for at least 10,000 years, according to the archaeological record, but little evidence of this ancient past remains. During the height of the last glacial period, about 18,000 years ago, the sea level was more than 300 feet lower than it is today. That put the shoreline many miles west of its present location—as much as 75 miles west at Heceta Head on the central coast. Melting glaciers caused the sea level to slowly rise over thousands of years, pushing settlement eastward. Archaeological evidence of these earliest coastal settlements has mostly been scattered or destroyed by waves.

The earliest known evidence of people on the Oregon coast comes from a bluff south of Bandon on the south coast, where remnants of a stone hearth, pieces of charcoal and flakes of stone seven feet below ground indicate that the area was inhabited about 10,000 years ago. Before this discovery in 2002, the oldest known settlement sites on the Oregon coast were at Tahkenitch Landing (near Hikes 78 and 79) and Indian Sands (Hike 113). The evidence was found in large middens, or refuse heaps, where people piled shells, fish bones, and other refuse from meals. Middens also reveal everyday objects, evidence of isolated houses, and burials. Radiocarbon dating has indicated these middens are about 8000 years old.

We know more about coastal dwellers from the past 1500 years, when the sea level and shoreline were about where they are today. During most of this period, people lived in rectangular houses built of split cedar planks. Some on the north coast were very large—up to 100 feet long and 40 feet wide—and were home to several families or even an entire village. On the south coast, each family in a village tended to have its own small plank house. These homes were clustered at the mouths of rivers and bays, where food was most plentiful. Many different languages were spoken by Oregon coast peoples, some similar to those of their neighbors but some entirely distinct. Linguistic differences suggest that, after crossing the Bering land bridge from Asia, some people probably migrated into the continent's interior, then south and finally west to the coast, while others may have migrated directly south down the coast.

are being loved to death—explored to death, anyway. Barnacles tend to be the first thing to go, rubbed off rocks by the trampling of many feet. Collecting intertidal animals is prohibited at several state-designated "marine gardens" and is prohibited to all but researchers with a permit at other sites. These same sites—among them, the marine gardens at Haystack Rock, Cape Kiwanda, Otter Rock, Yaquina Head, Yachats, Cape Perpetua, and Harris Beach—are also among the most popular spots for visitors, in part because they're easy to reach. To help preserve these areas, scan this book's chapters for suggestions of less well-known tide-pool areas.

Tips for tidepoolers. To help minimize disturbance to intertidal areas without giving up the treasure hunt entirely, keep the following in mind:

- Walk on well-worn pathways through the intertidal area, to avoid further damage. Mussels resist trampling better than other species and provide sure footing. Don't step in urchin beds, which are easily damaged.
- Don't pick up any rocks. If you inadvertently move a rock, carefully and slowly put it back exactly as you found it. Sea urchins and sea anemones are particularly dependent upon the shade of rocks and shells to keep them from drying out, and other

Gearhart Ridge path

Pelicans flying over the beach

plants and animals need exposure to light and food and will die if the rock they are on is overturned.

- Refrain from picking up any animals for a closer look, especially those clinging to rocks. If you do pick up something—a hermit crab, for example—put it back exactly where you found it. If it had been under cover, cover it again to protect it from exposure. If children in your party just have to touch something, take them to the Oregon Coast Aquarium or Mark O. Hatfield Marine Science Center in Newport; both have touch tanks for this purpose.

- If, where allowed, you gather any shellfish to eat, observe state fish and game regulations, usually posted at the site. Refrain from any collecting; the live plants and animals you take can't survive away from shore, and empty shells are recycled by hermit crabs, which need them for protection.

- Most of all, explore the intertidal zone slowly, for your own enjoyment and for the benefit of the creatures that live there.

- The best time for tidepooling is during the hour or so either before or after low tide, and the best tides for viewing the widest variety of intertidal creatures are those of 0.0 feet and lower, called "minus tides." (To avoid harming fragile creatures in the low-tide zone, avoid minus tides when taking school groups tidepooling, however.) The lowest daytime tides of the year generally occur in June and July. Morning low tides are better than afternoon ones because there's generally less wind to ruffle the surface of the water.

ACCESS FEES

Between the federal government's Recreation Access Tax at Forest Service–managed sites and state park fees at the more popular, developed parks, many (but not most) of the parks, waysides, and trailheads on the Oregon coast now charge a day-use fee (generally $5 when this book went to press). Self-pay stations are set up at most sites, and various one-day and annual passes are widely available. These fees are technically charged for use of the site, but you won't need to pay if you arrive by foot or bike.

THE OREGON COAST TRAIL

The Oregon coast offers long-distance hikers the opportunity of walking the entire coastline, border-to-border from Washington state to California. It's possible thanks to the still-evolving Oregon Coast Trail (OCT), which began as the brainchild of University of Oregon geography professor Sam Dicken in 1972.

It's an opportunity unique to Oregon, for several reasons. About 200 of the trail's projected 400 miles are on sandy beach (accessible to the public, thanks to the Oregon Beach Bill). Existing trails in state parks and national forests, plus links built specifically for the OCT, make up much of the remaining 200 miles. All of those trails are described in this book; each regional section of the book ends with a description of the OCT route transitions from beach to trail to highway stretches on that part of the coast. Be aware that this is not a detailed trail log, however; you will want to take more detailed maps, and expect the unexpected, including route changes, as the trail continues to evolve.

Though officially declared "hikeable" in 1988, the OCT is still a work in progress. Lack of funding slowed trail construction in the early 1990s, and there will probably always be some sections of highway hiking. The route isn't always obvious; look for wooden OCT signposts at transitions between beach, road shoulder, and trail.

The Oregon Coast Trail is certainly not a wilderness trail. US 101 hugs the beach closely in some places, and the trail cuts through, or just west of, many coastal towns. In some places, long walks along US 101 are required in order to cross river mouths on road bridges. At Gearhart and a few other spots, cars are allowed on the beach, making those stretches a little like roads as well. But much of the highway hiking can be eliminated by prearranging boat shuttles across rivers. And there are still long sections that offer plenty of solitude. You could easily find yourself completely alone on Netarts Spit, on much of the beach hike along the dunes between Florence and Coos Bay, or between Bandon and Cape Blanco.

A border-to-border hike, or just several days on the OCT, requires planning—and flexibility. Large rivers must be crossed, either by hiking around on the highway or by prearranging a boat shuttle. Many creeks and smaller rivers may be safely crossed or waded at low tide in summer, when water flows are low. Probably the most dangerous crossings, even in summer, are the Sixes and Elk rivers on either side of Cape Blanco on the southern coast, especially with a full pack. To make river crossings easier, you'll probably want to walk barefoot, tying your boots to the top of your pack. Be sure to unbuckle your backpack's waist strap (so that it will come off easily in case you fall), and use a walking stick to help you keep your balance.

Finding adequate sources of drinking water can be a challenge as well; carry a water filter and plenty of bottles to tide you over between watering holes. Camping is not allowed everywhere (see Camping at the Coast, above).

Suggested backpacking trips. Few people actually hike the entire Oregon Coast Trail border to border; more often, it's used for day hiking or for long weekend backpacks. In choosing a section to backpack, think about the kind of experience you want. Lots of beach walking? A mixture of headland hiking and beach walking? Total solitude, or in and out of civilization?

Following are a few varied choices for two- to five-day backpacking trips (assuming approximately 8 miles a day) that don't require much or any highway walking. These are only a few of many possible options for overnight hikes on the coast.

• Columbia River to Cannon Beach. A long beach hike followed by an ascent of Tillamook Head; approximates the route Lewis and Clark took from their winter quarters south of Astoria to an Indian village at the mouth of Ecola Creek. (See Oregon Coast Trail, North Coast.)

- Garibaldi to Pacific City. A boat ride across the mouth of Tillamook Bay to the tip of Bayocean Spit, then a hike over three capes with beach stretches, another bay-mouth crossing, and a short road stretch along the way. (See Oregon Coast Trail, North-Central Coast.)
- Siuslaw River's south jetty to Threemile Lake (or to Winchester Bay with a boat shut-

tle). Isolated dunes hiking all the way. (See Oregon Coast Trail, South-Central Coast.)

- Umpqua River's south jetty to Charleston. A long stretch of beach walking along the dunes, ending with a shuttle across the mouth of Coos Bay. (See Oregon Coast Trail, South-Central Coast.)
- Bandon to Cape Blanco. A long beach stretch (including isolated beach west of the New River) and an adventurous trek over Blacklock Point, crossing the Sixes River, to Cape Blanco. (See Oregon Coast Trail, South Coast.)

A NOTE ABOUT SAFETY

Safety is an important concern in all outdoor activities. No guidebook can alert you to every hazard or anticipate the limitations of every reader. Therefore, the descriptions of roads, trails, routes, and natural features in this book are not representations that a particular place or excursion will be safe for your party. When you follow any of the routes described in this book, you assume responsibility for your own safety. Under normal conditions, such excursions require the usual attention to traffic, road and trail conditions, weather, terrain, the capabilities of your party, and other factors. Keeping informed on current conditions and exercising common sense are the keys to a safe, enjoyable outing.

—The Mountaineers Books

the north coast

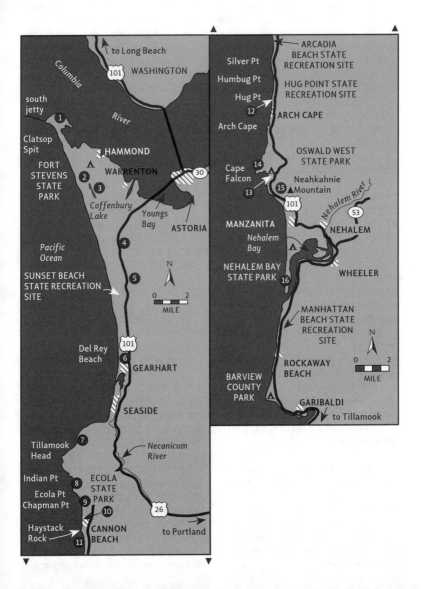

to Long Beach
Columbia
WASHINGTON
101
south jetty
River
1
Clatsop Spit
FORT STEVENS STATE PARK
HAMMOND
WARRENTON
2
3
Coffenbury Lake
Youngs Bay
30
ASTORIA
Pacific Ocean
4
SUNSET BEACH STATE RECREATION SITE
5
N
0   2
MILE
Del Rey Beach
101
6
GEARHART
SEASIDE
7
Tillamook Head
Necanicum River
Indian Pt
8
Ecola Pt
ECOLA STATE PARK
Chapman Pt
9
10
26
to Portland
Haystack Rock
CANNON BEACH
11

Silver Pt
ARCADIA BEACH STATE RECREATION SITE
Humbug Pt
HUG POINT STATE RECREATION SITE
Hug Pt
12
ARCH CAPE
Arch Cape
OSWALD WEST STATE PARK
Cape Falcon
14
Neahkahnie Mountain
13
15
101
Nehalem River
53
NEHALEM
MANZANITA
Nehalem Bay
WHEELER
NEHALEM BAY STATE PARK
16
MANHATTAN BEACH STATE RECREATION SITE
ROCKAWAY BEACH
N
0   2
MILE
BARVIEW COUNTY PARK
GARIBALDI
to Tillamook

IN SEARCH OF A WHALE

Passages from Lewis and Clark's journals about a trip over Tillamook Head to see a beached whale amount to the first written account of an Oregon coast hike. This fact, and William Clark's name attached to a viewpoint atop the head, conjure the Corps of Discovery every time I walk that trail. But as I slip up the trail—muddy, steep, and narrow, but a good deal easier than the "small Indian parth" Clark described—it's not so much Clark himself who comes to mind. Not Clark, not his dozen soldiers, nor the Chinook guide, nor Charbonneau.

It's Sacagawea, the Shoshone teenager, "wife" of Charbonneau, translator. She wasn't needed on the hike over the head; on the contrary, she had asked to go—insisted, it seems. A month and a half they'd been at Fort Clatsop, and she hadn't yet seen the Pacific Ocean twelve miles west. "The Indian woman . . . observed that she had traveled a long way with us to see the great waters," Clark writes, "and that now that monstrous fish was also to be seen, she thought it very hard she could not be permitted to see either." (The Journals of Lewis and Clark, New York: Houghton, Mifflin, 1953)

Captured by the Blackfeet as a girl, sold to Charbonneau when barely a woman, she made her way up the near-vertical trail, mute and resolute, with baby Jean-Baptiste strapped to her back, probably in the rain. Two centuries ago, two cultures; we have so little in common, she and I. Except for one thing. I, too, hear of great waters, and monstrous fish. I have walked a long way. I want to see them.

Long, wide beaches interrupted by a few tall, wild headlands characterize the northern Oregon coast. Sand has been flowing down the Columbia and settling onto the beaches at its mouth for eons. It's fifteen miles of open beach from the south jetty to Tillamook Head, and another seven miles of sand from Cannon Beach to Arch Cape.

You'll also find a lot of people. As the closest beaches to Portland, they're popular year-round, especially Seaside Beach and the beach right at Haystack Rock. But except during Cannon Beach's annual sand castle contest, it's never elbow to elbow. And it takes little effort to find quieter stretches. It's also easy to escape with a hike over Tillamook Head, Cape Falcon, or Neahkahnie Mountain.

The state parks on the north coast deserve special mention. From the south jetty of the Columbia nearly to Warrenton, most of the beaches, dunes, lakes, and forest are part of Fort Stevens State Park, one of the state's most diverse and interesting parks (see Hikes 1, 2, and 3). Between Seaside and Cannon Beach, Ecola State Park and adjacent Elmer Feldenheimer Forest Preserve comprise a large, contiguous tract of forest land draping Tillamook Head (see Hikes 7, 8, and 9). South of Cannon Beach, Oswald West State Park is a large, forested park incorporating two major north coast landmarks—Cape Falcon and Neahkahnie Mountain—as well as Short Sand Beach, popular among surfers year-round (see Hikes 13, 14, and 15). Nehalem Bay State Park occupies long Nehalem Spit (see Hike 16).

Interpretive centers. The Columbia River Maritime Museum (*www.seasurf.com/crmm* or 503/325-2323) on the river in Astoria is nationally acclaimed for its displays on boating, fishing, shipwrecks, and lighthouses. Moored just outside is the Lightship *Columbia*, a historic floating lighthouse that's also open for touring. Three miles off US 101 southwest of Astoria is a replica of Fort Clatsop, where the Lewis and Clark party spent the winter of 1805–6, in Lewis and Clark National Historical Park (*www.nps.gov/foc* or 503/861-2471). (The original replica fort burned down in fall 2005; its replacement opened a year later.) In the summer, period-dressed rangers help bring history alive with demonstrations and interpretive programs. At the north end of Seaside, just off US 101, the little Coastal Natural History Center (*www.nclctrust.org/gateway.html* or 503/738-5618) serves as a gateway to understanding and exploring the surrounding watershed and the adjacent Necanicum River estuary. Nature trails are being developed just outside.

Fort Stevens State Park, outside Warrenton, has an extensive historical area reflecting its role as one point in a "triangle of firepower" guarding the mouth of the Columbia during the Civil War and World Wars I and II. A replica of the original earthwork fortification still remains, along with six gun emplacements built just before World War I to guard the Columbia River. A World War I battery and a World War II gun emplacement are also open to the public. Adjacent to the main batteries is a military museum and interpretive center (503/861-2000) with displays and artifacts tracing the fort's history. A vintage army cargo truck can take visitors on forty-five-minute narrated tours of the historical area in the summer. Guided tours of underground Battery Mishler are also offered in the summer.

Wildlife-watching. Try the south jetty area at Fort Stevens State Park, where a wide variety of birds (often including some unusual species) may be seen on the ocean beach, dunes, or estuary. At Parking Area D, little trails lead down to the river, and a boardwalk leads to a concrete bird blind overlooking an estuary finger, where you may see nesting or wintering waterfowl.

In Seaside, Necanicum Estuary Park may offer decent bird-watching under the right conditions; it's directly across North Holladay Drive from Seaside High School (stairs lead down to the mudflats from the road).

Haystack Rock is a major nesting site for western gulls, pelagic cormorants, pigeon guillemots, and tufted puffins—in fact, it hosts one of the largest and most easily watched colonies of nesting puffins on the

Oregon coast. Spotting scopes are sometimes set up here in summer to give you a closer look at the birds. Look for seabirds at Ecola and Oswald West state parks; Nehalem Bay is a good site for spotting waterfowl, shorebirds, and seals.

Cape Falcon (Hike 14) can be a good vantage point for whale-watching, as are sites in Ecola State Park and at Neahkahnie Mountain (along the highway, not from the summit).

Tidepooling. (See Respectful Tidepooling, p. 31.) In Ecola State Park there's good tidepooling at both Indian Beach (Hike 8) and Crescent Beach (Hike 9). On Cannon Beach, Haystack Rock (Hike 11) has extensive—and extensively visited—tide pools; in summer, naturalists sometimes set up touch tanks at low tide to lessen human disturbance in the pools themselves. Tide pools form at both the north and south ends of Short Sand Beach as well (Hike 14).

Off-road cycling. Families enjoy the paved bicycle paths at both Fort Stevens (9 miles) and Nehalem Bay (1.5 miles) State Parks. Mountain bikes are allowed on the old roads on Tillamook Head, but not on its foot trails.

Camping/hostels. Fort Stevens State Park at Warrenton is a great choice for families; in addition to 596 campsites (and several yurts) it has historic sites, a lake, beach access, and miles of paved bike paths. Otherwise there are only private campgrounds (some close to the beach) in the Gearhart–Seaside–Cannon Beach area. In Seaside, International Hosteling–Seaside is one of two such hostels on the Oregon coast. Oswald West State Park south of Cannon Beach is unique among coastal campgrounds; it's a pack-in site, complete with wheelbarrows to help campers transport their gear 0.3 mile from highway to tent site. Use the southernmost of three parking areas to reach the campground (no reservations; closed in winter). Nehalem Bay State Park south of Manzanita has car camping, horse camping, and bike trails and is even accessible by air via the 2400-foot landing strip 0.25 mile from the campground entrance. Barview County Park (reservations 503/322-3522) north of Garibaldi offers rather spartan camping facilities, but dramatic views where the huge bay—fed by five rivers—meets the Pacific.

For reservations at state park campgrounds, call 800/452-5687.

Travelers' tips. Astoria is considered the northernmost town on the Oregon coast, though it's actually on the Columbia River some ten miles inland. With so many cafes and restaurants, a number of memorable hotels and B & Bs in restored Victorian homes, and a vibrant downtown with shops, galleries, and a restored movie palace, Astoria is well worth a visit. Quiet, sedate Gearhart has a single upscale cafe catering mainly to locals. Look for lodging and more restaurant choices in busy Seaside, whose popular beach boasts summer lifeguards (as does the one at Cannon Beach). Cannon Beach is small, arty, and busy, with perhaps the coast's best selection of restaurants, shops, and inns. Manzanita and Nehalem are smaller and quieter; enjoy browsing the shops along Nehalem's riverfront. It's fun to browse the curio shops and shell purveyors at Rockaway Beach, and the beach itself is long and lively, with kids, dogs, volleyball—and no cars. Arrange a charter boat fishing trip at the marina in Garibaldi.

Recommended hikes. In summer take a shuttle bus for a one-way hike on the Fort to Sea Trail (Hike 4). Each of the three headland ascents is awesome: Tillamook Head (Hike 7), Cape Falcon (Hike 13), and Neahkahnie Mountain (Hike 15), especially the south-to-north traverse if you have a shuttle car or don't mind walking the highway shoulder link. Favorite

beach trails are Crescent Beach (Hike 9) and Hug Point (Hike 12).

1 Clatsop Spit

RATING	DIFFICULTY	ONE-WAY	TERRAIN
★★	2	2.8 miles	Flat

Features: Beach, wildlife, ship traffic, adjacent to campground; **Contact:** Fort Stevens State Park, www.oregonstateparks.org or 800/551-6949

Call this the bird-watcher's special, though it offers good boat-watching and unstructured rambling as well. When Oregon birders talk about "the south jetty," however, it's this south jetty in Fort Stevens State Park they're referring to. The cast of characters changes season to season, even day to day. Bring binoculars to get the best views of passing pelicans or ocean-going container ships crossing the Columbia River bar.

GETTING THERE

Follow signs to Fort Stevens State Park from US 101 just south of the Youngs Bay Bridge at Astoria. As you head north on Ridge Road, turn left at the second park entrance (the day-use entrance) and follow it to its end at Parking Area D.

ON THE TRAIL

A short boardwalk leads south from Area D to a bird blind overlooking the tidal flats on a finger of the estuary. To start the beach walk, however, pick up the little trail leading north through the dunes toward the river, across the parking area from the boardwalk. Follow the hook of sandy river beach as it curves north and west. At 2.3 miles the beach ends at the south jetty; bear left, along the sand at the edge of the

Opposite: Riprap and viewing platform, Columbia River South Jetty

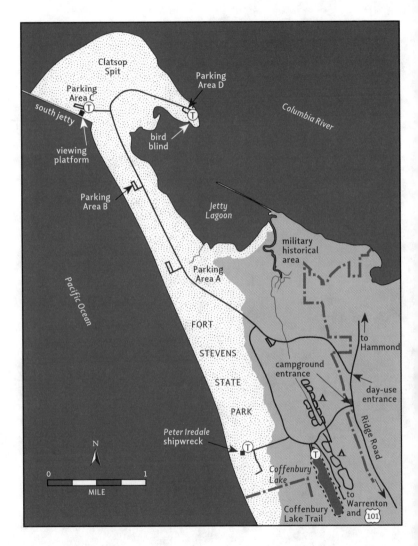

rocky jetty, for another 0.5 mile to the viewing platform at Area C, west of Area D 1.3 miles by road. Area C has a tall viewing platform overlooking river, jetty, and ocean beach, and is often staffed by naturalists in the summer. Return the way you came, or follow the road shoulder 0.4 mile to the junction, bear left, and continue another 0.9 mile back to Area D.

2 Peter Iredale

RATING	DIFFICULTY	ONE-WAY	TERRAIN
★★	1	Up to 4 miles	Flat

Features: Beach, shipwreck, adjacent to campground; **Contact:** Fort Stevens State Park, *www.oregonstateparks.org* or 800/551-6949

There's so much to see and explore in Fort Stevens State Park, from the parade of migrating birds at the estuary's edge to the extensive military reservation dating as far back as the Civil War. One of the most intriguing attractions is the rusting hulk of the Peter Iredale. *This English sailing ship ran aground in 1906; happily, no lives were lost. Visit in winter or spring, after storms have scoured the beach of much of its sand and exposed more of what's left of the boat's iron skeleton.*

GETTING THERE

Follow signs to Fort Stevens State Park from US 101 just south of the Youngs Bay Bridge at Astoria. As you head north on Ridge Road, turn left at the first park entrance (the campground entrance) and follow signs to the wreck of the *Peter Iredale*; the parking area is adjacent to the shipwreck.

ON THE TRAIL

An extensive network of bicycle paths at this park invites family touring without a car. There are footpaths as well, mostly in the military

Remains of the shipwreck Peter Iredale

areas and around the campground, useful for car-free exploration but otherwise not particularly noteworthy. (Detailed trail maps are available at the park.) Instead, walk the beach, beginning at the site of the *Peter Iredale.*

For a beach walk, the key is to head north. Cars are allowed on the beach year-round to the south of here, turning it into a bit of a highway at times. To the north they're prohibited May 1 through September 15 from noon to midnight. Enjoy the wide, wide beach, making either a round-trip or one-way walk. It's 2 miles to Area A, the next parking area north; from there it's 0.9 mile more to Area B and another 0.9 mile to Area C, start of the rocky south jetty.

3 Coffenbury Lake

RATING	DIFFICULTY	LOOP	TERRAIN
★★	2	2.2 miles	Flat

Features: Lake, swimming, fishing, wildlife, adjacent to campground; **Contact:** Fort Stevens State Park, www.oregonstateparks.org or 800/551-6949

Circumnavigating the lake makes a pleasant outing, especially early on a summer morning when you're likely to see water birds or hear songbirds in the brushy forest. On hot days Coffenbury Lake is appealing for swimming, since it's out of the wind that blows on the beach most afternoons. There are two sandy swimming areas on the lake. Motorboats are allowed, but a speed limit of ten miles per hour keeps wakes down and the atmosphere relatively tranquil. Most boaters on the lake are there to fish for perch, trout, crappie, and bass.

GETTING THERE

Follow signs to Fort Stevens State Park from US 101 just south of the Youngs Bay Bridge at Astoria. As you head north on Ridge Road, turn left at the first park entrance (the campground entrance). Past the campground entrance station, turn left into the parking area at Coffenbury Lake.

ON THE TRAIL

For a counterclockwise hike from the picnic area at the lake's north end, pick up the trail along the shoreline near the rest rooms. It follows the lake's edge and then ventures into the woods for a distance. At the far end the trail meets an old road; take a left onto it and across the lake's marshy south end, and then veer left where the footpath resumes. Walk through the picnic and swimming area on the lake's southeast side and drop back into the northeastern corner of the parking lot to return to your starting point.

4 Fort to Sea Trail

RATING	DIFFICULTY	ONE-WAY	TERRAIN
★★★★★	5	6.5 miles	Flat

Netul River Trail

RATING	DIFFICULTY	ONE-WAY	TERRAIN
★★★★★	1	1 mile	Flat

Features: Forest, creeks, lake, dunes, wildlife, historic site; **Contact:** Lewis and Clark National Historical Park, www.nps.gov/lewi or 503/861-2471

Fort to Sea Trail approximates the route the Lewis and Clark Expedition took from Fort Clatsop, the winter quarters they built in December 1805 on what is now called the Lewis and Clark River, to the Pacific Ocean to hunt, trade, and make salt. After more than ten years of planning, the trail was completed and dedicated in November 2005 as part of the Lewis and Clark Bicentennial celebration. Just a month before the celebration, the Fort Clatsop replica burned to the ground, but it was rebuilt—more historically accurate, and with better fireproofing—within a year. So much about the landscape has changed in 200 years—the surrounding hills are scarred by logging, and the dunes are now covered with fairways, dairy farms, and daffodils (blooming in early March). But parts of the trail have a timeless feel, such as the deep woods on the west slope of Clatsop Ridge and the dunes at the trail's end.

GETTING THERE

To reach the eastern trailhead, turn off US 101 south of Astoria, between mileposts 7 and 8, and follow signs 3 miles to Lewis and Clark National Historical Park, about 3 miles east of the highway. (Summer parking is at Netul River Landing day-use area, 1.25 miles south of the park entrance on Fort Clatsop Road.)

To reach the western trailhead at Sunset Beach State Recreation Site, turn west off US 101 on Sunset Beach Road (between mileposts 13 and 14) and follow it 1 mile to the trailhead parking area on the right, just before the road reaches the beach.

ON THE TRAIL

With trailheads at both ends, Fort to Sea Trail is ideally suited for a one-way hike; at this writing, the park was providing hourly shuttle buses to one-way hikers in summer. The eastern trailhead is at the visitor center for Fort Clatsop, though in summer visitors must park at Netul River Landing and either walk 1 mile to the fort (see Netul River Trail, below) or take one of the frequent shuttle buses. Two intermediate trailheads provide more options for shorter hikes: the parking area west of the visitor center off Fort Clatsop Road (only for vehicles with handicapped parking passes) and a midway point at the tunnel under US 101 (parking is allowed at

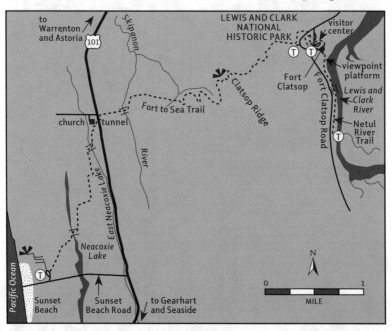

Pioneer Presbyterian Church any time except Sundays from 8:00 AM to 1:00 PM).

From the fort, pick up the Fort to Sea Trail between the main parking lot and the overflow lot. At the immediate junction, bear left to stay on the trail. (A right turn here would put you on the older Clay Pit Trail, narrow and root-bound; it passes a muddy pit where clay was once quarried for pottery works in Warrenton and Portland, then reunites with the Fort to Sea Trail to create a 0.5-mile loop.)

Continuing, the trail crosses the park access road and leads onto a long wooden boardwalk, then heads up a short distance to a handicapped parking area, 0.6 mile from the visitor center. A wide compacted gravel road picks up

Pilings in Lewis and Clark River, along Netul River Trail

SKUNK CABBAGE

Ever notice the sweet fragrance of skunk cabbage blossoms? Probably not. The blossoms' perfume tends to be overwhelmed by the decidedly rank odor emanating from the plant's stem and massive leaves.

As skunklike as its smell may be, *Lysichitum americanum* is one of the most reliable harbingers of spring on the Oregon coast, brightening shady forest bogs as early as February with bright yellow spathes hooding a pokerlike flower stem covered with hundreds of tiny greenish flowers, and large leaves measuring two, three, even four or five feet long. Perhaps it's an acquired affinity, but even the odor can be welcome after a long winter.

This tropical-looking Northwest plant is related to the taro root eaten in the South Pacific. Like taro, skunk cabbage root was reportedly roasted and pounded into flour by coastal natives (cooking neutralizes the toxic calcium oxalate contained in the plant). Various tribes also made medicines from the roots and leaves to ease childbirth, soothe cuts, and salve ringworm, among other uses. Bears and elk are fond of the roots, sometimes digging up whole bogs.

the route and leads through the woods, level at first and then ascending gently to reach an overlook at 1.6 miles atop Clatsop Ridge. From here the trail narrows to a forest footpath switchbacking down the hill and following the hill's contours above a creek. It's the trail's most remote section; I once saw a coyote trotting on the trail here. The trail crosses a couple of boardwalks leading over a wetland full of skunk cabbage before reaching a footbridge over the Skipanon River at 3.6 miles. In another 0.4 mile the trail turns briefly to asphalt and passes under US 101 at 4 miles.

From the highway, a footpath follows a wooden fence angling up a field past Pioneer Presbyterian Church, crests a low ridge, and drops down to East Neacoxie Lake at 4.2 miles, crossing it on a floating footbridge. For the next mile or so, the route zigzags over and along farmers' fields and right across a cow pasture, reaching the trail's longest bridge, crossing Neacoxie Lake (also called Sunset Lake), at 5.2 miles; look for waterfowl here. Head up over another couple of ridges, then zigzag down sand dunes and pass by a wetland at 5.7 miles. The trail drops down through dense shore pines to emerge (behind the rest rooms) at the western trailhead parking area at 6.2 miles. Pick up the last 0.3 mile of the Fort to Sea Trail at the far end of the parking lot; it leads through pines, over a pair of footbridges, and out through dunes to a platform overlooking the Pacific.

This is not where those nineteenth-century explorers made salt, however; they continued another 8 miles or so south to present-day

Seaside, to escape the diluting effect of the freshwater Columbia River.

Netul River Trail. From Netul River Landing, which has a picnic area and canoe/kayak launch, a path leads north to Fort Clatsop through a narrow corridor between the Lewis and Clark River and the park road, which is usually busy only in midsummer. Use it to get to the park or, especially in the quiet winter, to just enjoy the river and its winter waterfowl. At about 0.4 mile the trail crosses a finger of river on a footbridge. Nearing the fort it reaches an extensive boardwalk at the fort's own canoe landing, with a viewing platform and replica dugout canoes. From here (0.8 mile) walk up to the visitor center, or veer right to the fort. Return as you came.

5 Cullaby Lake

RATING	DIFFICULTY	LOOP	TERRAIN
***	2	1.3 or 1.4 miles	Flat to rolling

Features: Wetlands, ancient forest, lakeshore, wildlife; **Contact:** Clatsop County Parks, www .co.clatsop.or.us or 503/325-9306

This trail lies at the northern end of what's called the Gearhart Fen, one of the largest contiguous bogs on the Oregon coast. A hike here provides a snapshot of the temperate rainforest as you wind through bogs, along a stream and into old-growth forest. Visit in springtime late or early in the day to enjoy the frog chorus. Interpretive signs at various points along the trail describe the hydrology and plant and animal life that make up the wetlands ecosystem. The partly paved, partly gravel trail is doable with wheelchairs or strollers.

GETTING THERE

From US 101 between Gearhart and Warrenton, turn east between mileposts 13 and 14

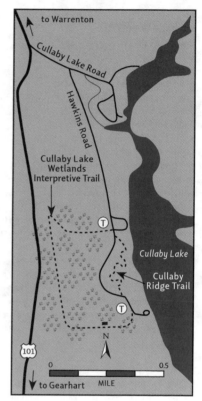

onto Cullaby Lake Road. Go 0.25 mile, turn right onto Hawkins Road, and continue about 0.6 mile to the main (north) parking area and boat ramp at Cullaby Lake Park.

ON THE TRAIL

Look for the Cullaby Lake Wetlands Interpretive Trail sign at the southwest corner of the north parking area and follow the wide gravel trail west through wetland bog teeming with salal, alder and spruce trees, and yellow skunk cabbage in spring. At 0.25 mile the trail turns south and rounds the shoulder of a hill dominated by old-growth spruce. At 0.5 mile the

Cullaby Ridge Trail

trail briefly turns to paved road as it follows an old roadbed, then curves east before turning to gravel again and reaching an elevated viewing platform overlooking the surrounding wetlands at 1 mile. The platform is a prime bird-watching and frog-listening post and has interpretive signs describing the wetland vegetation and bird life. In another 0.1 mile you'll reach the south trailhead and parking area.

Follow the park road 0.2 mile back to the north parking lot watching for the occasional slow car, or look for a sign to Cullaby Ridge Trail, on your right in 0.1 mile. This 0.3-mile return trail up and over a low ridge is somewhat rough with roots and rocks, but it gives you closer encounters with the big cedars and spruces in this remnant old-growth forest. The trail drops back to the south edge of the north parking area.

6 Gearhart Ridge Path

RATING	DIFFICULTY	ONE-WAY	TERRAIN
★★	1	0.7 mile	Flat

Features: Forest, neighborhood charm; **Contact:** Seaside Visitors Bureau, 888/306-2326

It's only 0.7 mile long, but this woodsy neighborhood path has a unique charm worth seeking out. It also serves as a link in the Oregon Coast Trail.

GETTING THERE

From US 101 north of Seaside, turn west at the sign to Gearhart and follow Pacific Way 0.5 mile to the stop sign at Cottage Avenue. Park on the street.

ON THE TRAIL

The easiest place to find the trail is in the center of town, at about the path's midpoint; walk behind the police and fire station at the intersection of Pacific Way and Cottage Avenue and look for the "No horses or vehicles on Ridge Path" sign. From here the level, elevated path extends north 0.4 mile and south 0.3 mile, winding among trees, crossing little streets, and passing shingled beach cottages tucked into the woods. Hike out and back

Gearhart Ridge Path

from your starting point for a 1.4-mile walk, or make a 1.6-mile loop with Cottage Avenue.

7 Tillamook Head

RATING	DIFFICULTY	ONE-WAY	TERRAIN
★★★★★	5	6 miles	900 feet elevation gain

Clatsop Loop

RATING	DIFFICULTY	ROUND-TRIP	TERRAIN
★★★★★	3	2.7 miles	750 feet elevation gain

Features: Forested headland, outstanding shoreline vistas, historic site, primitive camping, OCT; **Contact:** Ecola State Park, www .oregonstateparks.org or 800/551-6949

Tillamook Head dominates the north coast, especially from Seaside, where it forms a brooding backdrop to the lively beach scene. Signage along the trail that ascends the head reminds hikers of the Lewis and Clark Expedition's acquaintance with this landmark; in January 1806, members of the expedition hiked over Tillamook Head to the mouth of Ecola Creek (present-day Cannon Beach) to barter with locals for meat from a whale they had heard was beached there.

GETTING THERE

From US 101 take the northernmost Cannon Beach exit onto Cannon Beach Loop Road, turning right shortly at the sign to Ecola State Park and following signs about 4 miles, past

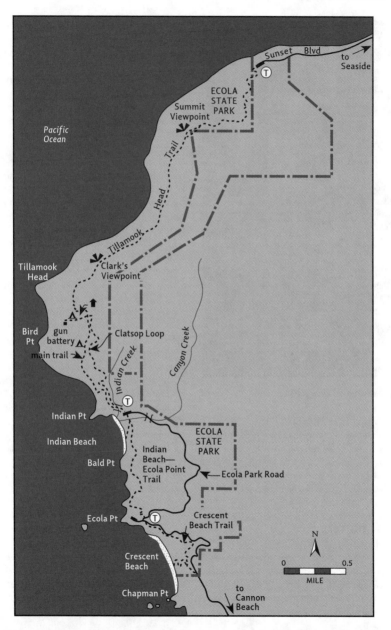

Campsite on Tillamook Head

parking at Ecola Point, to the road's end at Indian Beach. To reach the northern trailhead in Seaside, turn west off US 101 at the traffic light at Avenue U, drive 0.2 mile, turn left onto South Edgewood Road, and follow the road 1.2 miles (it becomes Sunset Boulevard) until it ends at a trailhead parking area.

ON THE TRAIL

The easiest way to see the headland today is via the Clatsop Loop trail, which starts and ends at Indian Beach in Ecola State Park, near Cannon Beach. It takes you up a trail near the bluffs above the ocean to a campsite atop the headland, returning you down an old forest road slightly inland. Alternately, with a shuttle vehicle you could make a one-way trek over the headland between Ecola State Park and Seaside.

To hike the entire trail north to south, park at the trailhead at the south end of Seaside and follow signs onto the main trail. (At about 0.25 mile, another trail comes in from the right—continue straight; shortly, at another unmarked junction, bear right.) After about 0.5 mile the trail steepens and begins switchbacking up the hillside. At 1.5 miles a spur leads to a gravel clearing at the summit of the headland—trees block the view west, but you can gaze east toward the Coast Range—and then loops back to the main trail. From here the trail rolls along the headland, offering occasional ocean views, including one at Clark's Viewpoint (3.7 miles). The trail then descends slowly, switchbacking briefly just before reaching the campsite at 4.4 miles. Continue south 0.2 mile to where the Clatsop Loop trail splits, and take either trail down the south side of the headland to Indian Beach.

Clatsop Loop: From parking at Indian Beach, walk north, cross Indian Creek on a footbridge, and immediately bear left for a clockwise walk on Clatsop Loop. The trail ascends steadily through the old forest, passing some very large, old trees, before topping out and descending briefly to a junction at 1.4 miles. Before returning on the loop trail, continue north 0.2 mile to reach a backpackers' campsite with a vault toilet and a covered picnic table as well as three three-sided log shelters arranged around a fire ring, each with four bunks and plenty snug in a storm. A short walk west leads to the ruins of a World War II gun battery, nearly obscured by vegetation; it was built as part of a series of coastal defense fortifications. Return to the trail junction and bear left to descend 1.3 miles to the Indian Beach parking area via an old road alongside Indian Creek.

8 Indian Beach–Ecola Point

RATING	DIFFICULTY	ROUND-TRIP	TERRAIN
**	2	3 miles	Rolling

Features: Outstanding shoreline vistas, forest, OCT; **Contact:** Ecola State Park, www.oregonstateparks.org or 800/551-6949

Ecola Point and Indian Beach are joined by a 1.5-mile section of the Oregon Coast Trail. It follows the scenic bluff 150 feet above the sea—pleasant for day trippers as well as long-distance hikers.

GETTING THERE

From US 101 take the northernmost Cannon Beach exit onto Cannon Beach Loop Road, turning right shortly at the sign to Ecola State Park and following signs about 4 miles, past parking at Ecola Point, to the road's end at Indian Beach.

ON THE TRAIL

For a north–south hike, drive to the end of the road at Indian Beach and pick up the trail toward the beach. After crossing Canyon Creek, veer left at the junction. The trail rolls along above the ocean, in and out of the woods, offering good views of the remote shoreline. It breaks out of the forest at the edge of the Ecola Point parking area. Return the way you came.

9 Crescent Beach

RATING	DIFFICULTY	ROUND-TRIP	TERRAIN
**	3	2.4 miles	100 feet elevation gain

Features: Hidden beach, forest; **Contact:** Ecola State Park, www.oregonstateparks.org or 800/551-6949

The route to remote Crescent Beach begins on an extension

Ecola State Park

of the Oregon Coast Trail, then drops down the hillside to the pocket beach bounded by Chapman Point.

GETTING THERE

From US 101 take the northernmost Cannon Beach exit onto Cannon Beach Loop Road, turning right shortly at the sign to Ecola State Park and following signs 2 miles to the first parking area in the park, at Ecola Point.

ON THE TRAIL

The trail begins near the rest rooms at the top of the parking area. After climbing some stairs you'll reach the park road; follow it for a few paces until the trail resumes, heading down the bank to the west. It rolls through ancient forest (muddy in places), crossing a creek on a footbridge at about 0.5 mile. At 1 mile you'll reach a junction; turn right, switchback down the steep forested hillside, cross another little bridge, and you're on Crescent Beach. (Bearing straight at the junction, you'll reach the park road in 0.1 mile.) Return the way you came.

10 Chapman Beach

RATING	DIFFICULTY	ROUND-TRIP	TERRAIN
★	3	1.5 miles	Flat

Features: Beach, creek, close to town; **Contact:** Cannon Beach Chamber of Commerce, *www.cannonbeach.org* or 503/436-2623

Most of Cannon Beach proper is clustered south of Ecola Creek, as are most beach goers. For a change, join the locals in a walk north from the creek to Chapman Point.

GETTING THERE

At the north end of Cannon Beach on Cannon Beach Loop Road, turn off heading toward

Chapman Beach with Haystack Rock beyond

TUFTED PUFFINS

Their bright red, triangle-shaped beaks led early coastal settlers to call them sea parrots. But it's their breeding plumage—white facial feathers with straw-colored plumes curving back behind the eyes, contrasting starkly with a glossy black body—that makes tufted puffins such recognizable summer nesters on Oregon's offshore rocks.

Tufted puffins range from northwestern Alaska to southern California; in Oregon they're estimated to be the sixth most common nesting seabird, with a population of about 5000. They're also among the most sensitive to intrusion or disturbance by humans or other land mammals.

Nesting puffins burrow in soil atop islands or in sandy bluffs above beaches. The female lays a single egg in early May; after the chick hatches, about six weeks later, it spends six to eight weeks in the burrow, daily gobbling a dozen fish delivered by both parents.

The best time to see tufted puffins is early in the morning during nesting season, from April through September; watch for short black wings flapping furiously as the birds fly to and from nests. Puffins prefer the seclusion of offshore rocks; the state's largest puffin colony (2000–4000 birds) is on the easternmost rock at Three Arch Rocks. They're easier to see at Haystack Rock at Cannon Beach, Yaquina Head, Cape Meares, Heceta Head, the highway turnout just north of Sea Lion Caves, and Coquille Point.

Ecola State Park Road, but rather than turning right toward the state park, continue straight and park at Les Shirley Park, just ahead on the left.

ON THE TRAIL

The easiest access is at Les Shirley Park. From the park, make your way down to the creek beach, then follow the ocean beach north to Chapman Point. At low tide you may even be able to get around the point, but take care with the tide and slippery rocks. Return the way you came.

11 Haystack Rock

RATING	DIFFICULTY	ROUND-TRIP	TERRAIN
★★★	2	1.5 miles	Flat

Features: Beach, wildlife, tide pools, dory-launching, close to town; **Contact:** Cannon Beach Chamber of Commerce, www.cannonbeach.org or 503/436-2623

A visit to Haystack Rock is almost a required pilgrimage, certainly if it's your first visit to this part

Tide pools at Haystack Rock

of the coast. It's perhaps the Oregon coast's best-known, most-photographed landmark. It's also an ecological gem, with the protection it deserves: The rock itself is protected as part of Oregon Islands National Wildlife Refuge, and the tide pools at its base are considered by the state to be a "marine garden." Take binoculars to get a good view of the seabird activity up high. In summer you might see fishing dories being launched here.

GETTING THERE

From downtown Cannon Beach, drive south to midtown. There's public parking near Gower and Second Streets.

ON THE TRAIL

From the parking area, walk between the motels to the beach access road (no cars allowed), then walk south and west to Haystack Rock. It's an easy walk to the rock. Return the way you came. (There's plenty more beach to the north and south if you care to stretch the outing.)

12 Hug Point

South to Arch Cape:

RATING	DIFFICULTY	ONE-WAY	TERRAIN
★★★	2	1.75 miles	Flat

North to Arcadia Beach:

RATING	DIFFICULTY	ONE-WAY	TERRAIN
★★★	2	1.3 miles	Flat

Features: Pocket beaches, onshore rocks, broad beach, waterfall, historic road; **Contact:** Hug Point State Recreation Site, www.oregonstateparks.org or 800/551-6949

A short drive south of Cannon Beach lies a quiet stretch of sand backed not by houses and motels but by forest and wave-sculpted rock. Visit Hug Point at mid- or low tide to keep your options open. With kids, a short walk north to the point and back with time to play on the beach may be enough. Passing a low point of land, you enter a rock-lined cove with a waterfall spilling onto the sand and caves carved into the cliffs. A road was carved into the rock at Hug Point early in the twentieth century to allow stagecoaches to pass, back when the beach was the Oregon Coast Highway. It's fun to follow on foot while waves splash just below where wheels once rolled.

GETTING THERE
From Cannon Beach, drive south on US 101 about 4 miles to Hug Point State Recreation Site (1.3 miles south of Arcadia Beach).

ON THE TRAIL
For walkers, the beach here offers relative solitude and outstanding views. It's actually on a 7-mile stretch of uninterrupted beach from Cannon Beach to Arch Cape. The walks described here are just two of many possibilities.

South to Arch Cape: Follow stairs onto the beach and head south. After passing through a garden of tall beach rocks, the beach widens, stretching all the way to the cliffs at Arch Cape.

North to Arcadia Beach: Follow stairs onto the beach, walk north past a low point of land, and take the rock "road" around Hug Point. From here Arcadia Beach stretches north to Humbug Point, a natural turnaround point. (If the tide is low enough and you've the energy, continue another 0.75 mile to Silver Point, marking the southern end of Cannon Beach.)

13 Cape Falcon

To Cape Falcon:

RATING	DIFFICULTY	ROUND-TRIP	TERRAIN
★★★★	4	5 miles	240 feet elevation gain

From Arch Cape to base of Neahkahnie Mountain:

RATING	DIFFICULTY	ONE-WAY	TERRAIN
★★★	5	8.5 miles	1200 feet elevation gain

Features: Headland, ancient forest, outstanding shoreline vistas, wildlife, OCT; **Contact:** Oswald West State Park, www.oregonstateparks.org or 800/551-6949

The longest unbroken forested stretch of the Oregon Coast Trail runs from Arch Cape to the highway below Neahkahnie Mountain. Arrange a shuttle car and hike it all, or make a shorter out-and-back hike from the park's parking area to the remote tip of the cape. Along the way you'll cross trickling creeks, listen to forest songbirds, and grab occasional ocean views. Carry binoculars not only to watch for whales but to watch the surfers far below off Short Sand Beach.

GETTING THERE
To park at Oswald West State Park, drive south from Cannon Beach on US 101 about 10 miles to Oswald West State Park. Park at the northernmost of the park's three parking areas along the highway. To park at the Arch Cape trailhead, drive south on US 101 about 5 miles from Cannon Beach. A short distance north of the US 101 highway tunnel, turn east onto Arch Cape Mill Road, turning left onto Third Street in a short distance. The trailhead, marked by a post, is on the south side of Third Street.

HEADLANDS, SEA STACKS, ARCHES, AND BLOWHOLES

About four-fifths of Oregon's shoreline consists of beaches; the remainder is rocky headlands, stalwartly resisting the pounding of countless waves. They and the many sea stacks standing just offshore exist because they're made of tougher volcanic rock, rather than the sandstone, mudstone, and siltstone that have already been eroded, or are in the process thereof, elsewhere on the coast.

Many of the north coast's most recognizable landmarks—Tillamook Head, Hug Point, Arch Cape, Cape Falcon—were formed by basalt flows sandwiched between layers of mudstone or sandstone. Neahkahnie Mountain, Cape Lookout, and Yaquina Head probably began as offshore islands some twenty million years ago. Cape Perpetua is formed of lava that flowed out of undersea vents some forty million years ago, hardening into a massive chunk of basalt that eventually uplifted to form the towering headland. Humbug Mountain is composed of gravelly conglomerate deposited more than a hundred million years ago. And Cape Kiwanda is a sandstone headland, sculpted but not yet destroyed by waves thanks to the protection of a basalt sea stack just offshore.

This same process—natural erosion of rocks of varying composition—is responsible for the many blowholes, spouting horns, cauldrons, and natural arches found along the coast. Some result from a particular pattern of erosion in a sandstone slab, such as the blowhole at Smelt Sands Wayside north of Yachats. Others, such as Devils Churn at Cape Perpetua, create a show when waves smash into an enlarged crack in ancient basalt. Devils Punchbowl, north of Newport, was formed when the roofs collapsed on sea caves formed of sandstone.

ON THE TRAIL

Round trip from Oswald West State Park to Cape Falcon: Follow the trail west from the parking area 0.5 mile to a junction. Bear right and follow the trail along the contours of the forested slope. At 1.8 miles it enters a clearing, offering good views south to Neahkahnie Mountain and Short Sand Beach. At 2.5 miles the trail emerges onto the cape's treeless tip; here a maze of trails cuts through the brush leading to various viewpoints north and south. Return as you came.

One-way from Arch Cape to base of Neahkahnie Mountain: Pick up the trail at the suspension bridge over Arch Cape Creek, next to its confluence with a cascading side stream. Follow the trail up about 0.1 mile, turning right at the trail post pointing toward Cape Falcon.

Here the trail carries hikers around the back side of Arch Cape, climbing gradually through a lovely climax forest. At about 1 mile the sight and sound of the ocean return; shortly the trail turns onto an old road and begins a descent toward US 101, hitting the highway at about 1.75 miles. Walk south about 50 yards and pick up the trail across the road.

The next mile or so stays within earshot, and sometimes sight, of US 101, rolling along through lovely old-growth forest and crossing the road into the community of Cape Falcon at about 2.5 miles. The trail eventually veers west, leaving the highway noise behind. It rolls along for a while and then begins an ascent, steep in places, to an old blowdown area that was logged over some years ago. As the trail starts to crest the ridge (at about 3.5 miles), look back toward the north for a glimpse up the coast and of Haystack Rock.

The trail now drops steadily until it reaches the sea cliff and begins rolling along the shoreline, offering occasional views. At 4.5 miles, a clear—but unmarked—spur trail leads to the cape's tip. Continuing south, the trail rolls along the hillside. At the trail junction at 7 miles bear right, following the sign about

Neahkahnie Mountain from trail to Cape Falcon

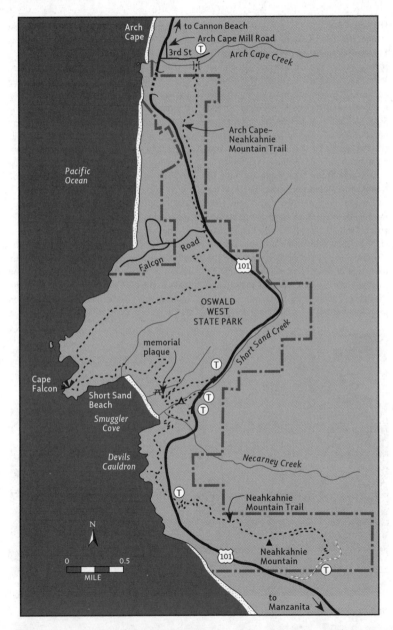

Arch Cape

to Cannon Beach

Arch Cape Mill Road

3rd St

Arch Cape Creek

Arch Cape–
Neahkahnie
Mountain Trail

Pacific
Ocean

Falcon   Road

101

OSWALD
WEST
STATE PARK

Short Sand Creek

memorial
plaque

Cape
Falcon

Short Sand Beach

Smuggler
Cove

Devils
Cauldron

Necarney Creek

Neahkahnie
Mountain Trail

N

0   0.5
MILE

101

Neahkahnie
Mountain

to
Manzanita

0.25 mile to the picnic area overlooking the beach. (A left turn leads to Oswald West State Park parking area in 0.5 mile.)

The trail resumes at the southeast corner of the picnic area. The route through the park is a little confusing due to a proliferation of trails, but signs (and the map accompanying this trail description) should help. Cross a bridge over Short Sand Creek, bear right at the next junction, continue west a short distance, cross a suspension bridge over Necarney Creek, and begin switchbacking fairly steeply up the hillside. About 0.5 mile from Necarney Creek the grade moderates, heading south not far

from US 101. Pass through a tunnel of vegetation and emerge onto a grassy hillside. Shortly you'll pass a spur trail (it leads west 0.1 mile to a fenced overlook above the churning sea, called Devils Cauldron) before the trail heads up to meet US 101 at a trailhead shared with Neahkahnie Mountain (Hike 15).

14 Short Sand Beach

RATING	DIFFICULTY	ROUND-TRIP	TERRAIN
**	2	1 mile	150 feet elevation gain

Tunnel-like trail between Short Sand Beach and Neahkahnie Mountain

Features: Pocket beach, forest, creeks, primitive camping; **Contact:** Oswald West State Park, www.oregonstateparks.org or 800/551-6949

Looking for a short leg-stretcher with the kids? Join the surfers and head out from Oswald West State Park to this crescent of beach backed by deep woods. Consider spending the night; in summer, carts are available to help you carry your gear 0.3 mile from car to campsite.

GETTING THERE

From Cannon Beach, drive south on US 101 about 10 miles to Oswald West State Park. Park at the middle of the park's three parking areas along the highway.

ON THE TRAIL

Follow trail signs down through the woods. (Either of the three will work; the trail from the middle parking area is the most direct route to the beach.) Bear right at the bridge to cross Short Sand Creek and you'll reach a picnic area just above the beach. Down on the beach there's good tidepooling if you time it right. If your party is game, explore a little farther on the network of interconnecting trails here; the bridge across Necarney Creek is just south of Short Sand Creek. When you're ready, return more or less as you came.

15 Neahkahnie Mountain

From south trailhead:

RATING	DIFFICULTY	ROUND-TRIP	TERRAIN
★★★★★	4	3 miles	890 feet elevation gain

From north trailhead:

RATING	DIFFICULTY	ROUND-TRIP	TERRAIN
★★★★★	5	9 miles	1200 feet elevation gain

Loop hike:

RATING	DIFFICULTY	ROUND-TRIP	TERRAIN
★★★★★	5	8 miles	1200 feet elevation gain

Features: Headland, ancient forest, outstanding shoreline vistas, wildflowers, OCT; **Contact:** Oswald West State Park, www.oregonstateparks .org or 800/551-6949

Neahkahnie Mountain was a vision-quest site for the original residents of this coastline, and still is—in a certain sense—for many contemporary hikers. Some seek inner visions, or the clarity that comes from maintaining target heart rate for a good, long period. Others are content with the magnificent views southward from Neahkahnie to the Nehalem River Valley. In spring look for white trillium, pink salmonberry, and other wildflowers along the trail; we heard the whump-whump of a grouse on a recent ascent.

GETTING THERE

To reach the south trailhead, turn east off US 101 about 1.5 miles north of Manzanita (or 13 miles south of Cannon Beach) at the hiker sign and drive 0.5 mile up a bumpy gravel road to a trailhead parking area. To reach the north trailhead, pull off the west side of US 101 when you see the OCT post on the highway's east side, 1 mile south of the southernmost parking area at Oswald West State Park.

ON THE TRAIL

The south approach is shorter, but you miss the magnificent old-growth forest blanketing the north slope. My preference: Get a friend to drive a shuttle car, then hike up the south trail and down the north (one way, 6 miles).

South approach: From the Oregon Coast Trail (OCT) marker post at the trailhead, the trail climbs steadily, varying between dark

View south from Neahkahnie Mountain

stands of Sitka spruce and open, brushy slopes with outstanding views. At 1.2 miles there's an OCT post on the summit ridge. To reach the summit, bear left up an old road toward a collection of telecommunications antennas; a rough trail continues around the building to the knobby summit. Return the way you came for 3 miles round trip.

Loop hike: To continue down the north side, return to the ridge-top junction and pick up the trail leading north at a slow descent around the back side of the mountain. About 0.5 mile beyond the junction the trail reaches the southern ridge, enters a clearing, and then begins dropping down through

gorgeous ancient forest, first with shorter switchbacks and later with long traverses. Minutes from the bottom it emerges from the woods and leads across the open hillside to end 4.2 miles from the ridge-top junction, on US 101 about 1.5 miles north of where the southern trailhead access road leaves the highway. Return to your car via highway shoulder and gravel road.

North approach: If you're starting here, look for the OCT post on the east side of US 101 about 1 mile south of the last parking area at Oswald West State Park. Follow the reverse of the loop hike description, for a 4.5-mile ascent.

16 Nehalem Spit

RATING	DIFFICULTY	ROUND-TRIP	TERRAIN
★★	3	4.2–5 miles	Flat

Features: Ocean beach, bay, dunes, wildlife, adjacent to campground; **Contact:** Nehalem Bay State Park, www.oregonstateparks.org or 800/551-6949

Nehalem Spit encloses Nehalem Bay with a long south-pointing finger of sand. If you walk to the tip, you can return via ocean beach, river beach, or sand trail. The trail isn't as scenic as the beach options—in fact, it's a little claustrophobic. But it can provide a welcome break from wet winds if the weather turns on you. For a one-way hike, prearrange a shuttle across the mouth of the spit.

GETTING THERE
From US 101 about 14 miles south of Cannon Beach, follow signs west and south through Manzanita to Nehalem Bay State Park. Drive to the day-use area, south of the campground.

ON THE TRAIL
You could start this walk in Manzanita, but an 8-mile round trip on soft sand is a bit much for most people. Instead, from the day-use area parking lot, walk past the rest rooms and over

Sailboarding on Nehalem Bay

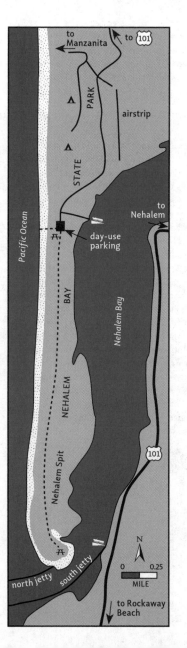

the dune to the beach, then head south. Keep your eyes open for shorebirds on the beach, especially in the spring and fall. After 2.1 miles of walking, you'll reach the rock-piled north jetty; you're likely to see harbor seals just outside the jetty.

From here you have three options: (1) return as you came; (2) follow the curve of the river beach to a little picnic site and outhouse (the beach here is a favorite haunt of harbor seals), then continue north along the bay another 2.2 miles to the park's boat ramp (if tide permits) and take the road 0.2 mile back to your car; or (3) follow a sandy horse trail that leads through the center of the dunes back to the parking area.

OREGON COAST TRAIL, NORTH COAST

Distance: About 66 miles, with boat shuttle at Nehalem Bay

Start at Parking Area C in Fort Stevens State Park, near the end of the road to the south jetty of the Columbia River, and follow the beach south for 16 miles. About 0.5 mile north of the Necanicum River in Gearhart, look for a path leading into the dunes and onto Third Street. Follow it east to the start of the Gearhart Ridge Path (Hike 6). Follow it 0.5 mile south to its terminus at F Street. Walk east along F Street, following the main road as it curves (and changes names) until it reaches US 101. Follow the highway into Seaside, then veer right onto North Holladay Drive. At 12th Avenue head west, crossing the Necanicum River, to where the road ends at the beach. Walk south on the beach toward Tillamook Head. Nearing the headland and the Lanai Motel, watch for an opportunity to walk up onto Sunset Boulevard, which ends on Tillamook Head. Follow Hike 7 (there's a great campsite with three-sided shelters and toilet at the summit), plus Hikes 8 and 9, bearing straight at the junction toward Ecola State Park Road.

Follow the road out of the park to the main road through Cannon Beach, cross Ecola Creek, and drop back onto the beach at the north end of town. Walk the beach 5.5 miles to Arch Cape (Silver Point, Humbug Point, and Hug Point can all be rounded at low tide). Leave the beach about 100 yards north of the cliffs and Arch Cape Creek on a

BEACHES AND SAND

Some 262 miles of Oregon's 326-mile coastline is sandy beach. Where'd all that sand come from? Mostly from the mountains that back the beach. Much of the Coast Range is built of sedimentary rock that itself began as sand sixty million years ago, when most of Oregon was under water. Geologic forces thrust the sea floor up to create a mountain range. Rain and rivers eroded the sandstone and other soft rock, carrying it out to sea and creating a huge reservoir of sand on the continental shelf.

Waves move sand toward the shore, and prevailing winds blow it farther inland except where its movement is blocked by harder volcanic headlands. Sand also moves north and south, within "littoral cells" of beach between headlands. During the last ice age the sea level was much lower than it is now and the shoreline was many miles to the west, allowing sand to move more easily south and, in larger quantities, north (pushed by winter waves from the southwest). That's why, today, you can find sand from southern Oregon's Klamath Mountains all the way up on the Clatsop Plains, north of Tillamook Head.

Every beach is constantly moving, shifting south in summer and back north in winter, growing and shrinking with the seasons. In winter the beach is cut back by high waves that push the sand into deeper waters, where it accumulates in offshore bars and creates two lines of breakers in winter. Come summer, low waves move the sand back onshore. The size of the sand grains on a particular beach helps determine the steepness of its slope: Very fine sand creates the almost level beaches of Clatsop County in the north, for example, while the gravelly beach at the end of Yaquina Head has a relatively steep slope. In between is the incline of fine gravel, sparked with bits of shell and jewel-like agates, found at places like Smelt Sands Wayside north of Yachats.

Bridge over Arch Cape Creek, Oregon Coast Trail

little trail that turns into Leach Street. Follow Leach Street east almost to US 101, turn right on Cannon Street, and follow it as it leads south and east, under the highway. At Third Street turn right; in one block, the OCT resumes; follow Hikes 13 and 15.

At the south end of Hike 15, follow the gravel road 0.5 mile down to US 101 and walk south on the road shoulder 1.3 miles. Turn west at the sign to Neahkahnie Beach, and walk down the road until you hit the beach and can resume beach walking to Nehalem Spit. Jetty Fishery (503/368-5746) routinely ferries hikers across the mouth of Nehalem Bay by prearrangement, and for a fee (otherwise, leave the beach at Nehalem Bay State Park and follow road signs to US 101). Continue down the beach past Rockaway to Barview County Park. Follow the park road to US 101 and walk along the highway shoulder to the boat basin at Garibaldi.

the north-central coast

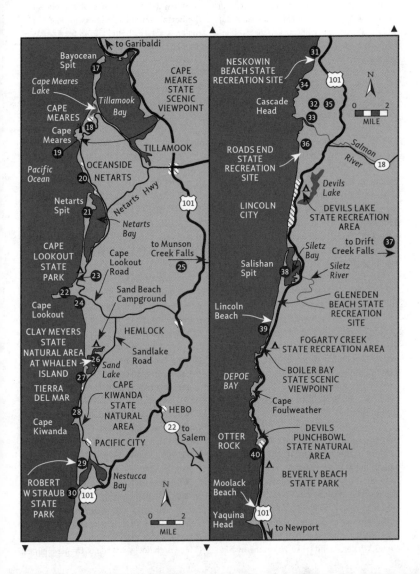

SPIT WALKING

To those called to the shore simply to walk on the sand, a beach is a beach—unless it's a spit. Looks the same at the start. But on a spit, each step you take propels you farther from the mainland, out to the unknown, where no one you meet—if indeed you meet anyone—comes from the other direction, and the only way out is the way you came. It could be a little intimidating. Or for some, a little compelling.

On a spit, the walk's end—or at least, the turnaround—comes gently: The spit simply narrows and narrows and the sand finally just runs out. But there's drama enough in the waters off the tip. Here river meets sea, and but for a brief moment of equilibrium at the turn of the tide, it's a constant battle for supremacy. It's in the weird angle of waves, the colliding swells, the tidal rips that run upriver with no loss of momentum, like wakes from invisible boats. The opposite shore may be just a stick's throw away, but with that wild water between, it could be another planet. It feels like the end of the earth, which it is, in a sense. It's windy out here, too, and a little bit lonely.

But beach walkers are suckers for solitude. And if you pay the slightest attention, it's clear you're not alone. There are the gulls, of course, and the shorebirds that hurriedly survey the tidal flats for food in a choreographed rhythm like a well-rehearsed avian corps de ballet. And if you look into the waves just inside the river's mouth, often as not a fellow mammal—fur sleek, dark seal head bobbing like flotsam—is looking back, eyeing you.

Oregon's coast has more small rivers than its neighbor states to the north or south, which means more river mouths, and more sand spits. On the north-central coast alone, there are four significant spits: Bayocean at the mouth of Tillamook Bay, Netarts (the longest of the four) north of Cape Lookout, Nestucca, and Salishan at the mouth of the Siletz. A trail circles Whalen Island (Hike 26) in the middle

of the Sand Lake estuary. The bays enclosed by these spits offer excellent opportunities for kayaking as well.

Spit walking is just one of the pleasures the north-central coast offers to hikers. The region is actually better known for a series of dramatic capes—Meares, Lookout, and Kiwanda—strung south from Tillamook Bay, followed by Cascade Head rising high above the Salmon River estuary. All four offer dramatic hiking trails: through forest, to wild cliff-top vistas, or between stretches of beach.

To reach what's known as the Three Capes area, leave US 101 at Tillamook (or Pacific City, northbound). Each of the three capes has its own personality and appeal. Cape Meares is topped by a historic lighthouse and surrounded by a federal wildlife refuge. The tip of fingerlike Cape Lookout is a good bet for spotting whales during the winter or spring migration. Sandstone Cape Kiwanda offers the best sand-dune sliding north of the Siuslaw River.

In earlier times, Cascade Head—like Neahkahnie Mountain to the north—served as a vision-quest site for indigenous people living near the banks of the Salmon River. Thanks to preservation efforts by both private and public agencies, its original magic remains. From the open meadows on its steep seaward face, you're treated to arguably the best view on the entire Oregon coast.

Interpretive center. The Tillamook Naval Air Station Museum (*www.tillamookair.com* or 503/842-1130) doesn't much concern itself with natural history; rather, it displays more than two dozen vintage flying aircraft in the world's largest wooden structure, a World War II blimp hangar.

Wildlife-watching. Good bird-watching sites include Bayocean Spit (bay, tide flats, and forest), the lighthouse viewpoint and trail at Cape Meares, and Devils Lake, especially by boat in winter; canoe and kayak rentals are available. (Three Arch Rocks, the site of Oregon's largest seabird colonies and the state's first coastal bird refuge, is off Oceanside, but you need a spotting scope for decent views.)

The US Fish and Wildlife Service has established a new national wildlife refuge at Siletz Bay and is in the process of acquiring lands around the bay for this refuge. Good spots to pause for some wildlife-watching are the public dock at the end of 51st Street, at the south end of Lincoln City, or the long highway turnout on the west side of US 101 about 1.5 miles to the south. Look for gulls, terns, and pelicans in summer and ducks, loons, and grebes in winter. Harbor seals can be seen hauled out near the water's edge across the channel from the dock year-round.

Boiler Bay State Scenic Viewpoint, just north of Depoe Bay, is known as one of the best mainland sites in Oregon for watching seabirds: brown pelicans August through October, Pacific loons in fall, marbled murrelets in spring and fall, and black oystercatchers year-round, as well as more unusual species.

To see seals and sea lions, try Oceanside Beach State Recreation Site, Nestucca Bay, and Siletz Bay. Best whale-watching spots are the tips of Cape Meares, Cape Lookout, and Cape Kiwanda, Boiler Bay, the seawall and the enclosed Whale Watching Center at Depoe Bay, and Cape Foulweather. Charter boats leave Depoe Bay all summer for whale-watching, but the viewing can be just as good from the seawall or from the town's sheltered Whale Watching Center, with its educational displays and fifty feet of ocean-facing windows. Orcas are sometimes spotted in Tillamook Bay.

Tidepooling. (See Respectful Tidepooling, p. 31.) The rocky coastline in the north-central region means lots of tide pools. Check out the south side of Cape Meares, accessible via the beach access at Short Creek (1 mile north of Oceanside). There's a small tide-pool area at the base of Maxwell Point, just north of Oceanside Beach Wayside, and a bouldery tide-pool area on the south side of Cape Lookout. You can do vertical tidepooling on tall rocks south of Cape Kiwanda. Boiler Bay has excellent tide pools, formed on bedrock shelves and between boulders, but access is tricky; park at the tiny, signed pullout 0.1 mile north of Boiler Bay State Scenic Viewpoint (or at the viewpoint itself) and follow a little scramble trail down the cliff. Otter Rock, just north of Devils Punchbowl State Natural Area, is one of the coast's premier intertidal habitats; do your best to limit your impact when visiting here.

Off-road cycling. Bayocean Spit trail (Hike 17) is open—and inviting—to cyclists. The route follows an old roadbed, making the cycling easy and leaving plenty of room for both hikers and bikers. You'll find bike tracks on the bayside of Netarts Spit (Hike 21), but it's rough going.

Camping/hostels. Cape Lookout State Park has a very appealing campground, well off US 101 and right on the beach. Among private campgrounds in the area, one in Netarts is right on the beach. There are more private and county campgrounds in the vicinity of Sand Lake, and one Forest Service campground, Sand Beach, used principally as a staging area for off-road vehicles. To the east, the Forest Service has three primitive campgrounds in the forest at Mount Hebo, catering mostly to anglers. From Lincoln City to Gleneden Beach, the coastline is extensively developed, with lots of motels but only one public campground: Devils Lake State Recreation Area, just outside Lincoln City. Beverly Beach State Park, just north of Yaquina Head, is large and right on the beach (and US 101).

For reservations at state park campgrounds, call 800/452-5687.

Travelers' tips. Oceanside is a lovely, tiny town and a good place to get a meal. Pacific City has a few small, good restaurants as well as grocery and hardware outlets where you can stock up for your trip. Little Neskowin has a well-stocked mercantile, motels, and an excellent neighborhood cafe. Lincoln City sprawls from Road's End to the mouth of the Siletz—some six miles of commercial development along US 101 (motels, dining and espresso, discount/variety stores, a large outlet mall) with six miles of nonstop, action-packed beach to the west. Gleneden Beach is the site of the coast's preeminent resort—Salishan—with golf, gracious accommodations, and excellent dining; across US 101 are shops and a noteworthy art gallery. Depoe Bay is a busy, touristy, fun little town arrayed along US 101 and around its tiny bay, where you can arrange a whale-watching boat tour.

Recommended hikes. Bayocean Spit (Hike 17) is wonderfully remote and varied; Netarts Spit (Hike 21) is even more remote, if you're up for a 10-mile round trip. Also recommended is the trail to the tip of Cape Lookout (Hike 22) and the beach walk over Cape Kiwanda to Tierra del Mar (Hike 28). For views, Cascade Head can't be beat (Hikes 32 and 33). If your timing's right (mid-July through December), check out Harts Cove (Hike 34). Drift Creek Falls, with its suspension bridge, is a great, short novelty hike (Hike 37).

17 Bayocean Spit

RATING	DIFFICULTY	ROUND-TRIP	TERRAIN
★★★★★	4	8 miles (beach trail loop, 7.3 miles)	Flat

Features: Ocean beach, bay, forest, wildlife, primitive camping, OCT; **Contact:** Tillamook Chamber of Commerce, 503/842-7525 or www.tillamookchamber.org

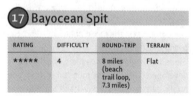 *In 1906 a real estate broker from Kansas City envisioned a second Atlantic City on the sand spit separating Tillamook Bay from the Pacific Ocean.*

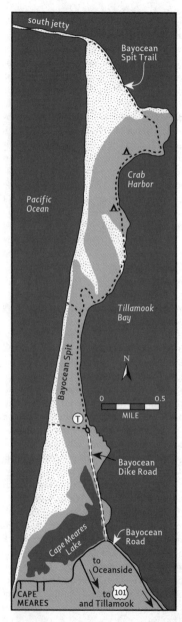

By 1914 as many as 600 building lots had been sold in what was called Bay Ocean Park, and it was becoming a bustling community. But the unstable spit couldn't support the development. Lots began eroding steadily, and in 1950 the last house on the spit washed into the sea. Today Bayocean Spit belongs to hikers, mountain bikers, and bird-watchers who wander the beach or the forested bay-side trail. A couple of campsites near the tip (protected from the wind by groves of trees) offer relatively remote overnight camping.

GETTING THERE

From US 101 in Tillamook, follow signs to Three Capes Scenic Route and head west and north about 8 miles. Watch for the big sign de-scribing the spit's history on the bay side of the road. Turn off the main highway and drive north 1 mile on graveled Bayocean Dike Road. Park at the road's end.

ON THE TRAIL

The main trail to the tip of the spit leads north out of the parking area; there's also a 0.3-mile trail to the beach that leads west through the dunes from the northwest corner of the parking area.

The main trail leads straight north, following the bay shore and offering expansive bay views. At about 1 mile the trail splits; bear right (a left turn leads 0.2 mile on a sandy trail over the foredune and down onto the beach). The Bayocean Spit trail passes a gate and enters the

BALD EAGLES

Stand alongside any bay on the Oregon coast and eventually you'll see a bald eagle. Every major estuary on the coast has at least one nesting pair of the huge birds, and those that nest here winter here as well. Winter is a good time to spot bald eagles on the coast, because in addition to the year-round residents, a number of birds migrate in from Alaska, Montana, and Canada to winter here too.

Bald eagles feed primarily on fish and waterfowl. As a result, they're never far from water. They nest high in large trees, building huge nests (seven to eight feet across) on a foundation of sticks and softening them with a lining of moss, grass, feathers, and pine needles. When they're not soaring high over a bay or above the ocean, bald eagles may be seen perched on tall snags over the water. When you're out on a high headland looking for whales, keep an eye peeled for a large bird with a bright white head soaring along the cliffs.

The bald eagle was removed from the federal endangered species list in 2007. Their reproductive success has not been as good on the Oregon coast as in other parts of the state, but these birds are holding their own here and even slowly increasing in number. Wildlife officials suspect that agricultural and industrial contaminants (such as dioxins, DDT, and PCBs) from the Columbia River may be a factor. Human disturbance near nests is another. Wildlife officials urge visitors to obey all trail-closure signs and to use only marked trails, particularly in or near refuges.

Trail on Bayocean Spit

forest. At about 1.4 miles it rises slightly, curves, and then drops back down to the bay shore. Near 2.5 miles, a cozy campsite appears in the trees off the trail to the left, and there's another campsite a short distance farther, near a rock with a plaque commemorating the completion of Tillamook Bay's south jetty in 1979. A couple of minutes farther down the trail there's a two-seater outhouse in a meadow off to the right. The last 0.6 mile of trail is along the windy tip of the spit, ending at the south jetty.

Cyclists, return as you came. Hikers have the option of making a loop by following the beach south about 2.3 miles to where the pine-topped dune to the left drops to merge with the grass-covered foredune. About 25 yards from the end of the forested hill, look for a trail (barely discernible) leading up and over the foredune to meet the main trail, and follow it south about 1 mile back to where you started.

18 Cape Meares

From beach to summit:

RATING	DIFFICULTY	ONE-WAY	TERRAIN
★★★	3	1.7–2 miles	800 feet elevation gain

High Tide Trail loop:

RATING	DIFFICULTY	ROUND-TRIP	TERRAIN
★★★	2	2.1 miles	100 feet elevation gain

To Big Spruce:

RATING	DIFFICULTY	ROUND-TRIP	TERRAIN
★★★	1	0.4 mile	Flat

Features: Headland, ancient forest, outstanding shoreline vistas, beach, landmark tree, OCT;

Contact: Cape Meares State Scenic Viewpoint, www.oregonstateparks.org or 800/551-6949

The section of Oregon Coast Trail stretching between the top of Cape Meares and the beachside community (also called Cape Meares) at the base of the cape offers day hikers several options. Make a one-way hike up (or down) between the town and the top of the cape, or make the same hike round trip. Or skip the heart-pounding walk up the cape by starting in town and making a gentle 2.1-mile low-elevation loop linking the High Tide Trail with a walk down the beach. Atop the cape, a short stroll leads to a massive example of the definitive north coast tree, the Sitka spruce.

GETTING THERE

To park at Cape Meares State Scenic Viewpoint trailhead, follow signs from US 101 in Tillamook to Three Capes Scenic Route, continuing on Cape Meares Loop Road about 10 miles to Cape Meares State Scenic Viewpoint. To park at the northern (beach) trailhead in Cape Meares, from Tillamook follow Three Capes

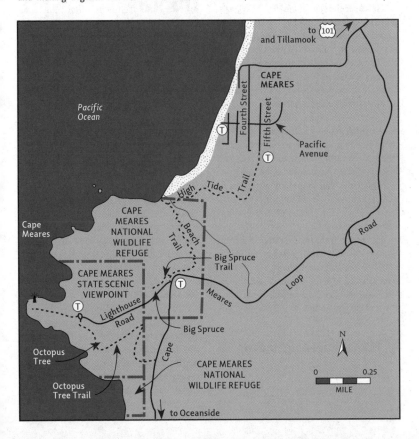

Scenic Route about 8 miles into the community of Cape Meares, turn left onto Fourth Street, then turn right on Pacific Avenue and continue to parking at the beach access.

ON THE TRAIL

Oregon Coast Trail from beach to summit:
From the Pacific Avenue beach access, follow the beach south 0.7 mile, picking up the Oregon Coast Trail at the base of the cliffs; follow it 0.2 mile up to a trail junction. If the tide is high, instead of hiking the beach walk up Pacific Avenue, turn left on Fifth Avenue, and walk about four blocks to the start of the High Tide Trail at a gate. (Don't be put off by "No Trespassing" signs here; vehicles aren't allowed, but hikers are.) Follow an old roadbed as it climbs about 100 feet in elevation through alder woods, then narrows to a footpath as it descends slowly to a small creek and rises again to the trail junction, 1.2 miles from the beach access.

From the junction the trail climbs, steeply in places, first through a logged area now dominated by alders and then into older Sitka spruce forest. At the top of the cape, turn left at the trail junction to reach the trailhead at the park road.

High Tide Trail loop: Park at the Pacific Avenue beach access in Cape Meares and follow the High Tide Trail as described above. Return on the beach.

Big Spruce Trail: The short trail to the "Big Spruce" starts at a parking area just inside the entrance to Cape Meares State Scenic Viewpoint, shared with the Oregon Coast Trail. At the immediate trail junction, bear left to follow the trail circling around to this very straight, very big spruce.

19 Cape Meares Lighthouse

Lighthouse Trail:

RATING	DIFFICULTY	ROUND-TRIP	TERRAIN
★★	1	0.5 mile	Flat

Octopus Tree and OCT:

RATING	DIFFICULTY	ROUND-TRIP	TERRAIN
★★	1	0.25 mile to Octopus Tree (0.75 mile one-way to end of trail)	Flat to rolling

Features: Ancient forest, landmark tree, lighthouse, OCT; **Contact:** Cape Meares State Scenic Viewpoint, www.oregonstateparks.org or 800/551-6949

The highlight here is the 1890 lighthouse atop the cape. Daily in summer and on spring and fall weekends, visitors can enter and get a close-up view of its huge crystal Fresnel lens, which was hand ground in France in 1887. It's no longer in service; instead, an automated beacon activated in 1963 shines from a concrete block house just behind the old lighthouse tower. The cape may be even better known for an oddity called the Octopus Tree: a massive Sitka spruce with six arms instead of a central trunk.

GETTING THERE

From US 101 in Tillamook, follow signs to Three Capes Scenic Route, continuing on Cape Meares Loop Road about 10 miles to Cape Meares State Scenic Viewpoint. Turn right at the park entrance onto Lighthouse Road and park at the end of the road.

ON THE TRAIL

From the road's end parking, a paved trail leads straight west, descending slightly to end at the lighthouse at the tip of the cape. The state park here is surrounded by Cape Meares National Wildlife Refuge, protecting important seabird nesting habitat; keep your eyes open for bald eagles hunting above the offshore islands, or for puffins flying in and out of nests on the south side of the cape. Return as you came.

Cape Meares Lighthouse

The trail to the Octopus Tree heads south past the rest rooms. It's a short stroll to the tree, enclosed by a wooden fence, presumably to discourage climbing. Return as you came. If you're hiking the Oregon Coast Trail, continue south, passing a stellar view southward of Three Arch Rocks and Maxwell Point. The trail gently descends to cross a creek and then gradually ascends to end at the highway about 0.6 mile south of the park entrance road.

20 Oceanside Beach

RATING	DIFFICULTY	ROUND-TRIP	TERRAIN
★★	2	3 miles	Flat

Features: Beach, wildlife, close to town; **Contact:** Oceanside Beach State Recreation Site, *www.oregonstateparks.org* or 800/551-6949

The beach at Oceanside has plenty of attractions: tide pools, seabirds, your own beach blanket perhaps. If you're in the mood for a stroll, consider a 1.5-mile walk to where North Fall Creek runs into the sea at the mouth of Netarts Bay, where you'll find more birds and fewer people than at the beach right in town.

GETTING THERE
From US 101 at Tillamook, take Three Capes Scenic Route west and south to the town of Oceanside and follow signs to Oceanside Beach State Recreation Area.

ON THE TRAIL
Walk on the beach, heading south from the parking area. In 1.5 miles the creek stops you, unless you're willing to wade. In that case you could continue another mile to the boat ramp at Netarts, if tide permits. Return as you came (or arrange a pickup at Netarts).

21 Netarts Spit

RATING	DIFFICULTY	ROUND-TRIP	TERRAIN
★★★	5	10 miles	Flat

Features: Ocean beach, bay, wildlife, adjacent to campground; **Contact:** Cape Lookout State Park, *www.oregonstateparks.org* or 800/551-6949

The simplest route on one of the coast's longest no-road, no-ORV (off-road-vehicle) sand spits is to start at Cape Lookout State Park campground and walk north up the beach until the sand runs out. Alternately, if the tide's low (or at least not high) walk north on the bay side and return via the beach.

GETTING THERE
From US 101 in Tillamook, follow signs west toward Three Capes Scenic Route. After crossing

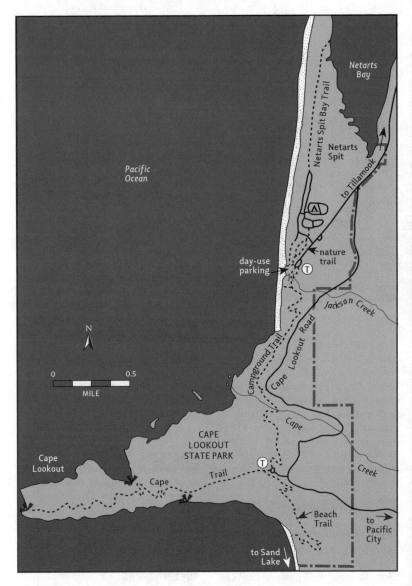

the Tillamook River, either turn north to loop around Cape Meares or turn south onto Netarts Highway to cut directly west toward Netarts and south to Cape Lookout State Park, about 10 miles from US 101 via the Netarts Highway. Park in the park's day-use area.

ON THE TRAIL

From the day-use area stroll north through the campground. The informal bayside trail starts next to campsite A-53 as a gated gravel road heading north. The road ends after about 0.5 mile and becomes a narrow trail, unmaintained (with overhanging scotch broom and shore pine) but easy to follow. At 0.7 mile the trail emerges from the woods onto the tidal flats along the bay. The trail continues north, cutting across mud and grass and cushiony pickleweed. You don't really need a trail here, but it tends to be the driest route, with the most solid footing. If you wish to shortcut the loop, do it before you've walked more than about 2 miles; beyond that point the forest in the center of the spit becomes impossibly dense with shore pine, salal, and huckleberry. Eventually the mudflats give way to open sand as you near the tip, across from Netarts and 5 miles from where you started. Return as you came or loop back down the long ocean beach.

Netarts Spit

22 Cape Lookout

RATING	DIFFICULTY	ROUND-TRIP	TERRAIN
★★★★★	4	5 miles	Rolling

Features: Outstanding shoreline vistas, forest, wildlife, adjacent to campground; **Contact:** Cape Lookout State Park, www.oregonstateparks.org or 800/551-6949

Cape Lookout, a steep-cliffed promontory extending nearly 2 miles due west into the Pacific, is a wonderful destination for hikers, with more than 7 miles of trail connecting miles of open beach. This hike to the tip of the cape and back is the most popular year-round. The 400-foot-high viewpoint at the end of the trail is considered one of the best sites for whale-watching on the Oregon coast. Gray whales may pass as close as 100 yards, but binoculars always improve viewing. Be prepared for mud on the trail in rainy periods.

GETTING THERE

From US 101 in Tillamook, follow signs west toward Three Capes Scenic Route. After crossing the Tillamook River, either turn north to loop around Cape Meares or turn south onto Netarts Highway to cut directly west toward Netarts and south to Cape Lookout State Park. Pass the park's campground entrance and continue another 2.8 miles on Cape Lookout Road to the trailhead parking area.

ON THE TRAIL

Two trails start side by side here. The Campground Trail, on the right, leads to the campground (Hike 23). To hike out to the tip of the cape, take the left-hand trail, Cape Trail, and at the junction with the Beach Trail (Hike 24), continue due west. The trail rolls west, gradually descending, passing a southward viewpoint at 0.6 mile and a northward viewpoint at 1.2 miles. The route returns to the south side of the cliffs, offering occasional views; listen for the moan of the

Cape Lookout

OREGON SILVERSPOT BUTTERFLIES

While wandering over salt-sprayed meadows on the north coast in the summertime, keep your eyes open for a medium-size orange butterfly flitting in the wind. It may be the Oregon silverspot, or hippolyta fritillary (*Speyeria zerene hippolyta*), a butterfly uniquely adapted to this harsh environment. Shrinking of its native habitat, due mainly to industrial and residential development as well as the spread of nonnative woody plants, has led to its listing as a threatened species. Habitat restoration efforts, however, are helping to stabilize its numbers.

Except at Mount Hebo in Tillamook County, the silverspot generally stays within a mile of the coast, frequenting open meadows touched by salt spray—the native coastal prairie atop Cascade Head, for example, and around Rock Creek and Big Creek north of Florence. While members of some butterfly species all emerge into adult form within days of one another and live for just a few weeks, Oregon silverspots seem to emerge from the larval stage over an extended period and to have an unusually long life span; they may be spied anytime from July through September if conditions are right. This evolutionary strategy has helped the Oregon silverspot survive. A slight wind or even a cloud cover may keep other butterflies from flying, but some Oregon silverspots are out mating or laying eggs almost all summer, regardless of conditions.

Note the dark brown coloration of its body and at the base of its wings; scientists believe this unusual coloration helps it absorb and retain heat where it's needed most. Its namesake spots are along the underside of the wings, visible only if the butterfly is poised on a plant with its wings folded.

offshore buoy as you approach the trail's end at the cape's tip. Return as you came.

23 Cape Lookout Campground Link

RATING	DIFFICULTY	ONE-WAY	TERRAIN
★	3	2.5 miles	840 feet elevation gain

Features: Forested headland, adjacent to campground, OCT; **Contact:** Cape Lookout State Park, www.oregonstateparks.org or 800/551-6949

This stretch of the Oregon Coast Trail serves day hikers as a link from the sea-level campground to trails taking off from atop Cape Lookout (Hikes 22 and 24). Between the campground and the picnic area is a 0.25-mile loop hike designed for young children, with sixteen marked stations identifying plants and forest processes. Pick up a trail guide brochure at the campground registration booth. A second short loop trail along Jackson Creek trail has a panel explaining fish habitat restoration efforts here; look for it off the park entrance road east of the RV dump station.

GETTING THERE

From US 101 in Tillamook, follow signs west toward Three Capes Scenic Route. After crossing the Tillamook River, either turn north to loop around Cape Meares or turn south onto Netarts Highway to cut directly west toward Netarts and south to Cape Lookout State Park. Continue to the park's campground, about 10 miles from US 101 via Netarts Highway. At the campground, follow signs to the picnic area at the park's south end (or follow the trail from your campsite).

ON THE TRAIL

Various spur trails through the day-use area make the trail's beginning a little confusing. Look for a gravel service road that eventually leads onto a narrow footpath. The trail winds up and up through the woods; at 1.2 miles you'll pass a spur road leading out to Cape Lookout Road. Stick to the main trail, crossing Cape Creek at about 1.6 miles. The trail continues along a rolling grade to emerge at the cape-top trailhead.

24 Cape Lookout Beach

RATING	DIFFICULTY	ROUND-TRIP	TERRAIN
★★★	3	4 miles (5.75 miles one-way to Sand Lake)	840 feet elevation gain

Features: Headland, ancient forest, ocean views, beach, adjacent to campground, OCT; **Contact:** Cape Lookout State Park, www.oregonstateparks.org or 800/551-6949

From the top of Cape Lookout you can hike 2 miles down to a secluded beach with a small tidepool area. Continue your hike down the beach before returning, if you like, or arrange for a shuttle car at Sand Beach Campground.

GETTING THERE

From US 101 in Tillamook, follow signs west toward Three Capes Scenic Route. After crossing the Tillamook River, either turn north to loop around Cape Meares or turn south onto Netarts Highway to cut directly west toward Netarts and south to Cape Lookout State Park. Pass the campground entrance and continue another 2.8 miles on Cape Lookout Road to the trailhead parking area.

ON THE TRAIL

Take the left-hand trail, Cape Trail, leading out of the trailhead parking area, but about 75 yards down the trail, make a sharp left turn down the hill at the junction with the Beach Trail. From here the trail descends gently through an old-growth Sitka spruce forest, crossing a creek at about the halfway point and switchbacking now and then. The trail ends close to the base of the cape. Continue down the beach if you like; the first mile or so is off-limits to vehicles, but you may encounter dune buggies past that point. Return as you came.

If you have a shuttle vehicle to pick you up, continue down the beach a total of about 3.75 miles to the outlet of Sand Lake and the ORV staging area at Sand Beach Campground, at the end of Galloway Road off Sandlake Road.

25 Munson Creek Falls

RATING	DIFFICULTY	ROUND-TRIP	TERRAIN
★★	1	0.5 mile	Flat

Features: Ancient forest, waterfall; **Contact:** Munson Creek State Natural Area, www.oregonstateparks.org or 800/551-6949

If you're bypassing Three Capes Scenic Route, traveling on US 101 instead, consider a forest walk and a picnic

at Munson Creek Falls, something of a sur-
prise along this route. Enjoy this relic of ancient rainforest, with its western red cedars
and, at 260 feet tall and 8 feet in diameter,
what may be the world's second-tallest Sitka spruce.

GETTING THERE
About 7 miles south of Tillamook on US 101
turn west at a sign to the falls and follow that
road 1.5 miles east to a gravel parking area.

ON THE TRAIL
From the parking area, the trail to the right
leads to a picnic spot at the base of the 319-
foot waterfall, the tallest in the Coast Range.
Return as you came.

26 Whalen Island

RATING	DIFFICULTY	ROUND-TRIP	TERRAIN
★★★	2	1.5 miles	Rolling

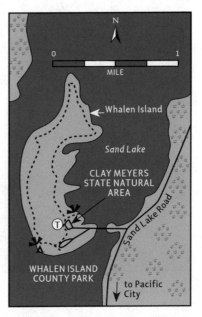

Features: Estuary views, forest, beach, adjacent to campground; **Contact:** Clay Meyers
State Natural Park at Whalen Island, www.oregon
stateparks.org or 800/551-6949

*Whalen Island is a tiny, dense-
ly forested island smack in
the middle of Sand Lake estuary. At high tide
it's surrounded by water; at low tide, by mudflats teeming with life. Forest borders the estuary to the north and south; to the west
waves pound the ocean beach at the entrance
to the shallow bay. The state acquired most of
the island and, in 2004, completed a delightful
loop trail circumnavigating the island.*

GETTING THERE
From the stoplight in the middle of Pacific City,
turn west, following signs to Three Capes Loop.
You'll cross the river and turn north, continuing
through the community of Tierra del Mar. At 5.5

miles from Pacific City, turn west at the sign to
Whalen Island. Go 0.2 mile, cross the estuary on
a bridge, and bear right into Clay Meyers State
Natural Area at Whalen Island.

ON THE TRAIL
From the parking area, take the trail north,
bearing left where a spur trail on the right
leads to an overlook at the edge of the estuary. The loop trail heads north, along the
estuary, but views are limited by the dense
tangle of shore pine, salal, and huckleberry.
The trail rises toward the island's north end,
where views open up of the water and hills to
the north. The trail then curves south, following the island's ocean side and offering opportunities to traipse down to the narrow sandy
beach, especially as you near the island's
south end. Finally the loop trail meets the
gravel wheelchair-accessible path from the
parking lot at a viewpoint overlooking Sand

Whalen Island

Lake. Follow it back to the parking lot, bearing left at the spur trail leading to Whalen Island County Park a rustic campground adjacent to the state natural area.

27 Tierra del Mar to Sand Lake

RATING	DIFFICULTY	ROUND-TRIP	TERRAIN
★	3	4 miles	Flat

Features: Beach, close to homes; **Contact:** Pacific City–Nestucca Valley Chamber of Commerce, *www.pacificcity.net* or 888/549-2632

In summer it's possible to walk on sand the entire distance from the base of Cape Lookout, wading the outlet to Sand Lake, over Cape Kiwanda, to Pacific City, even to Neskowin if you can arrange a boat shuttle at Nestucca Bay. With US 101 far inland, it's an appealing stretch of beach. More likely you'll walk only a portion of that

17 miles. The beachside community of Tierra del Mar is a good place to begin a short beach walk to Sand Lake.

GETTING THERE
From US 101 at the community of Hemlock, south of Tillamook, turn west on Sandlake Road and follow it, bearing left at the junction with Cape Lookout Road, to the community of Tierra del Mar. Best beach access is at the south end of town, where houses give way to dunes.

ON THE TRAIL
Heading north up the beach from the beach access, pass by beach houses, then open dunes; the outlet to Sand Lake is at 2 miles. Explore a bit, wade the lake's outlet if you like, but be aware that off-road vehicles frequent the beach and dunes north of the lake year-round. Return as you came (unless you arrange a shuttle at Sand Beach Campground, on the north side of the lake).

28 Cape Kiwanda to Tierra del Mar

RATING	DIFFICULTY	ROUND-TRIP	TERRAIN
★★	3	4 miles	120 feet elevation gain

Features: Outstanding shoreline vistas, beach, dune, tide pools, dory-launching; **Contact:** Cape Kiwanda State Natural Area, *www.oregonstate parks.org* or 800/551-6949

The highlight is the climb up Cape Kiwanda's sandy saddle—a 120-foot ascent that feels more like 300—and the sliding descent on the other side. Unlike its sister capes to the north, Cape Kiwanda is made of sandstone. It's eroding much faster than the coast's basalt capes, but along the way the waves are shaping its cliffs into gorgeous ocher sculptures. Minus tides in summer expose intertidal life on vertical surfaces of rocks at the cape's base.

GETTING THERE

Seven miles north of Neskowin on US 101, turn west at signs to Pacific City and continue 3 miles into town. Follow signs to the dory parking lot at Cape Kiwanda State Natural Area.

ON THE TRAIL

Walk this stretch of beach from either end, round-trip or one-way. For the most dramatic views of the cape's tip, climb up the steep sand slope toward the western end of the cape. Old fencing attempts to keep the curious

Low tide at Cape Kiwanda

away from the most dangerous cliffs on top. This is not a through route to the north side of the cliff, however.

To get through to the beach on the north, return to the dory beach and follow the gradual sand slope up the neck of the cape and over the top. Continue up the beach—a total of 2 miles to the beach access at the south end of Tierra del Mar. Return as you came. (Alternatively, you could combine this hike with Hike 27, and continue all the way to Sand Lake—an 8-mile round trip.)

If you're lucky you may get to watch dories launching or landing at the foot of the cape. This is the more heavily used of two sites on the Oregon coast where beach-launched motorized fishing dories still put in; the other is at Cannon Beach, alongside Haystack Rock. The boats are generally launched on an outgoing tide. The process requires considerable skill: back the trailered boat into the surf, gun the engine so the dory slides off into the shallows, drive quickly up the beach and park, run back to the boat and begin pushing it out through the surf from the stern, and then, at the right moment, give one last shove, wriggle over the transom, grab the wheel, fire up the engine, and gun it straight out through the surf.

29 Nestucca Spit

RATING	DIFFICULTY	ROUND-TRIP	TERRAIN
**	2	4 miles	Flat

Features: Ocean beach, bay, dunes, wildlife, adjacent to campground; **Contact:** Robert W. Straub State Park, www.oregonstateparks.org or 800/551-6949

Elbow-shaped Nestucca Bay is bounded on the northwest by Nestucca Spit, undeveloped and protected as a state park. Walk the beach to the

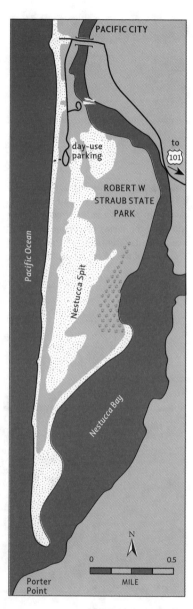

Baby harbor seal

spit's tip and back, or loop back along the bay, cutting back across the dunes to complete your return via beach.

GETTING THERE

Drive 7 miles north of Neskowin on US 101, turn west at signs to Pacific City, and continue 3 miles into town. Turn west at the stop light, cross the Nestucca River, then turn left again, following signs to Robert W. Straub State Park. The road ends at the park's beach-access day-use parking area.

ON THE TRAIL

From behind the rest rooms, cut over the short dune to the beach and head south. (Note what the trail looks like here, so you'll recognize it on the way back.) It's a straight shot to the end of the spit; enjoy the bird life, and possibly a seal's dark head in the waves. Return as you came, or continue around the tip of the spit along the dark Nestucca Bay for a distance. It may be possible to continue around

the bay at low tide, but not in my experience. Either backtrack around the spit or cut across the dunes to return to the beach, if it's not too marshy. You'll know you missed the trail to your car if you reach the more obvious beach access west of town, 0.7 mile farther north.

30 Porter Point

RATING	DIFFICULTY	ROUND-TRIP	TERRAIN
★	1	1 mile	Flat

Features: Beach, wildlife, solitude; **Contact:** Pacific City–Nestucca Valley Chamber of Commerce, www.*pacificcity.net* or 888/549-2632

A short walk, more like a stroll, leads around Porter Point to a secluded cove just inside the mouth of Nestucca Bay. It's a very quiet stretch of beach most of the year, not well-known (though I've never been there while the church camp at the end of the road was in full swing).

Porter Point

GETTING THERE

South of Pacific City, turn west off US 101, about 1.5 miles south of where the highway crosses the Nestucca River, onto Winema Road. Continue 0.5 mile to a beach access next to the church camp.

ON THE TRAIL

Walk north, around the point, where the beach widens at the river's turn to the sea. Return as you came. (Or for a longer walk, combine with Hike 31.)

31 Proposal Rock

Southbound to Cascade Head:

RATING	DIFFICULTY	ROUND-TRIP	TERRAIN
★★	1	1.4 miles	Flat

Northbound to Porter Point:

RATING	DIFFICULTY	ROUND-TRIP	TERRAIN
★★	4	8 miles	Flat

Features: Beach, onshore rocks, close to homes;
Contact: Neskowin Beach State Recreation Site, *www.oregonstateparks.org* or 800/551-6949

A turn-of-the-century marriage proposal here gave this tall, near-shore monolith its name. From the recreation site at Neskowin Beach, take a short walk to (and around, if tide permits) Proposal Rock, continuing south until the beach ends at Cascade Head. For a longer walk, head north up the beach, all the way to Porter Point (Hike 30) at the mouth of the Nestucca River.

GETTING THERE

At Neskowin, about 10 miles north of Lincoln City, pull off US 101 at signs to the Neskowin Beach State Recreation Site parking area.

ON THE TRAIL

Southbound to Cascade Head: Follow signs a short distance to the beach, crossing Hawk Creek then following an asphalt path and a gravel road to reach the beach alongside a cyclone fence. You can't miss Proposal Rock, so named at the successful conclusion to a turn-of-the-century coastal settler's courtship. The beach continues south for about 0.5 mile before running into Cascade Head. Return as you came.

Northbound to Porter Point: Long-distance walkers might choose to head north instead. It's about 4 miles from Proposal Rock to the mouth of the Nestucca by beach. Houses are strung along the beach for the first couple of miles; after that there's plenty of solitude until you reach the church camp at the end of Winema Road (see Hike 30). Unless you've left a shuttle vehicle here, return as you came.

32 Cascade Head—North Access

RATING	DIFFICULTY	ROUND-TRIP	TERRAIN
★★★★★	1	2 miles	Rolling

Features: Outstanding shoreline vistas, ancient forest, wildflowers, wildlife; **Contact:** The Nature Conservancy, *www.thenatureconservancy.org* or 503/230-1221; **Closed:** January 1–July 16

View south from Cascade Head

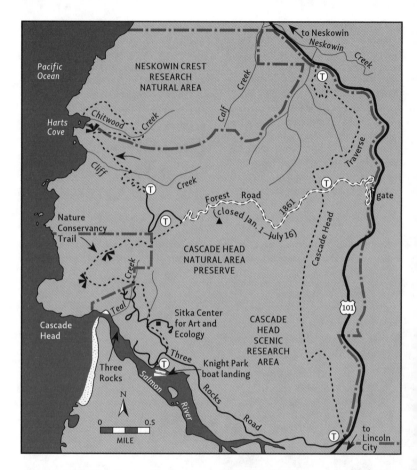

In 1966 The Nature Conservancy bought 300 acres at the western tip of Cascade Head, preserving the unique prairie and rainforest habitat there; this mellow stroll leads to and through the preserve. The road to this trailhead is closed from New Year's Day to midsummer to keep people out of Harts Cove (the south access trail, Hike 33, is open at that time). Enjoy this hike late summer through early winter.

GETTING THERE

Turn west off US 101 onto Forest Road 1861 (gated during the trail closure period) about 4 miles north of State Highway 18. Follow the gravel road west 3.2 miles to a trailhead pull-out on the left.

ON THE TRAIL

The trail begins as an old road following the hillside's contours through deep, cool woods.

After passing under a sign announcing your entry into The Nature Conservancy's Cascade Head Natural Area Preserve, you'll reach a signboard and kiosk with trail brochures at 0.6 mile. The nearly level trail emerges from the forest onto the grassy, open headland at 0.9 mile. From here it's a short walk to a benchmark signifying the summit knoll. Return as you came. (You can also continue down—straight down—to the south viewpoint, another 0.7 mile, and then return as you came, or—with a shuttle vehicle—walk out to the south access, Hike 33.)

33 Cascade Head—South Access

To south viewpoint:

RATING	DIFFICULTY	ROUND-TRIP	TERRAIN
★★★★★	3	4.6 miles	270 feet elevation gain

To summit knoll:

RATING	DIFFICULTY	ROUND-TRIP	TERRAIN
★★★★★	4	6 miles	1050 feet elevation gain

Boardwalk on southern Cascade Head Trail

Features: Outstanding shoreline vistas, ancient forest, wildflowers, wildlife; **Contact:** The Nature Conservancy, *www.thenatureconservancy.org* or 503/230-1221

Cascade Head is pure magic. Trails on the headland traverse old-growth forest as well as rejuvenating second growth and open prairie. Bobcats roam the forest, Pacific giant salamanders—the largest salamanders in the world—creep along the alder-shaded streambanks, chinook run up the Salmon River in the fall, and Oregon silverspot butterflies flit over the grassy headland in the summer. This hike, approaching the headland's tip from the south, is the most popular route on Cascade Head. Hikers often see hawks circling in the wind or deer grazing on the open headland late and early in the day. The view of the estuary and coastline to the south is awesome.

GETTING THERE

From US 101 (1.3 miles north of State Highway 18) turn west onto Three Rocks Road and drive 2.5 miles, just past Savage Road, to parking at Knight Park boat landing.

ON THE TRAIL

From Knight Park walk back up Three Rocks Road to Savage Road, watching for a boardwalk on the right signaling the start of a little access trail. Follow it 0.4 mile to the Sitka Center road and continue on Savage a short distance to where the trail resumes (roadside parking here is minimal).

The trail heads up a steep hillside, then levels off, crossing several small creeks on wooden footbridges and boardwalks. Gently ascending, the trail follows the hillside's contours through the forest, emerging onto the open prairie a short walk from the south viewpoint near a line

of fencing, 2.3 miles from the Knight Park trailhead. Return as you came, unless you're in the mood for some serious exercise in the form of a steep climb to the summit knoll, another 0.7 mile and 680 feet straight up. (The trail continues another mile to the north trailhead, 4 miles one way, inaccessible by car January through mid-July; see Hike 32.)

34 Harts Cove

RATING	DIFFICULTY	ROUND-TRIP	TERRAIN
★★★★★	4	5.8 miles	800 feet elevation gain

Features: Outstanding shoreline vistas, ancient forest, wildlife, primitive camping; **Contact:** Hebo Ranger District, *www.fs.fed.us/r6/siuslaw* or 503/392-3161; **Closed:** January 1–July 16

Forest Service Road 1861 is closed from New Year's to midsummer, to avoid disturbing certain easily ruffled residents, which means Harts Cove is hikeable only late summer through early winter. So you miss the spring wildflower bloom; you can still catch the noisy hordes of California sea lions riding the waves and lounging on offshore rocks at Harts Cove beginning in October. The trail winds through deep forest—some ancient, some younger—with occasional glimpses of ocean and, in season, a chorus of sea lion barks echoing through the trees.

GETTING THERE

Turn west off US 101 onto Forest Road 1861 (gated during the trail closure period) about 4 miles north of State Highway 18. Follow the gravel road west 4.1 miles, passing The Nature Conservancy trailhead, to where it ends at the Harts Cove trailhead.

Opposite: Harts Cove

ON THE TRAIL

The trail switchbacks down 1 mile to Cliff Creek, then ascends slowly as it follows the slope's contours north. A sign announces the trail's entry into Neskowin Crest Research Natural Area; just beyond the sign are a bench and a view of Harts Cove from the north. The trail continues, traveling deep into a ravine, crossing Chitwood Creek at about 2 miles, and emerging from the forest at 2.9 miles. Stroll down the open slope and settle into one of the informal viewpoints above Harts Cove. Be aware that there is no way to get into (or, rather, out of) the vertical-walled cove itself, so don't try. A couple of flat, protected spots in the forest above the meadow look appealing for overnight camping. Return as you came.

35 Cascade Head Traverse

RATING	DIFFICULTY	ONE-WAY	TERRAIN
★★★	5	6 miles	1120 feet elevation gain

Features: Headland, ancient forest, OCT; **Contact:** Hebo Ranger District, www.fs.fed.us/r6/siuslaw or 503/392-3161

Preservation of Cascade Head actually began back in 1934,

ESTUARIES

Estuaries are places, like the bays at river mouths, where freshwater running down rivers or streams mixes with saltwater pushed in by the tides. Oregon's bays amount to drowned river mouths, flooded by rising seas after the retreat of the last ice age. The complex environment in estuaries supports a wealth of plant life and creates important habitat for fish and shellfish, birds, and marine mammals. Compared with Washington and California, Oregon doesn't have many *large* estuaries, but lots of smaller ones: twenty-two formally classified estuaries, from the Columbia River's huge mouth to the tiny estuary at the outlet of the Winchuck River.

Hundreds of species depend upon estuaries for all or part of their life cycle. Among them are many full-time residents such as shrimp, crabs, and other invertebrates. Ocean-dwelling crabs return to estuaries to feed and breed. Ocean fish such as herring and anchovies use estuaries to spawn, and young salmon and steelhead migrating down rivers linger in the estuaries to gently acclimate to seawater before starting their ocean journeys. It's common to see harbor seals and sea lions bobbing in bays or lounging on bay shores or docks year-round.

A great variety of birds use estuaries for just a season. Shorebirds range the mudflats for a bite to eat in the spring and fall, when ducks bob on the swells or graze the shoreline. Pelicans dive for fish in summer. Other birds live by estuaries year-round, from great blue herons at the water's edge to bald eagles soaring high above.

when Congress set aside nearly 12,000 acres as an experimental forest. That tract stretches from the shoreline across US 101 into the Coast Range and includes the Salmon River estuary. This section of the Oregon Coast Trail traverses that tract and is well worth walking to enjoy the old-growth and second-growth forest through which it leads. Adjacent lands have since been set aside, protecting whole watersheds and forest ecosystems for research in applied forestry as well as studies of forest and estuary ecosystems, various animal species, and global climate change.

GETTING THERE

The north trailhead is on the west side of US 101 about 2 miles south of Neskowin; there's room for a few cars to park here. The south trailhead is on the north side of Three Rocks Road at its junction with US 101, 1.3 miles north of State Highway 18; here there's room for several cars.

ON THE TRAIL

Forest Road 1861 cuts across the trail at its high point, giving you options for shorter one-way hikes during the road's open season (mid-July to January 1). You could hike it round trip, but this hike really lends itself to a one-way hike with shuttle vehicle.

From the north trailhead, the trail follows a fairly level route west along an old road, above a melodious creek, for 0.4 mile. Reaching a trail post, it veers left onto a narrower forest path and heads uphill. It continues up, gradually switchbacking or following the contours of the hill, alternating between old-growth hemlock, second-growth forest, deep Sitka spruce forest, and salmonberry-filled clearings. Nearing Forest Road 1861, it tops out, drops through an alder grove, and meets the road at 2.5 miles.

The trail resumes across the road about

Shelf fungus, Cascade Head

50 yards to the west, immediately entering a lovely parklike ancient forest of hemlock, Douglas fir, and Sitka spruce. It follows the edge of a bog, filled with skunk cabbage blooming in March, then crosses a creek on a footbridge and stair-steps through the bog on a boardwalk. After moving into second-growth forest, the trail seems to split about 2 miles from Forest Road 1861; bear left on the more well-worn path. Soon the trail begins switchbacking down the hill, crossing creeks a few times and ending at the south trailhead 3.5 miles from the FR 1861 crossing.

36 Roads End

RATING	DIFFICULTY	ROUND-TRIP	TERRAIN
★	1	2.5 miles	Flat

Features: Beach, tide pools; **Contact:** Roads End State Recreation Site, www.oregonstateparks.org or 800/551-6949

It's a short but worthwhile walk north from Roads End Beach to the end of the sand "road." Once you're in the lee of the headland, a breezy summer day can quickly turn balmy.

GETTING THERE

From US 101 at the north end of Lincoln City, turn west at the sign for Roads End and follow signs 1 mile west and north to Roads End State Recreation Site.

ON THE TRAIL

Follow the beach north until you're stopped by the saddle-shaped headland. Houses line the bluff for about 1 mile; the end of the beach is rocky and more remote. Scramble around the point to find hidden realms of rock and pools if the tide permits, but watch the tide carefully so you don't get stranded.

Roads End Beach

37 Drift Creek Falls

RATING	DIFFICULTY	ROUND-TRIP	TERRAIN
★★★★★	3	3.2 miles (3.5 miles with North Fork Loop on return)	280 feet elevation gain

Features: Suspension footbridge, waterfall, forest; **Contact:** Hebo Ranger District, www .fs.fed.us/r6/siuslaw or 503/392-3161

This hike is named for the waterfall, and it's dramatic enough: an unnamed tributary pours over a mossy cliff and free-falls seventy-five feet into a pool in Drift Creek. But it's the suspension bridge near the trail's end that's the real draw—like nothing else on any Oregon trail. It hangs between support towers, each twenty-nine feet tall, and is anchored to the bedrock on either side of Drift Creek. From the middle of the bridge, you get a good look at the falls—if you dare. (Its gentle, swaying motion can be a bit unnerving.)

GETTING THERE

From US 101 at the south end of Lincoln City, 1 mile north of the Siletz River bridge, turn east onto Drift Creek Road, follow it for 1.5 miles, and bear right onto South Drift Creek Road. In 0.4 mile veer left at the sign to Drift Creek Falls Trail (Forest Road 17)

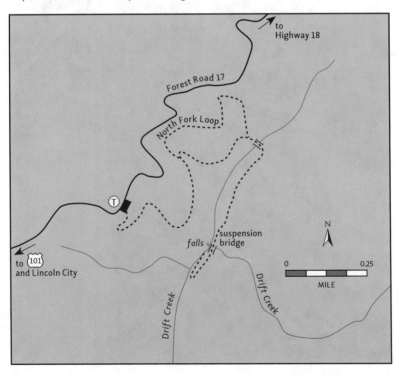

Bridge at Drift Creek Falls

and, in another 0.9 mile, left again. Continue another 3.3 miles and turn left. Follow the paved road 6.2 miles more to the trailhead parking area on the right. Alternatively, from State Highway 18 at Rose Lodge (just west of milepost 5), turn south onto Bear Creek Road (which becomes Forest Road 17) and follow the main road, bearing right at the fork at 4.6 miles and reaching the trailhead at 9 miles.

ON THE TRAIL

The trailhead is east of Lincoln City, a good twenty minutes off the highway from the north or south but well worth the drive. The route is paved and is well signed (but the signs are often vandalized; follow directions above).

The hike to the falls descends gently, mainly through former clear-cuts now growing trees ranging from about fifteen to fifty years old, plus a narrow band of century-old trees. Pass a bench at 0.5 mile, then at 0.7 mile the North Fork Loop takes off to the left

(see below). Continuing straight you'll pass the other end of the North Fork Loop and, at 1 mile, a small footbridge crossing an unnamed creek; at 1.3 miles the trail reaches the suspension bridge. To reach the trail's end, cross the bridge and follow the trail's switchbacks down 0.3 mile, dropping 100 feet in elevation to the creek's edge.

Return as you came, or take the North Fork Loop to wind up through a magnificent stand of old forest that has grown since a fire here more than a hundred years ago. The loop ascends, steeply in places, before leveling off and dropping to meet the main trail.

38 Salishan Spit

RATING	DIFFICULTY	ROUND-TRIP	TERRAIN
★	3	7 miles	Flat

Features: Ocean beach, wildlife, close to homes; **Contact:** Gleneden Beach State Recreation Site, *www.oregonstateparks.org* or 800/551-6949

Salishan Spit

Across the mouth of Siletz Bay lies Salishan Spit, a finger of land pointing north and lined most of the way with beach homes. Don't expect remoteness on this beach hike, but the reward at the spit's end is a wild realm of dunes, great for wildlife-watching.

GETTING THERE

From the south end of Lincoln City, continue south on US 101 about 3 miles and turn west at the sign to Gleneden Beach State Recreation Site, just south of Salishan.

ON THE TRAIL

The road up the spit is private, open only to homeowners and guests of Salishan Resort, and the nature trail that starts behind the service station at the shopping area, winding west between bay and fairway to the beach, is restricted to homeowners and guests as well. However, the beach itself—as everywhere on the Oregon coast—is open to the public.

From the recreation site, follow the beach north about 3 miles. At that point the narrowing spit becomes a wild realm of dunes covered with beach grass and scattered stands of shore pines. The Siletz River mouth is a good spot for seal- and bird-watching. Casual trails run through the dunes here—a good option if the weather turns on you. Otherwise, return via the beach to your starting point.

39 Fishing Rock

RATING	DIFFICULTY	ROUND-TRIP	TERRAIN
★★	3	4 miles	Flat (excluding 50-foot ascent at Fishing Rock)

Features: Beach, onshore rocks, close to homes;
Contact: Fogarty Creek State Recreation Area, www.oregonstateparks.org or 800/551-6949

Beach north of Fishing Rock

VELELLA VELELLA

If you spend any time strolling sandy Pacific beaches, especially in late spring or early summer, you're bound to stumble across corpses of *Velella velella*, or by-the-wind sailor, little jellyfish each an inch or two long, strewn sometimes by the tens of thousands along the tide line. Like other jellyfish, *Velella* have stinging cells in their tentacles, mild enough that you might not feel a sting if you handle them. But take care not to rub your eyes or touch your mouth after touching them.

In life, purple-blue *Velella* drifts the open ocean, like other jellyfish, on an air-filled elliptical float, a central feeding polyp and a fringe of tentacles dangling down to capture plankton. Its most recognizable characteristics are its brilliant blue-purple color and the "sail" that extends up from its oval float at a forty-five-degree angle.

The angled sail and prevailing northerly winds tend to hold *Velella* offshore, like a fleet of tiny sailboats; before a moderate wind, they tack at about forty-five degrees away from a following wind, and light southerly winds tend to blow them away from shore. Strong, prolonged winds from the south and west tend to spin *Velella* around, causing them to follow the wind at a closer angle and forcing scores of them up onto the beach, sometimes in vast swaths. There they perish and decay, their floats and sails diminishing from pliable blue boats to nearly transparent scraps of parchment.

Velella is found in temperate and tropical seas around the world, with slight variations. On the Asian side of the north Pacific, for example, the sail is angled in the opposite direction, corresponding with the wind patterns off those shores. Some scientists speculate that the two types occur together in midocean and are sorted, east and west, by the winds.

You can't see it from the highway, but Fishing Rock is worth seeking out. Watch waves crashing on the pocket beach to the south. Sheer cliffs add to the rock's drama, but take care with young children. Then clamber down the narrow trail on the rock's north face to access long Lincoln Beach. There are plenty of houses here; if you don't mind that, enjoy a northbound walk as far as Gleneden Beach, 2 miles to the north—or farther (see Hike 38).

GETTING THERE

Fishing Rock is at the west end of Fishing Rock Street in the town of Lincoln Beach (about 6 miles south of Lincoln City), across the highway just north of the northern entrance to

Fogarty Creek State Recreation Area. With the highway divider, the street is accessible only from the southbound lanes of US 101; if you're northbound, watch for the street sign and make a U-turn at the next opportunity. There's room for only two or three cars at the street-end beach access.

ON THE TRAIL

Crisscrossing trails, muddy and laced with roots, lead a short distance onto the windy top of the rock. To get to Lincoln Beach, follow the paths back east and north to a little draw that leads down to the beach, stretching north to the Siletz. Turning around at Gleneden Beach State Recreation Site results in a 4-mile walk. Return as you came (or leave a shuttle car here).

Wish you could get to that pocket beach you saw south of Fishing Rock? You can, through the park at Fogarty Creek. At the south end of Lincoln Beach, the park is an excellent place to picnic out of the wind, especially for families with children. The park is on the east side of US 101. Picnic tables are scattered along Fogarty Creek, which is spanned by several arching wooden footbridges. Asphalt paths on either side of the creek lead under US 101 to the pocket beach. From US 101, look for signed roads leading into the park from both the north and the south.

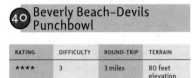

40 Beverly Beach–Devils Punchbowl

RATING	DIFFICULTY	ROUND-TRIP	TERRAIN
★★★★	3	3 miles	80 feet elevation gain

Features: Tidal punchbowl, tide pools, ocean vistas, beach walking, adjacent to campground, OCT; **Contact:** Devil's Punchbowl State Natural Area, www.oregonstateparks.org or 800/551-6949

Devils Punchbowl hosts a dramatic water show at high tide; a short walk to the north, extensive tide pools teem with life at low tide. The combination makes it an ideal destination for an out-and-back hike (or one way, with a shuttle car for campers at Beverly Beach State Park). Day visitors to Devils Punchbowl may take the beach walk after exploring the punchbowl area.

Otter Crest refers to the shoreline here; Otter Rock refers to the community at Devils Punchbowl as well as the rock 0.5 mile offshore at Beverly Beach. Place names are all that's left of the sea otter on the Oregon coast; history records that Otter Rock is the site where, in 1906, the last remaining sea otter in Oregon was shot. Successful reintroduction of sea otters off the Washington coast bodes well for plans to reestablish the species along Oregon's shore, too.

GETTING THERE

Devils Punchbowl is on Otter Rock Loop Road, off US 101 about 8 miles north of Newport or 5 miles south of Depoe Bay. Beverly Beach State Park is 3.5 miles north of Yaquina Head (north end of Newport) off US 101.

ON THE TRAIL

Starting at Beverly Beach State Park, walk north on the beach 1.25 miles until the cliffs stop you at Otter Rock. The beach here is popular with surfers. Stairs lead up the cliff, emerging across the access road from the rest rooms. Walk west a short distance to Devils Punchbowl, formed by the collapse of the roof over two intersecting sea caves in the sandstone just offshore. At high tide, water enters the bowl and churns wildly. It's particularly dramatic during winter storms. To see the tide pools (or pocket beach, if the tide's in), continue north from the rest rooms 2.5 blocks

Stairway to beach from Devils Punchbowl

on C Avenue to the start of a 0.1-mile asphalt path to the beach. At the far end of the beach, more stairs lead up to the Inn at Otter Crest resort complex.

OREGON COAST TRAIL, NORTH-CENTRAL COAST

Distance: About 70 miles, with boat shuttles at Tillamook, Netarts, and Nestucca Bays

From Garibaldi, either arrange a boat ride across Tillamook Bay to the tip of Bayocean Spit (Hike 17), following the beach to the base of Cape Meares, or walk the highway shoulder around Tillamook Bay to Tillamook and west to the community of Cape Meares. Follow trails over the cape (Hikes 18 and 19), then follow the road into Oceanside. Walk the beach to Netarts (Hike 20). Hitch a boat ride to the tip of Netarts Spit (Hike 21) following the beach to the base of Cape Lookout, or follow the road around Netarts Bay to the picnic area at Cape Lookout State Park. Follow trail over the neck of the cape and back down to the beach (Hikes 23 and 24).

Wade the outlet to Sand Lake and continue south to the dory parking lot in Pacific City, on the south side of Cape Kiwanda. You may be able to arrange a boat ride across the Nestucca River at a marina in Pacific City; if so, walk to the tip of Nestucca Spit and ferry across. If not, follow Cape Drive through town to US 101, walking the highway from Pacific City to Winema Road;

follow it west 0.5 mile to the beach and head south to Neskowin. Leave the beach and follow the highway 2 miles south to the trail over Cascade Head (Hike 35). Resume highway walking, returning to the beach next to the Shiloh Inn at the north end of Lincoln City.

Walk the beach to the mouth of Siletz Bay, returning to the highway at the gazebo at Siletz Bay Park to cross Schooner Creek and the Siletz River. Return to the beach at Gleneden Beach State Recreation Site, continuing to Lincoln Beach (Hike 39). Walk the highway to Otter Rock Loop Road; follow it to Devils Punchbowl, where stairs lead down the cliff to the beach (Hike 40). Pass Beverly Beach State Park and continue south another 2 miles to a scramble trail just north of Moolack Shores Motel, returning to the highway to ascend Yaquina Head.

HERMIT CRABS

Have you ever picked up an empty-looking snail shell that turned out to harbor a hitchhiking hermit crab? Once past the shock of that first pinch, kids may find that hermit crabs are their favorite seashore creatures, easy to spot as they scamper across a pool, hauling their houses with them. They're also one of the most common types of crab found in Oregon's intertidal areas; look for them between or under rocks, or under masses of seaweed.

Unlike their well-armored cousins, hermit crabs have no hard covering over their soft, coiled abdomens, forcing them to curl into abandoned snail shells to protect themselves. Eventually a hermit crab outgrows its shell and must find a new one, sometimes fighting other crabs for the right to occupy a particular shell if homes are in short supply. Once it finds a suitable shell, the crab stays put, leaving only when it's time to move into larger quarters. The most common type of hermit crab found in the midtide zone is *Pagurus hirsutiusculus*, as hairy as its name suggests.

Hermit crabs are exemplary recyclers. When one moves into a new shell, its old home is quickly occupied by a new resident, whose shell in turn is rapidly taken over by another hermit crab, and so on. Usually, the last move in a chain reaction like this is by a very small crab from a very dilapidated shell. To whom did the shell originally belong? Most often hermit crabs take up residence in shells from such common snails as *Nucella emarginata*—a pale, spiral-ribbed shell about an inch long. The smallest hermit crabs may inhabit old periwinkle shells.

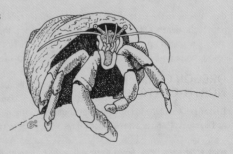

the central coast

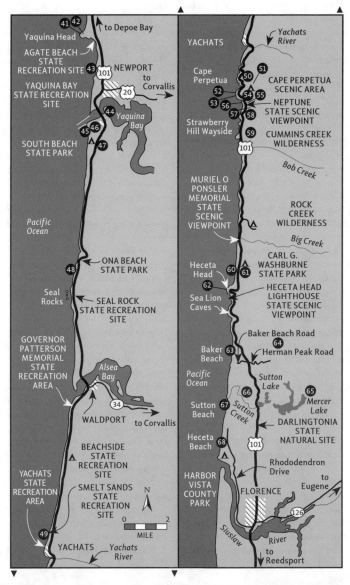

41 42
Yaquina Head
AGATE BEACH
STATE
RECREATION SITE 43
to Depoe Bay
NEWPORT
101 to
Corvallis
YAQUINA BAY
STATE RECREATION
SITE
20
44 Yaquina Bay
45 46
SOUTH BEACH
STATE PARK 47

Pacific
Ocean

ONA BEACH
48 STATE PARK

Seal
Rocks
SEAL ROCK
STATE RECREATION
SITE

GOVERNOR
PATTERSON
MEMORIAL
STATE
RECREATION
AREA
Alsea
Bay
34
WALDPORT to Corvallis

BEACHSIDE
STATE
RECREATION
SITE
YACHATS
STATE
RECREATION
AREA
SMELT SANDS
STATE
RECREATION
SITE
N
0   2
MILE
49 YACHATS
Yachats
River

YACHATS
Yachats
River

Cape
Perpetua
50 51
52 CAPE PERPETUA
SCENIC AREA
53 56 54 55
57 58 NEPTUNE
STATE SCENIC
VIEWPOINT
Strawberry
Hill Wayside 59 CUMMINS CREEK
WILDERNESS
101

Bob Creek

MURIEL O
PONSLER
MEMORIAL
STATE
SCENIC
VIEWPOINT
ROCK
CREEK
WILDERNESS
Big Creek

Heceta
Head
60 61
62
Sea Lion
Caves
CARL G.
WASHBURNE
STATE PARK
HECETA HEAD
LIGHTHOUSE
STATE SCENIC
VIEWPOINT

Baker Beach Road
64
Baker 63
Beach Herman Peak Road

Pacific
Ocean
Sutton
Lake
66 65
Mercer
Lake
Sutton 67 Sutton
Beach Creek
DARLINGTONIA
STATE
NATURAL SITE

Heceta
Beach 68
101
Rhododendron
Drive
to
Eugene
HARBOR
VISTA
COUNTY
PARK
FLORENCE
126
Siuslaw
River
to
Reedsport

LISTENING TO THE STORM

A storm is blowing out of the southwest, and a thousand feet high on Cummins Ridge, the whole world seems to be in motion: sword ferns rustling and alder branches flailing and cotton-soft green moss fluttering on tree trunks. Even the massive Sitka spruces are leaning slightly with the force of the gale. But what keeps grabbing my attention isn't so much the face of the storm but its voice: the sound of air moving over mountain and through forest, mercurial, from long sigh to deep groan, distinct from that other voice, the rhythmic roar of ocean meeting rocky shore fully three miles to the west.

The Nehalem Tillamooks used to tell tales about the owner of that voice—South Wind— tales told only in winter, of a spirit that traveled only in winter, during storms. He had several headbands, they said, one for every kind of mischief he made: for breaking off the limbs of trees, for breaking off the tops of trees, for felling whole trees. One headband he used sparingly. That one was for pulling up trees by the roots.

I've seen South Wind's handiwork before: skunk cabbage blooming in bogs of black earth where a century-old tree's roots once lay buried, ferns taking hold on that now-vertical wall of roots, the supine trunk nursing new tree seedlings. It's good to be on this ridge now, in the gray-green light of a winter afternoon, the whole world in motion. Soon South Wind will be choosing a headband for the night. I believe I'll go inside.

With its craggy punchbowl-strewn shoreline, intriguing tide pools, dramatic vistas, and deep Sitka spruce forest, Cape Perpetua (and neighboring Cummins Ridge) just south of Yachats is—for hikers—the centerpiece of the central coast. An extensive (about eighteen miles) and varied network of trails offers literally something for everyone, from paved, wheelchair-accessible paths along the shore to narrow forest trails traversing remote wilderness ridges. Cape Mountain, just north

of Florence, also offers longer trails, though they're designed more for horses than for hikers.

Otherwise the central coast offers mostly short hikes—a good variety, many of them excellent choices for kids. There's now a network of short trails at Yaquina Head Outstanding Natural Area north of Newport, though bird-watching, tidepooling, and lighthouse touring are the main attractions here. The central coast also offers some great beach walking; despite the proximity of US 101, there's a lovely remoteness to South Beach, to the beach north of Heceta Head, and to Baker Beach–Heceta Beach, the warm-up act for the extensive dunes south of the Siuslaw River.

Interpretive centers. Newport has a handful. The Oregon Coast Aquarium (www .aquarium.org or 541-867-3474) is not to be missed; exhibits introduce visitors to the varied life forms found at the Pacific's edge in Oregon. Next door is Hatfield Marine Science Center (www.hmsc.orst.edu/visitor or 541-867-0100); its public wing serves as a thinking person's boutique aquarium, nicely complementing its neighbor. (For more on both, see Hike 44). North of town, displays in Yaquina Head Interpretive Center detail local natural and human history (see Hike 43).

In Waldport, Historic Alsea Bay Bridge Interpretive Center (www.oregonstateparks .org or 541/563-2002) focuses on the coast's many historic (and new) bridges, along with anything involving bridges or the rivers they cross; displays and activities appeal to a wide range of ages and interests. Cape Perpetua Interpretive Center (541/547-3289) south of Yachats has well-presented displays dealing with local human and natural history; with its big west-facing picture windows, it's also a good spot from which to watch for whales during winter rains.

Wildlife-watching. Yaquina Head offers some of the closest mainland views of a seabird colony in the United States from spring through midsummer; among species nesting here are common murres, western gulls, Brandt's cormorants, and pigeon guillemots. Tufted puffins nest on the seaward side of the rock, though you may see them flying to and from their nests; brown pelicans can usually be seen in the area in summer and fall as well. Other good seabird-viewing spots are Seal Rock State Park, Cape Perpetua, and Heceta Head Lighthouse State Scenic Viewpoint. Yaquina Bay and Alsea Bay are good sites to see waterfowl and shorebirds.

Yaquina Head and Yaquina Bay are also good places to see seals and sea lions; scores of sea lions congregate on docks along Newport's bayfront. Look also at Seal Rock State Recreation Site, Alsea Bay, and Strawberry Hill Wayside, south of Cape Perpetua, where harbor seals congregate on a rock barely separated from the mainland by a moatlike channel.

Sea Lion Caves (*www.sealioncaves.com* or 541/547-3111), a commercial enterprise north of Florence, offers views into the world's largest sea cave, home to a large colony of Steller's sea lions in fall and winter (in spring and summer they loll on offshore rocks). Despite the hype and the unavoidable gift shop, a visit is well worth the admission price, at least once. You may see nesting pigeon guillemots and auklets inside the cave in spring and summer as well.

The best whale-watching sites are found at Yaquina Head, Seal Rocks, Cape Perpetua, Heceta Head, and near the turnout just south of the tunnel north of Sea Lion Caves.

Tidepooling. (See Respectful Tidepooling, p. 31.) The south side of Yaquina Head has extensive tide pools; use the stairs near the lighthouse. Most unusual—unique, perhaps—is the human-made, wheelchair-accessible intertidal area in what was the lower basalt quarry at Yaquina Head, completed in 1994.

It is slowly being colonized by intertidal plants and animals; among them, some nonnative invasive species, unfortunately. Seal Rock State Park also offers excellent tidepooling. Other good sites are Yachats State Recreation Area (be careful during heavy surf), the shoreline at Cape Perpetua (see Hike 54), Strawberry Hill Wayside, and the beach from Bob Creek south to Bray Point.

Off-road cycling. Bikes are welcome on the paved path through the dunes at South Beach State Park (Hike 45), allowing families to bike from their campground to the Oregon Coast Aquarium. Bicycles are not allowed on most of the forest trails on the central coast. One exception is Cummins Creek Trail (Hike 58). For a scenic and moderately challenging loop, ride 4 miles up Forest Service Road 55 to the upper Cooks Ridge trailhead. Pick up the trail and follow it uphill another 0.2 mile and then bear left onto Cummins Creek Trail. It's a steep, tricky descent for about 1.3 miles, then an easy 3.2-mile cruise along an old roadbed to the lower trailhead. Ride out to US 101 and head west along the highway back to your starting point.

Bikes are allowed on the Sutton trail system (Hike 66), but the trail is too sandy for good cycling in most places.

Camping/hostels. South Beach State Park, in the dunes just south of Newport, has a large campground; the campground at Beachside State Park, tucked between highway and high tide on the long beach between Waldport and Yachats, is relatively small. Small, woodsy Carl G. Washburne State Park (no reservations) is just north of Heceta Head. Between Yachats and Florence, the Forest Service has a string of campgrounds: Tillicum Beach (on the highway, catering to motor homes) followed by the more secluded, primitive Cape Perpetua, Rock Creek, Alder Dune, and Sutton Lake campgrounds. To reserve a site at Sutton Lake or Cape Perpetua campground, visit *www.reserveamerica.com* or call 877/444-6777. Harbor Vista County Park is just north of the Siuslaw River's north jetty; call 541/997-5987 for reservations.

For reservations at state park campgrounds, call 800/452-5687.

Travelers' tips. From its earliest days, Newport has been a popular tourist destination; services are arrayed along US 101, but browsing's best on the bayfront. Lodging ranges from romantic inns on Nye Beach to a large condominium complex on the bayfront; entertainment venues range from a community performing arts center to the bayfront wax museum. Waldport and Yachats both have smaller-town charm and plenty of lodging options in and around town. There's lodging on the river and on the beach north of Florence; seek souvenirs in Old Town, and get resupplied at the big stores along the highway.

Recommended hikes. The Cooks Ridge–Gwynn Creek loop (Hikes 55 and 57) at Cape Perpetua and the Cummins Creek loop (Hike 58) are my personal favorites at Cape Perpetua. The China Creek loop (Hike 61) makes a satisfying beach–forest hike, especially with the addition of the lush Creek–Valley

loop. The walk from Ona Beach to Seal Rock is a winter winner (Hike 48); on warmer days, enjoy the brisk creek crossing and solitude of Sutton Beach (Hike 67).

41 Salal Hill

RATING	DIFFICULTY	ROUND-TRIP	TERRAIN
★	2	0.6 mile	120 feet elevation gain

Features: Outstanding shoreline vistas, wildlife, lighthouse; **Contact:** Yaquina Head Outstanding Natural Area, www.blm.gov or 541/574-3100

A modest trail system has been developed at Yaquina Head, allowing visitors to explore the headland's varied attractions—an interpretive center, two tide-pool areas, a lighthouse and seabird observation platform, hilltop viewpoints—all by foot. Rising directly from the lighthouse parking lot at the end of the headland, Salal Hill Trail gets your heart pumping but is short enough for even reluctant hikers.

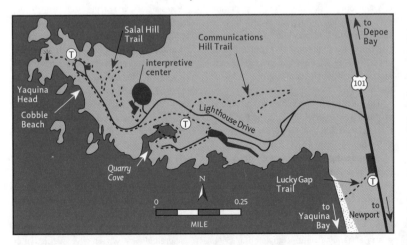

Yaquina Lighthouse from Salal Hill

GETTING THERE

From US 101 about 2 miles north of Newport, turn west on Lighthouse Drive at the sign to Yaquina Head and continue 1 mile to the parking area (or park at the interpretive center and walk to the lighthouse).

ON THE TRAIL

The trail begins behind the rest rooms, switchbacking up the steep hillside and ending with views of breakers rolling in to the shoreline to the north and south. Look for red-tailed hawks, kestrels, and peregrine falcons soaring overhead.

Yaquina Head was formed by Miocene-epoch lava flows; its hard volcanic basalt has endured the eroding effects of wind and waves while softer rock around it crumbled into the ocean. This basalt was also the headland's undoing, however; from 1925 to 1983, the area was quarried for local building and road construc-

tion material. The scars are still plainly visible on the drive out to the tip of the head. Quarrying was halted three years after the Bureau of Land Management took over the head in 1980; since then, the focus has been on developing interpretation and wildlife-watching opportunities.

42 Communications Hill

RATING	DIFFICULTY	ROUND-TRIP	TERRAIN
*	2	0.8 mile	180 feet elevation gain

Features: Outstanding shoreline vistas, wildlife, lighthouse; **Contact:** Yaquina Head Outstanding Natural Area, www.blm.gov or 541/574-3100

A short hike up the hill east of the interpretive center on Yaquina Head grants views of the shoreline. The trail's

SEA LIONS

There's no shortage of sea lions on the Oregon coast, though which species you're seeing (and hearing) depends upon season and locale. Thousands of adult male California sea lions, after spending the breeding season off California and Baja California, arrive off Oregon in October and remain through April; another 10,000 or more pass by the Oregon coast on their way to and from British Columbia in spring and fall. These are the sea lions of circus tradition; watch them lounging on offshore rocks or docks—Newport's bayfront and Astoria's East Mooring Basin are favorite hangouts—or listen for their signature bark on a late fall hike to Harts Cove or between Sunset Bay and Cape Arago.

A second species, Steller's (or northern) sea lions, live year-round in and around Sea Lion Caves north of Florence; elsewhere off Oregon, they're strictly summer visitors. They arrive in spring to breed, mainly at Rogue and Orford reefs on the southern coast (and at Sea Lion Caves), and stay through fall. Oregon's breeding population of 3000 or more is currently one of only two reproductive colonies of Steller's in the United States.

Which is which? The Steller's is lighter in color and may be three times the size of a California sea lion. (An adult male Steller's can be ten feet long and weigh 2000 pounds, while male California sea lions weigh in at about 700 pounds, the size of a female Steller's). The California sea lion also has a sagittal crest, or large forehead bump, contrasting with the rounder skull of the Steller's. To distinguish sea lions from seals, read about harbor seals and elephant seals on p. 180.

name refers to the congregation of Coast Guard navigation communications equipment at the summit of the hill.

GETTING THERE

From US 101 about 2 miles north of Newport, turn west on Lighthouse Drive at the sign for Yaquina Head. Park at either the interpretive center or Quarry Cove tide pools and follow the footpath a short distance (0.1 mile or less) to the base of the Communications Hill Trail; take care crossing Lighthouse Drive.

ON THE TRAIL

Pass by a gate and start up the wide gravel service road that serves as the hiking trail. It climbs through a Sitka spruce and shore pine forest, offering glimpses onto the shingled rooftops of a residential neighborhood. At the summit, take in views of the coastline and the forest (and clear-cuts) to the east.

43 Yaquina Head to Yaquina Bay

RATING	DIFFICULTY	ONE-WAY	TERRAIN
★★★	2	3.5 miles	180 feet elevation gain

Features: Beach, two lighthouses, outstanding shoreline vistas, wildlife; **Contact:** Yaquina Bay State Recreation Site, *www.oregonstate parks.org* or 800/551-6949

In 1871 a lighthouse was built at the entrance to Yaquina Bay, the first lighthouse north of the Umpqua River on the Oregon coast. Three years later it was mothballed

Yaquina Head Lighthouse

when the more effective Yaquina Head Light-house went into service just up the coast. Be-tween them stretch 3.5 miles of beach. Both lighthouses are accessible by car and are open for tours, daily in summer at this writing. If you're not in a rush, consider walking from one to the other, on what served as the main coastal highway in the 1870s and for several decades thereafter.

GETTING THERE

To park at Yaquina Head, take US 101 about 2 miles north of Newport, turn west on Light-house Drive at the sign to Yaquina Head, and continue 1 mile to the lighthouse parking area. To park at Yaquina Bay State Recreation Site, turn off US 101 just north of Yaquina Bay Bridge in Newport at the sign to the state rec-reation site.

ON THE TRAIL

To walk literally from lighthouse to light-house starting at ninety-three-foot-tall Ya-quina Head Lighthouse, which has been in continuous service since 1873, follow the roadside footpath east 0.25 mile to Yaquina Head Interpretive Center, worth a stop; inter-pretive exhibits range from a replica of the lighthouse's lantern room and keepers' quar-ters to an interactive fiber-optic panel show-ing where the Pacific coast's migrating gray whale population is at any time of year. Con-tinue on the path. At the Communications Hill trailhead, continue east on the shoulder of Lighthouse Drive another 0.5 mile to US 101. Walk along the highway shoulder a short way (or drive) to the beach access parking area off US 101 just south of Lighthouse Drive (about 2 miles north of Newport). From the lower corner of the parking lot, follow Lucky Gap Trail a short distance to the beach and head south.

You'll pass Agate Beach State Recreation Site and the point at Jumpoff Joe, below the artsy Nye Beach neighborhood. Approaching the north jetty, look east to spot the bottom few steps of a concrete stairway leading up a pine-covered hillside. The stairs lead into Yaquina Bay State Recreation Site, site of the oldest wood-frame lighthouse in the state. It functioned as lighthouse and keeper's quar-ters in one: A forty-foot tower rises above the roof of the Cape Cod–style house. The re-stored and period-furnished lighthouse now also houses a gift shop.

44 Yaquina Estuary

RATING	DIFFICULTY	ONE-WAY	TERRAIN
★★	1	0.5 mile	Flat

Features: Estuary, wildlife, access to two in-terpretive centers; **Contact:** Mark O. Hatfield Marine Science Center, *www.hmsc.orst.edu /visitor* or 541/867-0100; Oregon Coast Aquar-ium, *www.aquarium.org* or 541/867-3474

The Oregon coast's two premier marine science interpretive centers are both located along the south shore of Yaquina Bay. Linking the two is a paved trail winding along the edge of the bay. Interpretive signs de-scribe the dynamics of the estuarine system and identify many of its inhabitants; two ob-servation shelters allow you unobtrusively to watch the passing bird show. Use the path as an alternative to driving between the two centers, or add a short nature walk to a visit to one or both.

GETTING THERE

From US 101 just south of Yaquina Bay Bridge, follow signs to Hatfield Marine Science Center (or Oregon Coast Aquarium).

ON THE TRAIL

The estuary trail starts at the east end of the science center parking lot. (*Note: Dogs are*

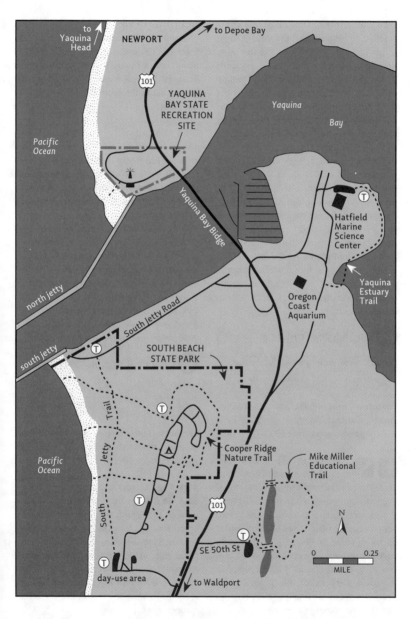

not allowed on the estuary trail.) It follows the mudflats ringing the bay; the view changes constantly with the seasons and the tides. Nearing the end, the trail crosses a wooden bridge over a finger of tidal marsh. The path ends at a service road; signs direct you a short distance to the Oregon Coast Aquarium. To find the trail from the road in front of the aquarium, walk north a short distance and watch for signs.

Hatfield Marine Science Center's public wing reopened in 1997 after a major renovation and is well worth a visit, especially by those school age or older. The touch pool, the octopus tank, and the dozen or more interactive displays on current marine science research are all organized around the theme "Searching for Patterns in a Complex World." Exhibits tap high-tech computer wizardry as well as "high-touch" experiential learning and help from friendly volunteers. (A donation is requested upon admission.)

45 South Jetty Trail

RATING	DIFFICULTY	ONE-WAY	TERRAIN
★	1	1 mile	Flat

Features: Dunes, wildlife, adjacent to campground; **Contact:** South Beach State Park, www.oregonstateparks.org or 800/551-6949

This wide, paved path leads from the day-use area at South Beach State Park to the road at the south jetty of Yaquina Bay, making it a very versatile trail. It's an accessible route through the grassy dunes, easy for wheelchairs and strollers. It allows families to bicycle from the state park to the Oregon Coast Aquarium and marine science center (about 4 miles round trip via South Jetty Road). Beach walkers at South Beach can use it to loop back through the dunes for a change of pace.

GETTING THERE

The south trailhead is at the South Beach State Park day-use area, off US 101 about 1.5 miles south of Yaquina Bay Bridge at Newport. The north trailhead is near the end of the road leading out to the south jetty under Yaquina Bay Bridge.

ON THE TRAIL

This straightforward trail follows a north–south route just inland from the beach grass–covered foredune. Along the way it crosses three paved spur trails between the beach and the campground. If you're starting at the trail's north end, bear left at the junction just beyond the start of the trail; a right turn leads out to the beach.

Take time to linger at the south jetty, which offers good bird-watching along with views of seals and sea lions swimming in the channel between the jetties; orcas are sometimes spotted in the channel in early summer. Look for large congregations of scoters just west of the bridge from September through early May, as well as a great variety of other ducks in the wintertime.

46 Cooper Ridge Nature Trail

RATING	DIFFICULTY	ONE-WAY	TERRAIN
★	2	1.5 miles	Rolling

Features: Dunes, forest, adjacent to campground; **Contact:** South Beach State Park, www.oregonstateparks.org or 800/551-6949

Numbered posts along Cooper Ridge Nature Trail are being reclaimed by the forest and are no longer recognizable, and there's no brochure available with descriptions corresponding to the numbered stations. No matter; it's still a pleasant trail for campers at South Beach State Park to stretch their legs on, particularly on a hot day (when it's cool under the Sitka spruce) or in the evening.

WAVES AND SPINDRIFT

Waves begin with the wind, though not with those winds blowing immediately offshore. More often they result from swells originating hundreds, even thousands of miles at sea. As wind blows over the ocean's surface it creates friction, as it transfers its energy from air to water. That friction stirs particles of water on the sea's surface to turn in a circular orbit, moving forward with the wind and then back under the sea's surface in a circular rolling motion.

Cresting waves take shape as swells approach the shore. Here the bottom of a wave's internal orbit begins to drag on the ocean floor, creating an elliptical rather than circular orbit and shortening the distance between waves, making them steeper. At this point the wave "trips" on the seabed. The wave front hollows out as the depth of water decreases, until the cresting wave finally crashes onto the beach.

Sometimes crashing waves leave great gobs of seafoam scattered across the beach like beaten egg whites or soap suds. It's not a sign of pollution, however; in fact, it usually signifies a healthy ocean. Salt and remains of dead microscopic plants in the water are whipped together by strong wave action to create the foam. In summer, northwest winds and the earth's rotation move warm surface water offshore, replacing it with cold water from the deep. The rising water brings nutrient-rich "fertilizer" to the ocean's surface, nourishing the plankton living there. The plankton multiply and, together with decaying plant matter, are stirred into the mix—which is why summer's spindrift can took so scummy.

GETTING THERE

From the Yaquina Bay Bridge at Newport, drive south 1.5 miles on US 101 to South Beach State Park and follow signs to the day-use area.

ON THE TRAIL

Those camping at the state park can walk through the campground to the northern-most beach access trail and head west, watching for the Cooper Ridge Nature Trail sign on their right as they head toward the beach. Otherwise, hikers can reach the trail via the South Jetty Trail (see Hike 45); take the northernmost campground spur trail and look for the Cooper Ridge sign as you near the campground.

The trail heads up a sand dune and then quickly becomes a bit obscure; try bearing right to stay on top of the forested ridge. The route becomes clearer as it gains the ridge and begins circling the campground. At about 0.5 mile there's a bench with a nice view of the south jetty; a few minutes farther along, the trail drops down to a pine woods and meadow before climbing back up on the ridge. About

when you start to hear the ocean again (about 1 mile), turn left at a junction to continue on the trail (going straight leads back into the campground) and proceed along the ridge until the trail ends near the registration booth at the campground entrance.

47 Mike Miller Educational Trail

RATING	DIFFICULTY	LOOP	TERRAIN
★	1	1 mile	120 feet elevation gain

Features: Forest, pond, nature trail; **Contact:** Lincoln County Parks, www.co.lincoln.or.us or 541/265-5747

Mike Miller Educational Trail

This short loop trail was designed to introduce Lincoln County schoolchildren to a variety of coastal forest habitats, including old growth, with huge stumps from long-ago logging and trees downed by the wind. The public is welcome on Mike Miller Educational Trail as well.

GETTING THERE

From Yaquina Bay Bridge at Newport, follow US 101 south 1.2 miles and turn east on Southeast 50th Street at the sign to the trail, just north of the entrance to South Beach State Park. The trailhead is on the left 0.2 mile ahead, where the road curves to the right; there is room for several cars to park on the trailhead side of the road.

ON THE TRAIL

Follow the trail uphill a short distance to where it splits into a loop; bearing left, the trail follows an old railroad bed for about 0.2 mile. It then veers right, drops down to cross the end of a long lake on a wooden boardwalk, and begins climbing through a Sitka spruce forest. The trail continues to climb slowly until it reaches the ridge top, from which it slowly descends to the edge of a blowdown area alongside a clear-cut at about 0.7 mile; it then drops down to a long footbridge across the other end of the lake, and completes the loop.

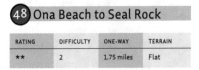

48 Ona Beach to Seal Rock

RATING	DIFFICULTY	ONE-WAY	TERRAIN
★★	2	1.75 miles	Flat

Features: Beach, tide pools, wildlife, adjacent to campground; **Contact:** Ona Beach State Park, *www.oregonstateparks.org* or 800/551-6949

In its understated way, Ona Beach State Park is one of the most appealing waysides on the Oregon

Seal Rock

coast. Beaver Creek curls languidly through the park, encircling a grassy picnic area far enough from the beach to be out of the wind; wooden picnic tables are scattered under tall spruces and pines. Big restrooms make for easy clothes changes before and after a day at the beach.

GETTING THERE

Ona Beach State Park is 7 miles south of Newport off US 101. Seal Rock State Recreation Site is off US 101 at the community of Seal Rock, between Newport and Waldport.

ON THE TRAIL

From the restrooms, look for the trail heading west. Follow it a short distance over a footbridge spanning Beaver Creek and to the beach.

Seal Rock State Recreation Site is 1.75 miles down the beach to the south. It's a great destination in its own right. Here are extensive tide pools (particularly south of the big rock) and opportunities to see nesting seabirds in summer, sea lions in winter, and harbor seals year-round. In recent years the large monolith of columnar basalt at the shoreline has come to be known as Seal Rock, though that place name comes from Seal Rocks, a 2.5-mile-long ledge of partially submerged rock about 0.1 mile offshore. That's where the pinnipeds tend to lounge; carry binoculars for the best views. In the winter at low tide there's even more to see between Ona Beach and Seal Rock; fossil-filled rocks are revealed on the beach after winter storms scour it of sand. For a one-way hike, leave a vehicle at Seal Rock State Recreation Site (just off US 101 at the community of Seal Rock, between Newport and Waldport); an asphalt path leads up the south side of the rock to the parking area.

Opposite: Yachats 804 Trail

49 Yachats 804 Trail

RATING	DIFFICULTY	ONE-WAY	TERRAIN
★★★	1	1.9 miles	Flat

Features: Blowholes, pocket beaches, broad beach, wildlife, close to town, OCT; **Contact:** Smelt Sands State Recreation Site, *www.oregon stateparks.org* or 800/551-6949

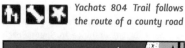 *Yachats 804 Trail follows the route of a county road*

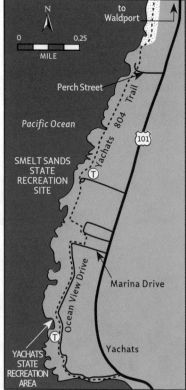

dedicated in 1890 but abandoned in the 1930s. Local residents fought all the way to the Oregon Supreme Court to return the portion north of Smelt Sands to public use in the late 1980s; in 2004, the southern section—mostly following Ocean View Drive—reopened to the public as well.

The trail's main attraction is a long, wave-sculpted shelf of sandstone north of Smelt Sands, with chasms and blowholes that, at high tide, shoot seawater into the air with the pulse of the waves. The trail's compacted gravel surface makes it passable for wheelchairs. The rocks and cliffs are fun to explore, though they're slippery when wet and potentially dangerous during storms.

GETTING THERE

From Yachats, drive 0.5 mile north on US 101 and turn west at the sign to Smelt Sands State Recreation Site.

ON THE TRAIL

Most visitors start at Smelt Sands and walk north 0.8 mile along the bluff, passing a pocket beach (where smelt have been dip-netted for years—hence the name) and rocky shelf to the west, motels and private homes to the right. The trail leads into a stand of shore pines, and skirts a narrow chasm at about 0.4 mile. Near the end it crosses Perch Street and drops down a sandstone bank to end at the beach, which stretches north 7 miles to Waldport. After as much beach walking as you like, return the way you came.

Southbound from Smelt Sands, the trail crosses a little footbridge, follows the grassy bluff in front of the Adobe Resort, and heads inland up a fence-lined *allée*. It turns right at the street and continues zigzagging on a gravel path along neighborhood streets until reaching Ocean View Drive, which it follows to US 101 at the south end of town (1.1 miles).

50 Cape Perpetua— Kittel-Amanda Trail

RATING	DIFFICULTY	ONE-WAY	TERRAIN
★★	3	2.2 miles	800 feet elevation gain

Features: Forested headland, ocean vistas, OCT; **Contact:** Cape Perpetua Scenic Area, www.fs.fed.us/r6/siuslaw or 541/547-3289

The main purpose of the Kittel-Amanda Trail, which leads up the north side of Cape Perpetua, is to get Oregon Coast Trail hikers, most of whom walk north to south, off the highway and onto a trail to ascend the cape. That's why the hike over Cape Perpetua is described here as a one-way traverse from north to south. Day hikers can make a round-trip hike on this trail as well, but they are more likely to start at the top and hike down (south to north) and back, as there is no trailhead parking along the highway at the north trailhead. The trail's name commemorates Joanne and Norman Kittel, who made the trail extension possible by allowing it to cross their private forest land, and Amanda, the last living member of a local Indian tribe.

GETTING THERE

Note: There is no trailhead parking along US 101 at the north end of the Kittel-Amanda Trail. To reach the southern trailhead, take US 101 about 0.25 mile north from the Cape Perpetua Interpretive Center road (about 3 miles south of Yachats) and turn east up Forest Road 55, then left onto Forest Road 5553, which ends at the viewpoint off US 101.

ON THE TRAIL

Walking south from Yachats (very carefully; there is virtually no highway shoulder), look for the wooden post marking the start of the trail on the left side of curving US 101 just 0.2

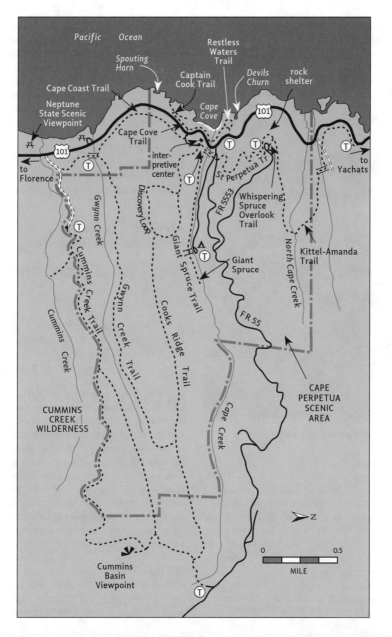

Pacific Ocean

Spouting Horn

Restless Waters Trail

Captain Cook Trail

Devils Churn

rock shelter

Cape Coast Trail

Neptune State Scenic Viewpoint

Cape Cove Trail

Cape Cove

101

interpretive center

St Perpetua Tr

to Florence

Gwynn Creek

Discovery Loop

FR 5553

Whispering Spruce Overlook Trail

to Yachats

Cummins Creek Trail

Gwynn Creek Trail

Cooks Ridge Trail

Giant Spruce Trail

Giant Spruce

North Cape Creek

Kittel-Amanda Trail

Cummins Creek

FR 55

CAPE PERPETUA SCENIC AREA

CUMMINS CREEK WILDERNESS

Cape Creek

N

0   0.5
MILE

Cummins Basin Viewpoint

Kittel-Amanda Trail, Cape Perpetua

mile south of the Yachats city limits sign (if you reach milepost 166, you've gone 0.3 mile too far). A few quick switchbacks get the trail up above the highway, then it heads south, passing a viewpoint, through a dark spruce forest. Bear right where a spur enters from above. At 0.25 you meet a gravel road; walk up it a few paces to where the trail resumes in a young forest and almost immediately crosses an unnamed creek on a substantial footbridge. It climbs steeply for about 0.5 mile, then moderates, continuing to climb

in deep forest. At about 1.5 miles a downed spruce log leads across North Cape Creek; look for elk tracks and skunk cabbage in the dark mud. Continue another 0.5 mile as the trail roller-coasters along the steep hillside. At 2.2 miles there's a trail junction; bear right to continue another 0.2 mile to the overlook on Whispering Spruce Overlook Trail, near the top of St. Perpetua Trail (Hike 51), which loops around a 1933 Coast Guard lookout. If you bear left, the trail quickly ends at the bottom corner of the first and lowest parking area at the top of Cape Perpetua (room for about ten cars).

51 Cape Perpetua— St. Perpetua Trail

RATING	DIFFICULTY	ROUND-TRIP	TERRAIN
★★★	3	3 miles	800 feet elevation gain

Features: Outstanding shoreline vistas, forested headland, adjacent to campground, OCT; **Contact:** Cape Perpetua Scenic Area, *www.fs.fed.us/r6/siuslaw* or 541/547-3289

Steep, forested Cape Perpetua dominates the coastline south of Yachats. It's formed of layers of lava that cooled into basalt and were uplifted millions of years ago. This trail up and even over the cape's tip is one of several options available to hikers in Cape Perpetua Scenic Area. It's hiking for hiking's sake; you could drive to the top of the cape, but then you'd miss the slow unfurling of the view to the south and the deep forest quiet on the north side of the cape.

GETTING THERE

For the lower trailhead, turn off US 101 at Cape Perpetua Interpretive Center, about 3 miles south of Yachats. To leave a shuttle vehicle at the upper trailhead, turn east off US 101 onto Forest Road 55 about 0.25 mile north from the Cape Perpetua Interpretive Center road, then bear left onto Forest Service Road 5553, which ends at the cape's summit viewpoint.

ON THE TRAIL

From the lower trailhead at the interpretive center, follow an asphalt path down to Cape Creek, cross the creek, and continue across the campground road and Forest Service Road 55. Steep at first, the trail switchbacks through forest up the cape's south side. About 0.2 mile from the top, a spectacular view opens to the south. Continue up the grassy hillside to the rock-walled viewpoint at the top. Extend your outing with a stroll around the paved, 0.25-mile Whispering Spruce Overlook Trail. It loops around the summit, with links to the Kittel-Amanda Trail (Hike 50). The rock shelter on the west side, built in 1933 by the Civilian Conservation Corps and used as a Coast Guard lookout during World War II, is a good spot for whale-watching. Unless you've left a second car at the top for a one-way hike, return as you came.

52 Giant Spruce Trail

RATING	DIFFICULTY	ROUND-TRIP	TERRAIN
★★	2	2 miles	140 feet elevation gain

Features: Ancient forest, creek, landmark tree, adjacent to campground; **Contact:** Cape Perpetua Scenic Area, *www.fs.fed.us/r6 /siuslaw* or 541/547-3289

A good choice with young children is the 2-mile round-trip walk to the Giant Spruce at Cape Perpetua. It leads into a lovely old-growth forest; markers are keyed to an interpretive brochure—one of the simplest, best explanations I've read for a very complex subject, old-growth forest ecology—available at the interpretive center.

GETTING THERE

Turn off US 101 at Cape Perpetua Interpretive Center, about 3 miles south of Yachats.

ON THE TRAIL

From the interpretive center, follow the asphalt path down to Cape Creek, but rather than crossing the gurgling creek, walk up its south bank, listening for northern spotted, great horned, and pygmy owls. You'll pass (but not cross) a second footbridge at 0.8 mile, leading to the end of the campground road. (For a shorter hike, you can cut the whole walk

Sculpture at Cape Perpetua Interpretive Center

Giant Spruce

to just 0.4 mile round trip by starting here at the end of the campground road rather than at the interpretive center.)

From here it's 0.2 mile to the trail's namesake, a huge, 500-year-old Sitka spruce. Return as you came.

53 Restless Waters Trail

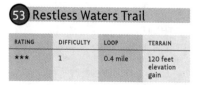

RATING	DIFFICULTY	LOOP	TERRAIN
★★★	1	0.4 mile	120 feet elevation gain

Features: Blowhole, beach, tide pools adjacent to campground; **Contact:** Cape Perpetua Scenic Area, *www.fs.fed.us/r6/siuslaw* or 541/547-3289

The best time to take this short, scenic trail is at high tide, when the water show at Devils Churn is most spectacular. With long, gradual switchbacks ascending the short but steep seaside bluff, this is an easy walk or roll (it's wheelchair-accessible) for nearly everyone.

GETTING THERE
Turn off US 101 at the Devils Churn parking area, just north of the Cape Perpetua Interpretive Center (about 3 miles south of Yachats).

ON THE TRAIL
The trail starts at the lower parking area. It switches down the hillside toward the ocean, as highway sounds gradually give way to the crashing of the surf, to a viewpoint above Devils Churn, a dead-end rock chute where waves rush in, smash the wall, and shoot seawater into the air when the tide is high enough. Stairs lead down to the rock shelf, which is fun to explore (with caution).

To complete the 0.4-mile loop, continue south on the trail (still paved, but no longer considered wheelchair-accessible). Around the point, a spur trail leads to stairs onto the rock ledge above Cape Cove Beach. At the junction, bear left to return to the parking lot.

Alternatively, you could continue south on Cape Cove Trail. Just a few paces past the junction mentioned above, look for a faint footpath leading north, under the limbs of a large spruce, to a wooden barrier protecting ancient shell middens; clamber down it to reach the beach (or continue on the main trail and take the spur trail just south of where the trail crosses Cape Creek). Continuing on, Cape Cove Trail leads up to the highway, along the highway shoulder briefly, and back down to link with Captain Cook Trail (Hike 54) after 0.3 mile. If you go all the way to Spouting Horn and back to the Restless Waters trailhead, it's 1.3 miles round trip.

Restless Waters Trail is also accessible by

Restless Waters Trail

GULLS AND THEIR COUSINS

Just a seagull? Look closer. Eight different kinds of gull commonly inhabit or visit the Oregon coast. It can be tough to tell one from another, even if you know what you're looking for. Species are similar to begin with. Then their plumage changes as they age and when they breed. Some interbreed, further muddying the picture. Then there are the gull-like jaegers and terns.... Understand why serious bird-watchers shun the overly general term, "seagull"?

Still, most common on the Oregon coast year-round is the western gull, characterized by its pink legs, white breast, dark back, and darker tail feathers. Also pink-legged but with a somewhat darker head is the herring gull. Look for the soft gray, red-billed Heermann's gull August through November.

In spring and especially fall, you might see a fancy-flying parasitic jaeger harassing gulls just offshore; it's about the same size as a gull, but darker in color, with falcon-like wings and flying pattern. The terns you may see along Oregon's shore spring through fall are a bit smaller than most gulls, with a black cap and orange-red bill tipped with black.

Gulls seem the most ubiquitous of coastal birds. But that's just their gregarious nature and tendency to be where you are, on the beach. In fact, western gulls represent fewer than 2 percent of the breeding seabirds on the Northwest coast. Train your binoculars on an offshore rock this summer and you'll see that the common murre, in the same family as penguins, is by far the most common of all.

---

foot from the Cape Perpetua Interpretive Center (see Hike 54).

54 Captain Cook Trail

RATING	DIFFICULTY	ROUND-TRIP	TERRAIN
★★★	1	0.6 mile	120 feet elevation gain

Features: Blowholes, beach, tide pools, adjacent to campground; **Contact:** Cape Perpetua Scenic Area, www.fs.fed.us/r6/siuslaw or 541/547-3289

Cape Perpetua was "discovered" and named by Captain James Cook in 1778, but shell middens found along Captain Cook Trail indicate that Alsi Indians discovered the cape much earlier, camping here and gathering shellfish in summers between about A.D. 450 and 1620. With tide pools at low tide and the dramatic Spouting Horn at high tide, a walk on this short trail is appealing nearly any time of day.

GETTING THERE

Turn off US 101 at Cape Perpetua Interpretive Center, about 3 miles south of Yachats.

ON THE TRAIL

Follow the paved path west under the highway (or, from the adjacent highway turnout, take the footbridge and path south and west). At the trail junction, bear left onto Cape Cove Trail (the right-hand trail is Restless Waters Trail). A second junction marks the start of a loop with Captain Cook Trail; bearing left, it first leads past Spouting Horn, a hole in the top of a sea cave at the end of Cook's Chasm where, at high tide, air and water spout when incoming waves build pressure inside the cave. Continue along the trail to reach the bedrock shelves revealed as tide pools at low tide. A ranger is frequently on duty, especially on weekends and in summer, to talk with visitors about what they see in this state-protected marine garden. Return as you came. (Alternatively, you can link this hike with Hike 53, Restless Waters Trail, for a 1.3-mile round trip.)

Twenty-four-rayed sea star

55 Cooks Ridge

RATING	DIFFICULTY	ONE-WAY	TERRAIN
★★★	4	3.7 miles	1200 feet elevation gain

Discovery Loop:

RATING	DIFFICULTY	ROUND-TRIP	TERRAIN
★★★	3	2 miles	400 feet elevation gain

Features: Ancient forest, ocean views, adjacent to campground; **Contact:** Cape Perpetua Scenic Area, *www.fs.fed.us/r6/siuslaw* or 541/547-3289

Cooks Ridge Trail is one of several forest hikes in Cape Perpetua Scenic Area, and the one most convenient to the interpretive center. Start at the interpretive center and follow signs to the mid-trail Discovery Loop for a short out-and-back hike into an old-growth grove on the forested hillside. The upper end of the trail is also accessible by road, allowing a one-way, 3.7-mile hike (with shuttle car) as well. Links with other hikes in the scenic area offer more loop options.

GETTING THERE

For the lower trailhead, take US 101 about 3 miles south of Yachats and turn in at Cape Perpetua Interpretive Center. For the upper trailhead, turn off US 101 just north of the interpretive center onto Forest Service Road 55, go 4 miles, and park at the signed trailhead.

ON THE TRAIL

The lower trailhead for Cooks Ridge Trail starts at the upper end of the parking lot above the interpretive center. The trail begins in dense Douglas fir and spruce and then leads into a stand of old-growth Sitka spruce at about 0.7 mile, where a junction signals the start of the 0.6-mile mid-trail Discovery Loop. (Hike the loop and return as you came for a 2-mile round-trip short forest hike.)

Continuing beyond the loop, the trail slowly ascends Cooks Ridge through a mixture of old growth and younger forest. Listen for the sound of the waves crashing far below, and look for occasional ocean vistas through the trees. After 2.4 miles, the trail meets the top of Gwynn Creek Trail; stay left (or bear right to make a 6.4-mile loop with the Gwynn Creek Trail, Hike 57, down Gwynn Creek, and back to the interpretive center). Cooks Ridge Trail continues gently up and meets the top of Cummins Creek Trail at 3.5 miles; stay left. (Another option is to bear right to make a 9.3-mile loop with the Cummins Creek Trail, Hike 58, up to Cummins Basin Viewpoint and then down Cummins Creek.)

Cooks Ridge Trail ends in 0.2 mile at Forest Road 55 at 3.7 miles. Return as you came.

56 Cape Coast Trail

RATING	DIFFICULTY	ONE-WAY	TERRAIN
★	2	1.3 miles	Rolling

Features: Forest, adjacent to campground, OCT; **Contact:** Cape Perpetua Scenic Area, www.fs.fed.us/r6/siuslaw or 541/547-3289

From the cape's interpretive center, the Oregon Coast Trail rolls south through the forest 1.3 miles along the route of the old stage road. Follow it to access Gwynn Creek or Cummins Creek Trails, or just for an easy, short walk in the woods.

GETTING THERE
Northern access is at Cape Perpetua Interpretive Center, off US 101 about 3 miles south of Yachats. Middle access is at a wayside parking area 0.3 mile north of Neptune State Scenic Viewpoint off US 101. Southern access is off

the road to Cummins Creek Trail, 1.3 miles south of Cape Perpetua Interpretive Center.

ON THE TRAIL
Pick up the Oregon Coast Trail at the interpretive center. At 1 mile Gwynn Creek Trail (Hike 57) comes in from the left. Continuing south, the trail crosses the creek on a footbridge; cut down the grassy opening and across the highway to the wayside here, or continue south another 0.3 mile to the trail's end, 0.1 mile off US 101 up a gravel road leading to the trailhead for Cummins Creek Trail (Hike 58). Return as you came. (To reach the trailhead for Cummins Creek Trail, go left on the gravel road and walk 0.2 mile.)

57 Gwynn Creek

RATING	DIFFICULTY	ROUND-TRIP	TERRAIN
★★★★★	4	6 miles	1200 feet elevation gain

Features: Ancient forest, creeks, adjacent to campground; **Contact:** Cape Perpetua Scenic Area, www.fs.fed.us/r6/siuslaw or 541/547-3289

The trail up Gwynn Creek may be the prettiest on Cape Perpetua. It follows the hillside above the creek, gently climbing through deep forest, much of it old growth. It's lovely all by itself or linked with Cooks Ridge Trail for a loop hike.

GETTING THERE
From Yachats, drive 4 miles south on US 101, passing Cape Perpetua Interpretive Center, and park at a wayside on the highway's west side (0.3 mile north of Neptune State Scenic Viewpoint).

ON THE TRAIL
The Gwynn Creek Trail begins off the Cape Coast Trail (Hike 56); hike here from the

Gwynn Creek Trail

interpretive center, or start at a wayside off US 101. Cross the highway, walk around the gate and up a grassy clearing, and look left for the footbridge crossing Gwynn Creek. The trail begins at creek level but immediately begins a slow climb up the hillside on the north bank of the creek. The trail crosses several side creeks; one at about 1.5 miles is especially pretty, cascading in a fan down a rock face. At about 2.5 miles the trail switches left, leading out of the protected valley and onto windier Cooks Ridge. The trail ends at its junction with Cooks Ridge Trail, at 3 miles. Return as you came (or follow Cooks Ridge Trail, Hike 55, 2.4 miles back down to the interpretive center for a 5.4-mile loop).

58 Cummins Creek

RATING	DIFFICULTY	LOOP	TERRAIN
★★★★	5	9 miles	1150 feet elevation gain

Features: Ancient forest, adjacent to campground; **Contact:** Cape Perpetua Scenic Area, *www.fs.fed.us/r6/siuslaw* or 541/547-3289

Most of Cummins Creek Trail follows an old road, making it inviting for off-road cycling and easy for hikers and bikers to share the trail. (Despite the name, the trail stays well above the creek.)

View near top of Cummins Creek Loop

It passes through some gorgeous old forest, though forest tends to form a wall on either side of the roadbed, making it feel a little less intimate than forest footpaths. The addition of a scenic loop at the upper end has really enhanced the trail.

GETTING THERE

From US 101 about 4 miles south of Yachats, turn west at the sign to Cummins Creek trailhead and drive 0.3 mile to the road's end.

ON THE TRAIL

The trail travels a gentle uphill grade following the old roadbed. At 0.25 mile an unsigned, unmaintained trail takes off to the right and leads 0.25 mile to a lovely spot on Cummins Creek, shallow and tranquil in late summer (but no doubt boisterous in December). Continuing on, the main trail enters a beautiful grove of old-growth Sitka spruce at about 0.5 mile and goes in and out of old growth, passing the end of the Cummins Creek loop spur on the left at about 1.5 miles. At 3.2 miles the trail leaves the old road and bears left up a narrower, rockier, steeper footpath. At 3.8 miles a spur on the right leads 0.1 mile to a viewpoint overlooking a sea of trees in Cummins Basin. A short distance farther, the trail splits at a junction marked by a rock cairn; to complete the 9-mile Cummins Creek loop, bear left here. The trail soon emerges onto a grassy ridge, revealing a blue-green panorama of forested ridges to the south. It returns to forest—big Douglas fir and cedar—and winds downhill, steeply in places, to meet the main Cummins Creek Trail 1.5 miles from the cairn. Follow the main trail back to the trailhead.

For a longer loop hike, go straight (rather than left) at the rock cairn and continue to the junction with Cooks Ridge Trail (Hike 55) at 4.5 miles. Bear left and walk 1.1 miles down Cooks Ridge Trail to the junction with Gwynn Creek Trail (Hike 57). From here, bear right down Cooks Ridge, then (at the interpretive center) left on Cape Coast Trail and left up the Cummins Creek Trail road 0.2 mile for a 9.5-mile loop. Or bear left at the junction with Gwynn Creek Trail, left on Cape Coast Trail (Hike 56), and left up the Cummins Creek Trail road for a 9.1-mile loop.

59 Cummins Ridge

RATING	DIFFICULTY	ONE-WAY	TERRAIN
****	4	6.2 miles	1360 feet elevation loss/gain

Features: Ancient forest, wilderness; **Contact:** Mapleton Ranger District, www.fs.fed.us/r6/siuslaw or 541/ 902-8526

Cummins Creek Wilderness, adjacent to Cape Perpetua Scenic Area, and Rock Creek Wilderness a few miles south were created to preserve some of the last major virgin stands of Sitka spruce, western hemlock, and Douglas fir in the coastal forest. The only trail through Cummins Creek Wilderness is Cummins Ridge Trail, a 6.2-mile route whose lower 3.5 miles originated as a logging road in 1968. Some 2.7 miles of footpath were added to the upper end of the old road to stretch the trail all the way to the edge of the wilderness. Though it's a rather long drive to the upper trailhead, the upper few miles are the most appealing part of the trail, where it winds through the old growth on a narrow footpath; once the trail leads onto the old road, you feel somewhat walled off from the forest by the thick growth of alders on either side of the road-trail.

GETTING THERE

For the lower trailhead, from US 101 turn east on Forest Road 1051 at the sign to Cummins Ridge trailhead (2 miles south of Cape Perpetua Interpretive Center and about 5 miles south of Yachats) and drive 2.2 miles to the trailhead at the end of the road. (The road actually continues northward a short distance, though it's narrow and virtually impassable to vehicles.) To park at the upper trailhead, turn off US 101 about 7 miles south of Yachats on gravel Forest Road 56 just north of Tenmile Creek Bridge. At 2 miles, turn left onto paved Forest Road 5694. Where a spur road comes in from the right in 7.8 miles, continue straight on Forest Road 5694; shortly after the road turns to gravel, turn left on Forest Road 515 and follow it about 0.2 mile to where it ends at the trailhead.

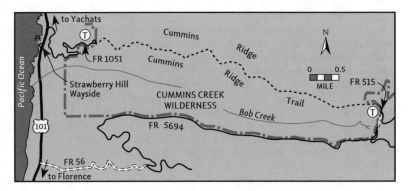

ON THE TRAIL

If possible, leave a shuttle vehicle at the lower trailhead and hike the trail one way downhill (if you hike it as a round trip, the difficulty rating increases to strenuous).

From the upper trailhead, the trail begins as a narrow path through the woods, following the ridgeline. At 2.7 miles it leads onto an old roadbed, easy to follow and well maintained but somewhat brushy for lack of hikers. Watch as the predominantly Douglas fir forest slowly gives way to Sitka spruce as you near the coast. The trail continues on the old road all the way to the lower trailhead.

60 Hobbit Beach

RATING	DIFFICULTY	ROUND-TRIP	TERRAIN
★★★	1	0.5 mile	200 feet elevation gain

Features: Hidden beach, forest, adjacent to campground; **Contact:** Carl G. Washburne Memorial State Park, *www.oregonstateparks.org* or 800/551-6949

Follow a short, twisting trail through a deep, dark forest of Sitka spruce, then down a tunnel of tall salal, to emerge at a secluded beach at the base of Heceta Head; if you don't see Bilbo Baggins scurrying along the trail just ahead of you, you aren't looking hard enough. A steep hill of sand, and the rivulets of a freshwater seep, keep kids entertained for hours.

GETTING THERE

North of Florence, look for trailhead parking (shared with China Creek Trail, Hike 61) in a wide turnout on the east side of US 101 just south of milepost 177, across the highway from a trail sign and 1.2 miles south of the entrance to Carl G. Washburne State Park.

Trail to Hobbit Beach

ON THE TRAIL

From the parking turnout, cross the highway and enter the woods at the wooden post, continuing past the junction with the Heceta Head Lighthouse Trail (Hike 62). The Hobbit Trail winds gently downhill through a dense forest of pine, spruce, and tall rhododendron, closing in tunnel-like near the end. It then opens up into a narrow corridor of salal before ending at Hobbit Beach just north of towering Heceta Head.

Just south of the trail's end, another trail leads up off the beach to some wooded campsites, but a sign warns that the area is for day use only (6:00 AM to 9:00 PM). Return as you came (or combine with a beach walk or with the China Creek Trail, Hike 61, across the highway to make a 3- or 4-mile loop).

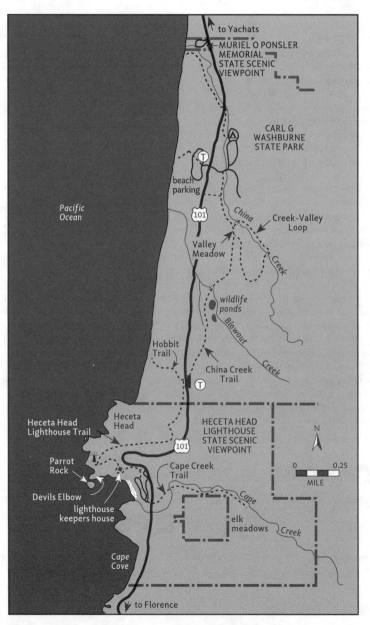

SHORE PINES

It's hard to believe that the short, twisted shore pines that help define Oregon's coastal landscape are actually the same species as the ramrod-straight lodgepole pines found high in the mountains. Botanists have argued for years about whether these two varieties of *Pinus contorta* are actually two different species or, at least, subspecies; generally they're recognized as two varieties of the same species.

Inland, lodgepole pines grow fifty to a hundred feet tall, with a high crown of boughs clustered near the top of the tree. On the coast, the shore pines growing atop sea cliffs or on dunes average twenty-five to thirty feet in height, with a rounded crown of limbs sometimes beginning at the ground. Wherever it grows, *Pinus contorta* is distinguished from other Northwest pines by its short needles, which grow in bundles of two, and its short (about two inches), round, hard, prickly cone. Shore pines may be found in either dry areas or bogs, and they're particularly common in the dunes of the central and southern Oregon coast. But their range is limited to the narrow (in places barely a mile wide) transition zone between the ocean and the start of the coastal forest.

Though they often grow in dense groves, it's not unusual to find a contorted shore pine standing alone, looking like the wind-sculpted *krummholz* you find at timberline, high in the mountains. But these trees' distortion is caused not from blowing wind (pushing foliage toward the leeward side) but from moisture; there's more foliage on the weather side, so the tree grows toward the rain, not away from it.

61 China Creek

RATING	DIFFICULTY	ROUND-TRIP	TERRAIN
★★★★	2	3.2–4 miles	120 feet elevation loss

Features: Forest, meadow, creeks, optional beach walking, adjacent to campground;

Contact: Carl G. Washburne Memorial State Park, *www.oregonstateparks.org* or 800/551-6949

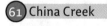 *A perfectly lovely trail system, often overlooked in favor of the Hobbit Trail across the highway, follows China Creek through Carl G. Washburne State Park. There are almost too many*

Opposite: China Creek Trail

choices, all through gorgeous coastal forest, with the option of a beach walk to complete a loop.

GETTING THERE

North of Florence, look for trailhead parking (shared with Hobbit Beach, Hike 60) in a wide turnout on the east side of US 101 just south of milepost 177, across the highway from a trail sign and 1.2 miles south of the entrance to Carl G. Washburne State Park.

ON THE TRAIL

The trail starts near the parking on the east side of the highway. It drops down briefly, then levels off, following the route of the old coast highway north along slow-moving Blowout Creek. At 0.5 mile the trail passes a couple of ponds; look for evidence of beavers. It crosses the creek and then continues north through the woods. A few steps before the trail emerges from the trees and drops down into sunny Valley Meadow at 1.3 miles, look for a trail spur to the right—the start of the Creek-Valley Loop.

The Creek-Valley Loop is a relatively recent addition to the trail system; it leads into a gorgeous Sitka spruce forest with inviting creek crossings. To make this 0.8-mile side trip, from the main trail just north of Valley Meadow take the spur trail to the right and cross a small creek on a culvert. The trail heads up briefly, then zigzags south and east across a carpet of moss, to the accompaniment of the ocean's roar. It drops down and veers north, crossing babbling China Creek at 0.5 mile, then follows the creek's east bank to Valley Meadow and a second footbridge at 0.8 mile, where it rejoins the main trail.

From Valley Meadow, the main trail continues north, climbing onto an old road lined with shore pines, passing a short spur (leading west to the highway), and meeting the paved road into Washburne State Park at 1.6 miles. If

you brought a shuttle vehicle to the state park, your hike ends here; you can also return the way you came.

To make a 3-mile beach loop with the Hobbit Trail, Hike 60, turn left on the campground road and follow it out to US 101, cross the highway, and pick up a beach trail, which cuts across the parking loop at the park's beach access area. At the beach, turn south and walk 1.2 miles to the west end of the Hobbit Trail. To make a 4-mile beach loop with the Hobbit Trail, follow the paved campground road north to the end of the campground and pick up the paved path heading north. It leads 0.3 mile under the highway along China Creek and emerges near the creek at the beach. Turn south and walk 1.7 miles on the beach to the end of the Hobbit Trail.

62 Heceta Head Lighthouse

South access from Heceta Head Lighthouse State Scenic Viewpoint:

RATING	DIFFICULTY	ROUND-TRIP	TERRAIN
★★★	2	1 mile	200 feet elevation gain

North access from Hobbit Beach trailhead:

RATING	DIFFICULTY	ROUND-TRIP	TERRAIN
★★★	4	3 miles	400 feet elevation gain

Features: Forested headland, outstanding shoreline vistas, lighthouse, forest, beach, wildlife, OCT; **Contact:** Heceta Head Lighthouse State Scenic Viewpoint, *www.oregonstateparks .org* or 800/551-6949

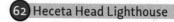 *Heceta Head is a great place for a day at the beach. The small, enclosed cove is fun for wading, but*

it's big enough to fly kites. Children enjoy "sailing" driftwood boats down Cape Creek, which empties into the ocean at the south end of the beach; at the beach's north end is a rock formation known as Devils Elbow. To get out of the wind, consider hiking up the creek: Follow a gravel road under the highway bridge, past a gate, and over a plank bridge spanning the creek, and immediately bear left on Cape Creek Trail, which follows an old road alongside the creek another 0.6 mile or so to a wide elk pasture.

The main attraction of this park, in addition to the beach, is 1893 Heceta Head Lighthouse and the classic Queen Anne–style light-tender's house (now managed as a bed and breakfast, under contract with the Forest Service). The lighthouse is open for tours every afternoon, March through October.

GETTING THERE

For the trail's south access, turn off US 101 at Heceta Head Lighthouse State Scenic Viewpoint, about 11 miles north of Florence. (For driving directions to the trail's north access, see directions to Hike 61.)

ON THE TRAIL

The lighthouse is accessible to the public only by trail, traditionally via the beach at Devils Elbow. Recently the lighthouse trail was extended to intersect Hobbit Trail (Hike 61) near US 101 to the north, adding a link to the Oregon Coast Trail. Start at either end, or link it with trails in Washburne State Park (see Hike 61).

From the south, follow the trail out of the parking lot at the state scenic viewpoint, passing picnic tables and up the hill following an old wagon road. At about 0.25 mile you pass

Lighthouse keeper's house at Heceta Head

the lighthouse keeper's house; a spur trail leads east to a viewpoint overlooking Parrot Rock (so named in the late 1800s for the tufted puffins—"sea parrots"—that have since abandoned the island). Continue on the main trail another 0.25 mile to reach the lighthouse itself. From the grassy flat at the base of the lighthouse, hikers can look east to watch for fishing boats, whales, or seabirds nesting on the offshore rocks, or look back west to watch the huge original Fresnel lens still turning slowly in the lighthouse tower.

From the north at the Hobbit Beach trailhead, cross the highway to the beach trail, but at the immediate junction, head south (left). The trail runs parallel to the highway for a short distance, then it veers away into a draw and starts up the airy forested hillside, first on steps and then on a series of switchbacks. At 0.75 mile it levels off at a view of the coastline to the north, then drops down into a dark spruce forest, switchbacking before meeting the southern lighthouse trail just east of the light.

63 Baker Beach

RATING	DIFFICULTY	ROUND-TRIP	TERRAIN
*	2	0.8 mile	Slight ascent on soft sand

Lily Lake loop

RATING	DIFFICULTY	ROUND-TRIP	TERRAIN
*	1	1 mile	Rolling

Features: Beach, dune, forest; **Contact:** Mapleton Ranger District, *www.fs.fed.us/r6/siuslaw* or 541/902-8526

In addition to the trail leading through the dunes to Baker Beach (used mainly by a local outfitter

Baker Beach Trail

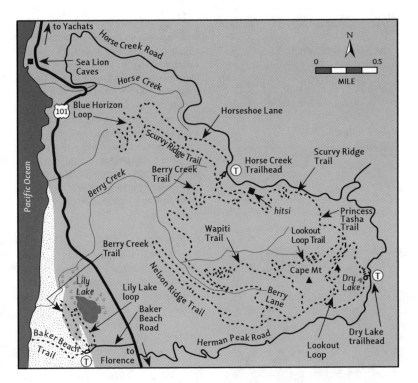

for horseback beach rides), *additional short trails have been developed here for riding and walking. The trail closest to the creek (Berry Creek Trail) isn't very appealing, but two trails between the creek and Lily Lake combine to make a pleasant short loop hike.*

GETTING THERE

About 6 miles north of Florence on US 101, turn west on Baker Beach Road and continue 0.5 mile to the large parking area at the road's end.

ON THE TRAIL

To Baker Beach: Follow the sand trail across a small creek and over the foredune. The dunes here are mostly open sand with a little vegeta-

tion; expect slow going in the soft sand. Reach the beach in 0.4 mile. For a longer walk, head north up the beach, crossing the mouth of Berry Creek in 0.25 mile and reaching the end of the beach at the base of Heceta Head in another 1.5 miles. Or walk south 2.75 miles to Sutton Beach and Sutton Creek (Hike 67).

Lily Lake loop: Pick up the trail heading north at the east end of the parking lot and follow it up to a junction; go straight. Continue along a forested sand ridge 0.4 mile to the junction with Berry Creek Trail; turn right and wind down to a view of Lily Lake through the trees. Follow a sandy forested path to another junction just before reaching the road; go right, up the hill, then left at the final junction to end where you started.

64 Cape Mountain

Cape Mountain summit:

RATING	DIFFICULTY	ROUND-TRIP	TERRAIN
★	3	2.2 miles	400 feet elevation gain

Nelson Ridge:

RATING	DIFFICULTY	ROUND-TRIP	TERRAIN
★	5	6.75 miles	800 feet elevation gain

Features: Forest, ocean views, solitude, adjacent to campground; **Contact:** Mapleton Ranger District, www.fs.fed.us/r6/siuslaw or 541/902-8526

Hitsi (traditional Siuslaw Indian hunting shelter) on Cape Mountain

In the early 1990s the Forest Service and volunteers, mainly from equestrian clubs, built a network of trails called the Coast Horse Trail System on Cape Mountain, just a few miles east of US 101 above Baker Beach. They were built mainly with equestrians in mind, but hikers can use them too. They're not the most appealing trails in the Coast Range—you're never far from a clear-cut, and ocean views are few. But some trail stretches pass through beautiful old-growth stands, and you're far from the highway; the roar you hear may be the ocean or, deep in a canyon, Berry Creek rushing to the sea.

GETTING THERE

From US 101, turn east on Herman Peak Road about 6 miles north of Florence (just south of Baker Beach Road) and drive 3 miles to the Dry Lake trailhead, on the left. The Horse Creek trailhead is 1.5 miles farther.

ON THE TRAIL

Here are a couple of the many options for day hikes on the Cape Mountain trails:

To Cape Mountain summit: This short loop to a former fire lookout site offers the best ocean views on this trail system. From between the horse corrals at the Dry Lake trailhead, start up Princess Tasha Trail, ascending for 0.5 mile to a four-way junction; take the first trail on your left (Lookout Loop Trail) and follow a fairly level route another 0.5 mile, bearing left at a junction, to a second junction where a combination of old road and trail lead left and up a short distance to the old lookout site in a (logged) clearing. Return from the spur trail to the Lookout Loop Trail (the first junction) and go left to follow it south. In 0.5 mile it crosses an old road and veers east, parallel to the road, for another 0.5 mile to swing around Dry Lake and end back at the Dry Lake trailhead.

To Nelson Ridge: This substantial day hike,

also from the Dry Lake trailhead, stretches far out a woodsy ridge and cuts through forests of every age, from ancient to just planted. A footpath takes off along the east side of Dry Lake and tends up, then down, for 0.5 mile, emerging onto an old road and bearing left. Follow it (or what's marked as "trail" along the roadside) down, into replanted clear-cut at about 1.5 miles, and back into forest on Nelson Ridge, bearing left at all trail junctions on the ridge. At about 2.5 miles the trail doubles back on itself and heads down to cross Berry Creek at 3.3 miles. Hop across the rocks and head up Wapiti Trail, bearing straight at the four-way junction. The trail switchbacks up at a gentle grade through the forest, reentering that clear-cut about 0.75 mile above the creek. Back in the forest, follow switchbacks up to the four-way junction with Princess Tasha Trail; the middle path descends slowly 0.5 mile back to the trailhead.

65 Enchanted Valley

RATING	DIFFICULTY	ROUND-TRIP	TERRAIN
★★★	1	0.8 mile or more	Flat

Features: Creek valley, wildlife; **Contact:** Mapleton Ranger District, www.fs.fed.us/r6/siuslaw or 541/902-8526

A wide, plush valley extending from an arm of Mercer Lake, drained by a gurgling creek, Enchanted Valley is a good choice for a picnic, a short summer walk out of the wind, or a blood-warming stroll on a misty winter day. What had served for many years as pasture for dairy cattle is being returned to its natural state, with a creek that again meanders through the valley rather than alongside it, and a grassy meadow that serves as winter range for some 250 wild elk. Eventually, trails here may be extended to link with those at Cape Mountain to the north (Hike 64).

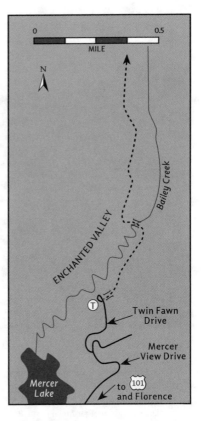

GETTING THERE

From US 101 about 6 miles north of Florence, just north of Sutton Beach Road, turn east on Mercer Lake Road and follow it about 4 miles (it becomes Mercer View Drive), then veer left onto Twin Fawn Drive and continue 0.3 mile to the trailhead parking area at road's end.

ON THE TRAIL

Start up the valley on an old road that's been converted to a footpath. A couple of small bridges cross rivulets along the way, then at 0.4 mile a more substantial footbridge crosses Bailey Creek. For a short hike, this is a good

Enchanted Valley

turnaround point. But the old road continues west and north, just inside the forest at the valley's edge. You can walk it for miles. The open valley extends another 1 mile north. Return as you came.

66 Sutton Trail

RATING	DIFFICULTY	LOOP	TERRAIN
★	3	5 miles	Flat or rolling grade

Features: Forest, dunes, creeks, adjacent to campground; **Contact:** Mapleton Ranger District, *www.fs.fed.us/r6/siuslaw* or 541/902-8526

Between campgrounds at Alder and Dune Lakes and at Sutton Creek, north of Florence, there's an interesting and relatively little-used trail system that winds through forest and dune and along the creek. The trails are mostly level, though they climb and drop slightly in a few places. They traverse terrain ranging from dense forest to lush creekside meadows and pockets of open sand dunes, providing opportunities for wildlife-watching and quiet forest wandering, especially for families camping in the area.

GETTING THERE

Sutton Beach Road heads west off US 101 about 6 miles north of Florence. The road to Sutton Campground is on the right in about 1 mile; the main road ends in another 1.5 miles at Sutton Day Use Area. Sutton Boat Launch is 0.5 mile north of the beach road on the east side of US 101.

ON THE TRAIL

This loop hike takes in most of the trail system from the highway to the beach, with opportunities for further exploration. Follow this hike description, or use the map (page 144) to pick a route and head out for as long an outing as you like. Trail junctions are generally clearly marked with destinations, though individual trails have not been named.

The trails may be accessed at any of several points, but the main trailheads are at Sutton Boat Launch (the trail leads under US 101 along Sutton Creek); Sutton Campground (two footbridges provide access to the trail across the creek); Sutton Day Use Area (see Hike 67); and Alder Dune Campground, 1 mile north of Sutton Boat Launch on US 101 (closed in winter, but accessible by foot).

From Sutton Boat Launch, it's 0.25 mile to the lower campground road. Follow it around until the trail resumes and immediately meets the Sutton Campground Loop trail. Bearing

INSECT-EATING PLANTS

Two species of insectivorous plants can be found in bogs on the southern half of the Oregon coast.

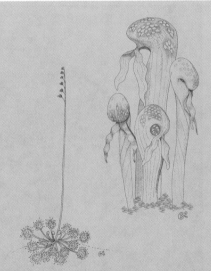

The greenish-purple leaves of the pitcher plant (*Darlingtonia californica*) look a little like mustachioed cobras jutting up anywhere from six inches to three feet out of their crowded bogs. The leaves are what lure, capture, and digest the insects the plant uses to supplement its diet with nitrogen; bugs fly into the tubular, hooded leaves, are caught by a sticky secretion, and are digested by enzymes. The leaves are the most morbidly fascinating feature of *Darlingtonia*, but look also for the plant's nodding purple flower topping a slender stalk during the blooming season, June through August.

Harder to spot is the much smaller sundew (*Drosera rotundifolia*). Its rounded leaf blades, fanned out close to the ground, are covered by fine hairs tipped with digestive glands. Insects get trapped in the hairs—and the rest is dinner. The plant's small, white flower blooms atop a two- to twelve-inch stalk in summertime.

The best place to see the pitcher plant on the Oregon coast is the Darlingtonia State Natural Site, on the east side of US 101 a short distance north of Florence. Across the highway, a boardwalk viewing area at the entrance to Sutton Campground winds past a smaller *Darlingtonia* bog. To spot sundew along the trail at South Slough (Hike 86), pick up an Estuary Study Trail guide at the visitor center and follow it to the sundew bog near the dikes at the trail's end.

left you'll follow the creek, passing first one footbridge and then, at 0.5 mile, another. Cross it to begin the Middle Loop, hugging the creek's west shore for 1.25 miles to a third footbridge. Rather than cross it, bear left and walk 0.5 mile to the day-use area (the starting point for Hike 67).

To continue the full loop hike, bear right along the creek's estuary and then follow the sinuous creek itself back to the third footbridge, at 3.5 miles. Cross it this time, and follow the east side of the loop back through the heart of the brushy dunes. (About 0.75 mile past the third bridge you'll meet a 0.75-mile spur trail leading east to Alder Dune Campground; it leads to another 1-mile trail circling Alder Lake.) Continuing on the Middle Loop, at the next junction bear left (the right-hand path heads toward the second footbridge and the campground) to follow the east side of the Sutton Campground Loop trail through the dunes to the end of the lower campground loop road. Cross the campground road and follow the trail back to the boat launch.

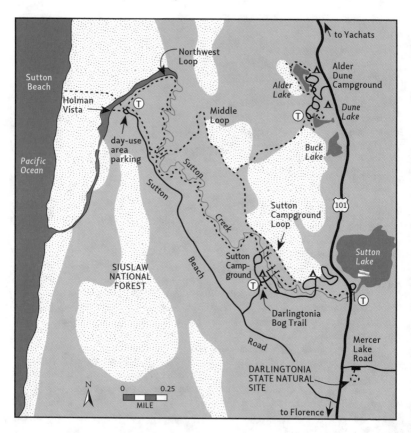

Deer tracks along Sutton Trail

67 Sutton Beach

RATING	DIFFICULTY	ROUND-TRIP	TERRAIN
★★	2	2.5 miles	Flat

Features: Beach, creek crossing, adjacent to campground; **Contact:** Mapleton Ranger District, *www.fs.fed.us/r6/siuslaw* or 541/902-8526

The quickest way to Sutton Beach is to wade Sutton Creek. That fact keeps this beach fairly secluded (though it's accessible by beach from the north—see Hike 63, Baker Beach). The creek may be waded any season of the year, even midwinter, when the chilly water may hit mid-thigh. On a mild winter day, however, it can be a not-unpleasant start to a beach outing; in summer the creek is lower, and wading with children is easier and safer.

GETTING THERE
About 6 miles north of Florence, turn west off US 101 onto Sutton Beach Road and follow it 2.5 miles to where it ends at Holman Vista.

ON THE TRAIL
A wooden boardwalk and raised viewing platform (wheelchair accessible) at Holman Vista grants a good view of the dunes and Sutton Creek estuary. To get to the beach, take the asphalt trail just north of the viewpoint trail and follow it a short distance to the creek. Blue-ringed trail posts mark the crossing, but you may have to veer up or down the creek a bit to find the shallowest route. Across the creek, posts continue to mark the way 0.25 mile to the beach. You might just leave your shoes off; water can cover the sandy trail at several points. Heading south on the beach, you'll meet the creek again in about 1.25 miles, where it runs into the ocean; return as you came.

Cape Lookout Beach

Alternatively, you could cross the creek and continue south to Heceta Beach or even the Siuslaw North Jetty (Hike 68). But south of the creek, civilization resumes with houses and people and a large motel. To the north it's just wild beach. Another option is to head north from the creek to Baker Beach (Hike 63).

68 Siuslaw North Jetty

RATING	DIFFICULTY	ROUND-TRIP	TERRAIN
*	1	1.25 miles	Flat

Features: Beach, wildlife, close to town; **Contact:** Florence Area Chamber of Commerce, *www.florencechamber.com* or 541/997-3128

The beach north of the north jetty at Florence is wide, windy, and wild. Check out the action at the river's mouth—seals, sea lions, and seabirds—before heading north on Heceta Beach.

GETTING THERE

From US 101 north of the junction with State Highway 126, turn west on 35th Street at the sign for the north jetty. In about 1 mile, turn right onto North Rhododendron Drive and follow it just past Harbor Vista County Park. Turn left onto North Jetty Road and continue to the road's end. Heceta Beach Access is about 1.25 miles farther north on Rhododendron Drive, or watch for signs to it on US 101 about 3 miles north of State Highway 126.

ON THE TRAIL

From the jetty, walk north along the beach for 0.75 mile, enjoying its wildness. At 1.25 miles you'll reach Heceta Beach Access; leave a car here for a one-way walk, or return as you came. You can also continue past this stretch of development to the wild shore of Sutton Creek, another 0.75 mile north (see Hike 67, Sutton Beach).

OREGON COAST TRAIL, CENTRAL COAST

Distance: About 64 miles

 Follow US 101 over Yaquina Head; walk the beach to Yaquina Bay (Hike 43). Cross the bay on the highway bridge; at the end, walk a short distance and turn right at the sign to the Oregon Coast Aquarium. Turn left onto Southwest 26th Street and walk west to the south jetty. Head south on the beach (or South Jetty Trail, Hike 45); ford Beaver Creek. At Seal Rock, scramble up the steep sandstone cliff and follow the asphalt path out to US 101. Follow the highway for about 1 mile, then turn west on Quail Street to the beach. Approaching Waldport, follow the beach around into the mouth of Alsea Bay. At the mouth of the bay, leave the beach and follow the main road back up to US 101 and across the bridge; return to the beach at the south end of town.

CROWS AND RAVENS

In coastal Indian mythology, Raven is the trickster: self-serving, often sneaky, plenty smart. Spend some time watching ravens or their cousins, the crows, on the beach, and you'll see those character traits come alive. They're bold, brainy, curious, and clever enough to have figured out the easy way to open a mussel or clam: Fly up high and drop it on a rock or, better yet, drop it on a paved road and let a passing car's tires do the work.

Both American crows and common ravens can be found year-round on the beaches, dunes, tree islands, and transition forests of the Oregon coast. Look for them scavenging for food at low tide—or, in the spring, ferreting out other birds' nests to snack on the eggs or babies there. Their harsh voices are pretty unmistakable, a familiar *caw, caw, caw* from the crow or the gravelly *cr-r-ruck* of the raven. In flight they range from straightforward to wildly acrobatic, especially the raven, and especially during spring courtship: soaring, tumbling, barrel-rolling, alone or with a mate.

Crows are gregarious, more likely to flock together than the often solitary ravens. Ravens are also substantially larger than crows, have a characteristic "goiter patch" (a ruffle of feathers at the throat), and have a stouter and slightly hooked bill. In flight, the raven's tail feathers form a spade shape; the crow's tail is squared off.

Approaching Yachats, the beach ends at a headland topped with houses. Look for a trail running up the sandstone slope (Hike 49) and follow the 804 Trail through Smelt Sands State Recreation Area and beyond, along the bluff and through the neighborhood, to its end on Ocean View Drive at US 101. Cross the Yachats River bridge, turn right on Yachats Ocean Road and follow it for a mile to US 101. Walk cautiously on the narrow highway 0.4 mile to the start of the Kittel-Amanda trail (Hike 50), marked with a small sign on the east side of the highway. Take it up Cape Perpetua, take Hike 51 down the other side, and follow Hike 56 to the Cummins Creek road. Follow the highway south for about 7 miles (Caution: little or no road shoulder). Where the beach widens at Big Creek or at Muriel O. Ponsler Memorial State Scenic Viewpoint,

walk down to the sand and follow the beach south.

Approaching Heceta Head, watch for an OCT trail post in the brush at the end of Hike 60; take it to the lighthouse trail, Hike 62, over Heceta Head. At Heceta Head Lighthouse State Scenic Viewpoint, return to the highway (caution: narrow tunnel), passing Sea Lion Caves. Descending the headland, with Florence in the distance, look for railroad tie steps leading down the hill below the guardrail, just south of milepost 181 and the sign for the Southview housing development. Follow a mowed path that zigzags down to the beach. Continue south, wading Sutton Creek. At the north jetty of the Siuslaw River, walk North Jetty Road to Rhododendron Drive, turn south, and follow it into Florence, continuing south on US 101 to cross the Siuslaw River.

the south-central coast

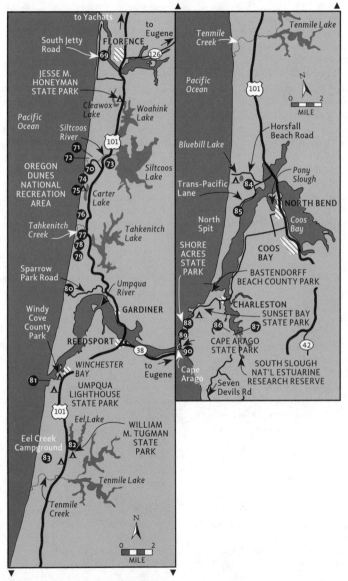

DUNE HELL

Rarely have I actually been weathered out of a hike at the beach. It happened on Umpqua Dunes. It was raining in the Willamette Valley that morning, raining in the Coast Range, still raining when we pulled up to the trailhead. "We" was my dad the Mountain Man (who, to add to the drama, doesn't much like the beach anyway) and me. We suited up. We started across.

Usually in a rain like this, there are breaks, long enough to sneak in a hike. Not this day. Couldn't see, for one thing; I figured that dark shape ahead on the left was a tree island, maybe. But blindness we could handle. It was the horizontal, sand-laden rain that did us in. Imagine a pressure washer loaded with liquid cement pointed at you. We trudged on, fueled by the same genetically encoded stubbornness. I forget who gave up first. But well before we reached the tree island, we realized it was time to get off Umpqua Dunes. The nickname I'd heard for the trail fit: Dune Hell.

So there was that history when, three years later, I finally tried it again. A day in April, as pleasant, it turned out, as a good day in June: blue sky, sun, barely windy; sunglasses and windbreakers. We were surprised, after sauntering across the open dunes, how soggy the trail from dune to beach was, and we laughed about how we thought we'd need a camel on Umpqua Dunes, but what we really needed was scuba gear. By the time we headed back from the beach, the afternoon winds had picked up and it was a grittier return, but still not unpleasant. Dune Heaven? Well, close to it. The same hill of sand—just a matter of how the winds are blowing.

The longest stretch of Oregon beach unbroken by headlands is the fifty-two miles of sand running from Heceta Head to the mouth of Coos Bay. South of Florence, most of the land between the shore and highway belongs to Oregon Dunes National Recreation Area. It's the largest expanse of coastal sand dunes in the United States, with some dunes as tall as

500 feet. But numbers can't express the essence of the dunes' appeal: the play of light and shadow across the open sand, the lazy curve of a tannin-stained creek through the forest, the stillness found in the lee of a hummock on a blustery day.

There's road access through dunes to beach at several points; in between, hiking trails provide access to more remote stretches of beach, often with good opportunities for wildlife-watching along the way.

First-time visitors to the dunes are sometimes taken aback by the presence of off-road vehicles breaking the silence of the dunes. Dune buggies have been a fixture on the dunes for years, fiercely defended by a contingent of local residents. But their use is restricted to certain parts of the dunes, generally well away from hiking trails. Among the areas where ORVs are allowed are the beaches immediately north of the Umpqua River and Coos Bay.

The dunes end at hook-shaped Coos Bay, the second-largest estuary in Oregon, smaller only than the Columbia River's mouth. Much of the salt marsh that used to surround the bay has been destroyed in favor of agricultural or industrial interests, but the bay's many sloughs and inlets still provide important habitat for a variety of plants, fish, birds, and mammals. Best access is at South Slough National Estuarine Research Reserve south of Charleston, where interesting loop trails lead down to the edge of the salt marsh.

South of Coos Bay, US 101 follows an inland route that doesn't return to the shoreline until Bandon. Detour west through Charleston to take in one of the most dramatic, intriguing sections of the coast. Cape Arago Highway leads past a lighthouse-topped island followed by an idyllic crescent-shaped bay, formal public gardens, broad tide pools, fantastic wildlife-watching, and a sculpture garden of offshore rocks—all strung together by a 3.5-mile section of the Oregon Coast Trail.

Interpretive centers. The Umpqua Discovery Center (541/271-4816) on the river in Reedsport has displays featuring the natural and human history of the nearby dunes and lower Umpqua River area. A small interpretive center at South Slough National Estuarine Research Reserve (541/888-5558) introduces visitors to estuarine ecology in displays geared to children.

Wildlife-watching. A variety of birds nest, rest, or winter in the dunes, from tiny snowy plovers and songbirds to swans, ospreys, and bald eagles. Among the best hikes for bird-watching are Siuslaw South Jetty Dune (Hike 69), Waxmyrtle Trail (Hike 70), Lagoon Trail (Hike 71), and Taylor Dunes (Hike 74). The river mouths are always good bets for shorebirds as well as seals and sea lions.

Drive 3 miles east of Reedsport on State Highway 38 for a good chance at seeing Roosevelt elk. A frontage road leads off the highway at Dean Creek Elk Viewing Area (541/756-0100), so you can safely stop and watch the large herd of elk that frequents the meadow here. The Bureau of Land Management has also built an open-sided shelter for wildlife-watching in any weather; interpretive signs describe the elk and other animals that inhabit the meadow.

Off Coos Bay, South Slough offers excellent wildlife-watching (see Hike 86). Pony Slough is an easily accessible spot for bird-watching just off US 101. From downtown North Bend, take Virginia Avenue west 0.7 mile to Marion Street and turn right, following the paved road 1 mile to where it ends in a large parking area with a boat launch, wind-sheltered picnic tables, and rest rooms. In winter look for egrets and large concentrations of shorebirds here, while big "birds"—orange-and-white Coast Guard helicopters—take off and land at the adjacent airport.

Cape Arago offers the best whale-watching on the south-central coast, along with views of seabirds, sea lions, harbor seals, and even elephant seals. The roadside viewpoint overlooking Shell Island, a scant 0.5 mile north of the park's loop at the end of Cape Arago Highway, is the best viewpoint.

Tidepooling. (See Respectful Tidepooling, p. 31.) With dunes comprising most of the south-central coastline, there's no tidepooling until you get south of Coos Bay. Tide pools form on rock shelves and among boulders at the north and south ends of crescent-shaped Sunset Bay; those to the north are the more extensive and appear to be the safest as well. Immense tide pools form in the North Cove at Cape Arago, and also at the South and Middle Coves (Hike 90).

Off-road cycling. Most of the trails in the Oregon Dunes are too sandy for cycling. An exception is Siltcoos Lake Trail (Hike 73), but look out for the stairs on the south side of the loop.

Camping/hostels. Jessie M. Honeyman State Park is huge, with nearly 400 campsites tucked among the rhododendrons, shore pines, and Douglas firs. In summer the water of sand-bottomed Cleawox Lake is relatively warm; you'll find a sandy, roped-off swimming area and swimming platform at one of the park's day-use areas, plus boat rentals (canoes, rowboats, and pedal boats), a snack bar, and a small grocery. To the south there's a collection of primitive Forest Service campgrounds along Siltcoos Beach Road and one each at Carter Lake, Tahkenitch Lake, and Eel Creek. (Those off Horsfall Beach Road north of Coos Bay cater to ORV and horse owners.) Sites at several of these Forest Service campgrounds may be reserved at www.*reserve america.com* or 877/444-6777.

Windy Cove A (541/271-4138) and Windy Cove B (541/271-5634) are a pair of large county parks at Winchester Bay well equipped for RVs; call at least two weeks in advance for reservations. South of the Umpqua River are a pair of small state park campgrounds—Umpqua

ROOSEVELT ELK

The second-largest members of the deer family in North America, elk are a fixture of Oregon's Coast Range and its lowlands. Early settlers killed the native Roosevelt elk rather indiscriminately, and much of their habitat was destroyed. But limits on hunting (imposed beginning in 1904) and transplantation efforts by wildlife officials have allowed the animals to become reestablished along virtually the entire coastline (to the chagrin, at times, of coastal gardeners).

With their tall stature and long, dark hair encircling their thick necks, contrasting with gray or paler brown bodies, elk are easy to distinguish from deer. In the forest they're most active at dawn and dusk, moving almost silently among the trees. Around midday they tend to rest or graze. You're not likely to see an elk while hiking, but you'll know they're near from their deep hoof prints and their droppings, like a deer's but larger.

Oregon wildlife officials manage five elk foraging areas comprised of hayfields, clearings, and meadows on the coast and in the Coast Range. The largest is 1200-acre Jewell Meadows Wildlife Area, on the north coast near Jewell in the interior of Clatsop County. Closer to US 101 is 1040-acre Dean Creek Elk Viewing Area, developed by the Bureau of Land Management on pastures just three miles east of Reedsport on State Highway 38. You can see animals at either site year-round, though they're most numerous in winter, when the weather is cool, and early and late in the day. During calving season in late spring, female elk tend to seek seclusion in the forest.

Lighthouse and William M. Tugman—located on lakes with swimming beaches. Out Cape Arago Highway, camping is available at Bastendorff Beach County Park (to reserve a "camping cabin," call 541/888-5353) and at Sunset Bay State Park, popular in summer for its lovely ocean cove with a gradually sloping sandy beach and relatively warm water.

For reservations at state park campgrounds, call 800/452-5687.

Travelers' tips. The headquarters for Oregon Dunes National Recreation Area is in Reedsport, where you'll find some respectable restaurants; a bit south is Winchester Bay, where a large marina sits near the mouth of the Umpqua. North Bend and Coos Bay form a continuous strip of development for some five miles of US 101; gas up, grab some fast food, overnight at a motel, resupply at the mall. The little fishing town you were hoping to find is southwest of Coos Bay at Charleston on the Cape Arago Highway.

Recommended hikes. There's not a bad trail in the dunes, though my favorites are Oregon Dunes Overlook (Hike 76), the Threemile Lake–Tahkenitch Dunes loop (Hikes 78 and 79), and—when conditions are right—John Dellenback Trail across Umpqua Dunes (Hike 83). In winter, when most dunes trails are at least partially under water, Waxmyrtle Trail (Hike 70) is a good choice. Walk the Hidden Creek Trail at South Slough (Hike 86) while the skunk cabbage is blooming in early spring. Take all day to walk the Cape Arago Shoreline Trail (Hike 88), stopping to watch wildlife.

69 Siuslaw South Jetty Dune

RATING	DIFFICULTY	ROUND-TRIP	TERRAIN
★	1	1 mile	Flat

Features: Wetlands, dunes, wildlife; **Contact:** Oregon Dunes National Recreation Area, *www.fs.fed.us/r6/siuslaw* or 541-271-3611

 A little-known, unsigned path follows an old dike through the marshes east of the road on the Siuslaw River's South Jetty. Birdwatchers and others who enjoy a little solitude close to town will find this trail worth seeking out.

GETTING THERE

From the Siuslaw River Bridge at Florence, drive 0.6 mile south on US 101 and turn west on South Jetty Road. A half-dozen parking lots are strung along the road, ending about 0.25 mile south of the jetty itself.

ON THE TRAIL

To reach the beach here, pick any of the parking lots on South Jetty Road, park, climb over the foredune, and you're there. For this hike, park at the third beach parking lot, just north of a little viewpoint facing the marsh, and follow the brushy dike-top trail leading east across the dune. Almost any time of year you'll see waterfowl of one kind or another in the wetlands to the north and south; large flocks of swans frequent the area in the winter. After 0.5 mile the dike falls away to a small creek;

Beach strawberry

wade it to climb onto a fantastic landscape of contorted dunes above thick forest bordering the Siuslaw River below. The formal trail is over, but the landscape invites further exploration. Return as you came.

70 Waxmyrtle Trail

RATING	DIFFICULTY	ROUND-TRIP	TERRAIN
★★★★★	3	2.5 miles	Slight incline

Features: Estuary, forest, beach, wildlife, adjacent to campground; **Contact:** Oregon Dunes National Recreation Area, www.fs.fed .us/r6/siuslaw or 541-271-3611

Follow a woodsy trail above the Siltcoos River to a quiet stretch of beach near the river's mouth. The trees provide a natural blind behind which to observe the bird life in the estuary. A large marsh near the trail's end is closed to hikers mid-March through mid-September to protect any snowy plovers that may be nesting there, but an alternative trail to the south still gets you to the beach year-round. Dogs are allowed on the beach trail but restricted in the estuary.

GETTING THERE

From US 101 about 7 miles south of Florence, take Siltcoos Beach Road west 1 mile to the Stagecoach trailhead parking area just west of the entrance to Waxmyrtle Campground.

ON THE TRAIL

From the trailhead parking area, follow the trail 0.1 mile east to the Waxmyrtle Campground road, cross the Siltcoos River, and turn west where the trail begins following the river's south bank. Climb stairs up a short hill forested with shore pines, continuing along the bluff to a junction at about 0.4 mile.

Bear right to follow the Estuary Trail on a riverside route out to the beach. (It is closed March 15 to September 15 to protect nesting plovers; in winter, when it's open, dogs must be on leash.) Otherwise, bear left at the junction on the beach access trail, which goes a short distance before joining an old sand road that skirts the plover nesting area and ends at the beach. Dogs are allowed here year-round as long as they stay south of the beach access trail; humans can walk north up the beach but are asked to stay out of open sand at the mouth of the creek during nesting season. Return as you came.

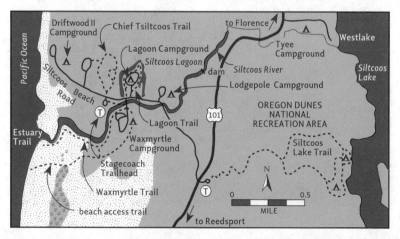

71 Lagoon Trail

RATING	DIFFICULTY	LOOP	TERRAIN
★★	1	1 mile	Flat

Features: Wetlands, forest, wildlife, adjacent to campground; **Contact:** Oregon Dunes National Recreation Area, *www.fs.fed.us/r6/siuslaw* or 541/271-3611

Lagoon Trail follows an old arm of the Siltcoos River that was cut off when Siltcoos Beach Road was built, hence the nickname: The River of No Return. If you're very lucky and very observant you might see a bittern in the lagoon during nesting season.

GETTING THERE
From US 101 about 7 miles south of Florence, take Siltcoos Beach Road west 1 mile to the Stagecoach trailhead parking area just west of the entrance to Waxmyrtle Campground.

ON THE TRAIL
The trail begins on the north side of the road directly across from the entrance to Waxmyrtle Campground; follow the trail parallel to the road 0.1 mile east. Cross Siltcoos Beach Road to the boardwalk along the lagoon. It turns quickly into a footpath, marshy in spots, following the water's edge. Walk quietly, watching for waterfowl and songbirds. After 0.25 mile the trail leaves the lagoon's edge but quickly returns, following the lagoon to loop around Lagoon Campground and end where the campground road meets Siltcoos Beach Road.

72 Chief Tsiltcoos Trail

RATING	DIFFICULTY	LOOP	TERRAIN
★	2	1.25 miles	100 feet elevation gain

Features: Dune forest, adjacent to campground; **Contact:** Oregon Dunes National Recreation Area, *www.fs.fed.us/r6/siuslaw* or 541/271-3611

For those camping in one of the campgrounds on Siltcoos Beach Road, this short, woodsy trail up an old tree island characteristic of the dunes landscape makes a nice outing, especially early or late in the day. Walk from your campsite or park at the Stagecoach trailhead.

GETTING THERE
From US 101 about 7 miles south of Florence take Siltcoos Beach Road west 1 mile to the Stagecoach trailhead parking area just west of the entrance to Waxmyrtle Campground.

ON THE TRAIL
Cross the beach road to the trail, which quickly splits to form the loop. Taking the right fork,

Lagoon Trail

follow the trail up into the woods, listening for the many songbirds that inhabit the forest. A 0.1-mile spur to the left loops to the top of the knoll and back to the main trail. Otherwise, continue on the main trail. At about 0.6 mile a spur to the right leads to Driftwood II Campground (primarily for ORV users); to complete the loop, stay to the left on the main trail back to your starting point.

Siltcoos Lake Trail

73 Siltcoos Lake

RATING	DIFFICULTY	LOOP	TERRAIN
★★	3	5 miles	600 feet elevation gain

Features: Lake, forest, primitive camping; **Contact:** Oregon Dunes National Recreation Area, *www.fs.fed.us/r6/siuslaw* or 541/271-3611

On a warm summer's day, there's nothing like hiking a couple of miles through deep coastal forest, then plunging into freshwater Siltcoos Lake, the largest lake on the Oregon coast. There are several campgrounds on the lakeshore, often occupied by boaters arriving by water.

GETTING THERE

From Florence, take US 101 south about 7 miles and turn east at the sign to the Siltcoos Lake trailhead, across the highway from Siltcoos Beach Road.

ON THE TRAIL

Begin hiking up a steady incline through dense shrubbery. The trail levels off and then splits into two trails at 1 mile. Either direction leads to the lake in a little more than 1 mile. Taking the left-hand trail, the route drops slowly through second-growth forest logged long ago (look for old-time loggers' springboard notches in stumps). At 2.2 miles a spur trail leads left to a group of five lakeside campsites; stay right to continue around the lakeshore to a single (lovely) campsite to the south. (On our last visit there were outhouses at both campsites, but both were in very bad condition.) The campground loops are a bit confusing here, but bear left and you'll eventually wind around to the return trail. It leads over a boardwalk and up a set of stairs, then skirts the bottom of a clear-cut 0.3 mile before completing the loop. Bear left to return to the trailhead.

74 Taylor Dunes

RATING	DIFFICULTY	ROUND-TRIP	TERRAIN
**	2	2 miles	Slight ascent

Features: Dunes, forest, wildlife, adjacent to campground; **Contact:** Oregon Dunes National Recreation Area, *www.fs.fed.us/r6/siuslaw* or 541/271-3611

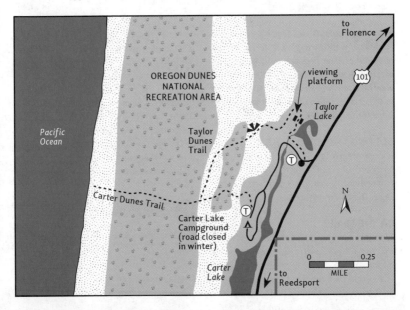

Tracks across the Oregon Dunes

Taylor Dunes Trail offers a 1-mile walk through the forest to the open dunes. The first 0.5 mile, to a scenic overlook, is wheelchair-accessible. As a short view hike, it's fine all by itself; to reach the beach (3 miles round trip), link it with Carter Dunes Trail (Hike 75).

GETTING THERE

From Florence take US 101 south about 8 miles and turn west at the road to Carter Lake Campground; immediately turn left into the Taylor Dunes parking area.

ON THE TRAIL

Cross the campground road and begin walking along Taylor Lake. A boardwalk viewing platform invites hikers to pause at the pond and watch for osprey and other birds. Continue as the trail climbs up the hillside at a gentle grade. At 0.5 mile the trail splits; bear left a short distance to a viewpoint at the edge of the forest. Bear right to continue on the trail route, now on open sand.

Follow trail posts another 0.5 mile through the dunes to where the trail intersects Carter Dunes Trail. The intersection may not be well marked; look for a trail marker to the east or, to the west, a footpath entering a shrubby pine grove. Return as you came. (Or go to the right on the Carter Dunes Trail to reach the beach in 0.5 mile.)

75 Carter Dunes

RATING	DIFFICULTY	ROUND-TRIP	TERRAIN
★★★★	3	1.5 miles	Slight ascent

Features: Dunes, forest, beach, solitude, adjacent to campground; **Contact:** Oregon

Dunes National Recreation Area, *www.fs.fed.us/r6/siuslaw* or 541/271-3611

![hiker][dog][kids] *It's just 0.75 mile across the dunes to the beach on Carter Dunes Trail to one of the quietest, loneliest beaches in the Oregon dunes. (In winter, when the campground and its access road are closed, use Taylor Dunes Trail, Hike 74.)*

GETTING THERE
From Florence take US 101 south about 8 miles and turn west at the road to Carter Lake Campground; follow the road 0.4 mile to the trailhead parking area.

ON THE TRAIL
Walk west 0.1 mile up through dense forest to the edge of the open dunes. Follow blue-topped trail posts across the sand past the junction with Taylor Dunes Trail at 0.25 mile

to where the trail resumes at a grove of pines. Continue through the trees and follow marker posts across more open sand. Cross the deflation plain on a distinct but sometimes soggy trail, then head up and over the foredune to the beach. Return as you came.

76 Oregon Dunes Overlook

RATING	DIFFICULTY	LOOP	TERRAIN
★★★	3	2–4.5 miles	140 feet elevation loss

Features: Dunes, forest, creek, beach; **Contact:** Oregon Dunes National Recreation Area, *www.fs.fed.us/r6/siuslaw* or 541/271-3611

![icons] *Tourists traveling the Oregon coast can stop at this day-use area for a quick overview of the dunes before motoring on. Better yet, park*

Oregon Dunes Overlook Trail

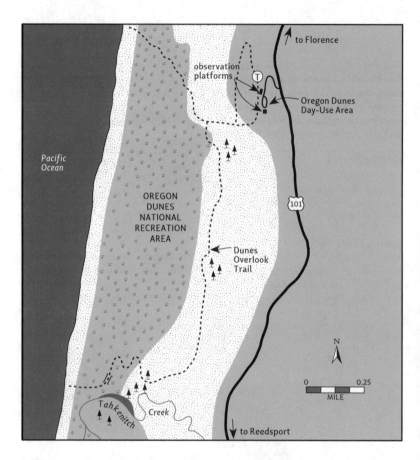

and walk to the beach on one of the most in-teresting short trails in the dunes. Return as you came, or walk down the beach to make a loop return on an alternate trail.

GETTING THERE

Take US 101 about 10 miles south of Florence (and about the same distance north of Reed-sport) and turn west at the sign to Oregon Dunes Day Use Area (formerly Oregon Dunes Overlook).

ON THE TRAIL

You can reach the main trail from one of two directions. From the covered viewing platform off the parking area, walk north on an asphalt trail, past several picnic tables, and make a sharp left turn at the start of a gravel path gently descending the hillside. Alternately, walk south up the stairs or ramp to the upper viewing deck off the parking area and follow a winding, sandy trail a short distance through the trees, then walk or slide to the bottom of a tall sand dune. Both approaches take you to the middle of an open dune in about 0.25 mile; from here, posts mark the route west across another 0.25 mile of open sand. To reach the beach, bear right with the posts to enter the deflation plain, which the trail crosses with help from small bridges. Climbing over the foredune, the trail reaches the beach at 1 mile. Return as you came.

For a longer 4.5-mile loop hike, walk south along the beach for 1.5 miles until you see a trail post (if you reach Tahkenitch Creek, you've gone too far). Follow the trail as it climbs over the foredune, crosses a footbridge, and leads up into a tree island of shore pines. From here, posts mark the way north across open dunes to another tree island about 1 mile from the beach and then back on open sand. Skirt just west of a third tree island (the post, nearly buried in sand, may be a little hard to see). Continue following posts until you reach the open sand just below the overlook, 2 miles from where you left the beach; climb up the sand hill to the right or go up the trail ascending to the left.

77 Tahkenitch Creek

RATING	DIFFICULTY	LOOP	TERRAIN
★★★	3	1.5, 2.5, 3, or 4 miles	Flat to modest incline

Features: Dunes, forest, creek, beach, wildlife;
Contact: Oregon Dunes National Recreation Area, www.fs.fed.us/r6/siuslaw or 541/271-3611

On its way from Tahkenitch Lake to the ocean, Tahkenitch Creek twists and turns through the dunes, curving north and then south before meeting the sea. A trail system has been built inside the embrace of Tahkenitch Creek. Anglers use it to get to the creek's bank; for others, it provides easy walking through a dramatic landscape of forest, marsh, and

open dunes. At the south end of the longest loop, the trail meets Tahkenitch Dunes Trail (Hike 78), offering the option of an even longer loop hike to Threemile Lake (about 11 miles total) or a one-way trek (with a shuttle car) ending at Tahkenitch Campground.

GETTING THERE
The signed trailhead is just west of US 101, 1.6 miles south of the Oregon Dunes Day Use Area and about 8 miles north of Reedsport.

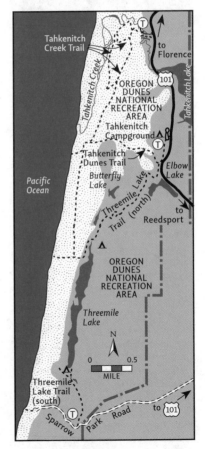

View of Tahkenitch Dunes

ON THE TRAIL

From the parking area, the trail descends 0.1 mile to a footbridge at a bend in the sinuous creek. Continue a short distance to a junction, the first of several; bear right to peek at a particularly gorgeous creek beach, otherwise bear left with the main trail.

To make a counterclockwise, 4-mile round trip, bear right at upcoming junctions or follow signs pointing to "beach." For shorter loops, circle back to the left at one or another junction. The trail winds in and out of vegetated and open dunes. Though the path is clear most of the way, wooden posts mark the route across stretches of open sand. Note that the trail on the eastern side of the loop is apt to be covered with standing water much of the way in winter; we've waded here barefoot in January, through pools the color of French onion soup. The western trail stretches are drier.

At 1.4 miles from the trailhead, signs point you east for a short distance to a junction, where you bear right and continue 0.9 mile more to reach the junction with Tahkenitch Dunes Trail and a view of the ocean. Continue 0.5 mile more on the dunes trail to reach

the beach, or backtrack not quite 0.9 mile on the Tahkenitch Creek Trail to the last junction. Bear right at this and the next two junctions to return to the trailhead.

78 Tahkenitch Dunes

RATING	DIFFICULTY	ROUND-TRIP	TERRAIN
★★★	3	3.5 miles	240 feet elevation gain

Features: Forest, dunes, adjacent to campground; **Contact:** Oregon Dunes National Recreation Area, *www.fs.fed.us/r6/siuslaw* or 541/271-3611

The trail from Tahkenitch Campground to the beach is one of many—a bit longer than most—leading across the dunes to the beach. Its main appeal is the link it provides to Threemile Lake Trail (see Hike 79).

GETTING THERE

From US 101 about 7 miles north of Reedsport, turn west at the sign to Tahkenitch Campground.

ON THE TRAIL

From the trailhead parking area, follow the trail 0.25 mile to a junction and bear right (left leads to Threemile Lake). The route takes a fairly level course through the forest until the trees give way to open dunes at 0.75 mile. Look to the southwest to see posts marking the route. Cross a swath of pines leading to the soggy deflation plain, where it meets the southern end of Tahkenitch Creek Trail (Hike 77), on the right. Just ahead, at a fenced ocean viewpoint, the trail veers south. Follow the wide sandy path another 0.5 mile south to where it ends at the beach just south of the ever-moving creek mouth.

79 Threemile Lake Trail— North Access

RATING	DIFFICULTY	ROUND-TRIP	TERRAIN
★★★★★	4	6 miles (beach–lake loop 6.75 miles)	400 feet elevation gain

Features: Lake, ancient forest, dunes, beach, adjacent to campground, primitive camping; **Contact:** Oregon Dunes National Recreation Area, *www.fs.fed.us/r6/siuslaw* or 541-271-3611

The trail to the north end of hidden Threemile Lake leads through lush forest, some of the most gorgeous woods on the coast. Hike it round trip, or combine it with a long amble on a remote stretch of beach for one of the most appealing hikes on the Oregon coast.

GETTING THERE

From US 101 about 7 miles north of Reedsport, turn west at the sign to Tahkenitch Campground.

ON THE TRAIL

From the trailhead parking area, follow the Tahkenitch Dunes Trail (Hike 78) with a 0.25-mile uphill stroll to a trail junction; bear left. The route

Threemile Lake

mostly ascends for about 1 mile to a bench with a view of the mouth of Tahkenitch Creek; then it gently descends through deep forest. Listen for the buzz of the rufous hummingbird flitting through the forest. In the early spring, bright yellow skunk cabbage blossoms fill lush creekbeds. Flying squirrels inhabit the shrubby forest understory here, and the creeks are home to eight different species of salamander.

Nearing the lake, the trail crosses a narrow log bridge and then ascends to a rise at the forest's edge, where there's a small campsite. Continue a short distance along the sand, bearing left to see, and drop down to Threemile Lake at 3 miles. Return as you came.

For a loop hike, follow trail posts across the dunes 0.5 mile west to the beach. Hike north on the beach 1.5 miles and look for trail posts mark-

THE DUNE LANDSCAPE

Take a hike across Oregon's coastal dunes and you'll quickly recognize a particular pattern of landforms. Following are some definitions to help you identify the most easily recognizable elements of this unique geography.

Foredune: The big sand seawall behind the beach looks natural enough, but it is actually a relatively new phenomenon, resulting from the introduction of European beach grass at the turn of the century. The foredune blocks the movement of sand eastward. Behind it forms . . .

Hummocks: These are knoblike mounds behind a foredune. Some are dry, composed mainly of open sand. Others are wet, supporting many plant species. Behind them you may need to take off your shoes and wade through the . . .

Deflation plain, the wet, vegetation-rich depression inland from the foredune. As a foredune grows, winds scour lighter-weight sand particles out of the sand bed behind it, effectively deflating it down to the water table and allowing it to support a wealth of plant life.

Tree islands: These are steep-sloped miniforests isolated by shifting sands. The same trees and understory plants found in the inland transition forest are generally found here.

Transition forest is an approximately mile-wide plant community between the dunes and the coastal forest. Plants common to the transition forest include Sitka spruce, western hemlock, and Douglas fir, plus rhododendron, evergreen huckleberry, and salmonberry. The most common tree is the shore pine, which is not found in the coastal forest. The density of some plant species creates a virtually impenetrable thicket in places.

ing the western end of Tahkenitch Dunes Trail (if you reach the mouth of Tahkenitch Creek, you've gone too far); follow it 1.75 miles back to the campground. (Wooden posts also mark a route through the dunes parallel to the beach walk, but they're not always easy to follow.)

80 Threemile Lake Trail—South Access

RATING	DIFFICULTY	ROUND-TRIP	TERRAIN
★★	1	1.5 miles	160 feet elevation gain

Southern trail to Threemile Lake

Features: Lake, ancient forest, solitude, primitive camping; **Contact:** Oregon Dunes National Recreation Area, *www.fs.fed.us/r6/siuslaw* or 541/271-3611

A relatively little-used trail leads to the south end of Threemile Lake. The forest through which the trail leads is deep and lush, and the quiet beach at the lakeshore is tempting for overnight camping. Be aware, however, that the trailhead is on a remote road not regularly patrolled, and vandalism (especially to cars left overnight) is more likely to be a problem

here than at more well-used trailheads such as that for the north access to Threemile Lake (Hike 79).

GETTING THERE

From US 101 about 3.5 miles north of Reedsport, turn west on bumpy gravel Sparrow Park Road and follow it 3.3 miles to the trailhead, marked with a small trailhead sign nailed to a tree at a wide spot in the road just west of a sign indicating the national forest boundary.

ON THE TRAIL

Follow the trail through the forest uphill about 0.25 mile and then gently downhill, glimpsing a pond on the right at about 0.5 mile. Immediately there's a trail junction. A left turn leads 0.2 mile up a trail to the edge of the dunes and down a sand trail to a campsite, where the marked trail ends. Or, back at the junction, you can continue on the main trail down to a log footbridge (slippery when wet) and back up a short distance to a gentle, sandy beach at the south end of the lake. Either way, return as you came.

81 Lake Marie

RATING	DIFFICULTY	LOOP	TERRAIN
★	1	1 mile	Nearly flat

Features: Lake, swimming, lighthouse, adjacent to campground; **Contact:** Umpqua Lighthouse State Park, *www.oregonstateparks.org* or 800/551-6949

This is a good choice for those with children, because it's short, it's level most of the way, and it has views of Lake Marie the entire distance. In summer, end your hike with a dip at the little lake's swimming area, and plan a visit to the lighthouse.

GETTING THERE

Turn off US 101 at the sign to Umpqua Lighthouse State Park, about 4 miles south of Reedsport. Follow signs to trailhead parking at the east end of the lake, off the lighthouse road.

ON THE TRAIL

Begin walking either from your campsite (access trails from the park campground connect with the lake trail) or from the trailhead parking area. As you walk clockwise, the trail begins as a paved path, turning to dirt as it approaches the marshy south end of the lake. It climbs a bit on the west side of the lake, descending again and meeting a spur trail about 0.2 mile before completion of

View west from Lake Marie

SNOWY PLOVERS

To the untrained eye the snowy plover doesn't look much different from any number of small shorebirds you may see feeding along the beach, following the advance and retreat of the waves. What sets it apart is a sharp decline in its numbers, enough to have it officially listed as a threatened species in 1993.

Why the decline? Habitat loss is a part of the story. Unlike other shorebirds, the snowy plover nests on flat, open, sandy beaches at the high-tide line around active sand dunes, especially where there are also estuaries or backwater ponds. The introduction of European beach grass on the Oregon coast has stabilized the dunes, diminishing the availability of open dunes. Even sand spits at the mouths of creeks and small rivers have been stabilized, leaving less open sand for plovers to nest upon. Residential and industrial development has gobbled up prime plover habitat as well.

Nesting on the open beach, snowy plovers are particularly vulnerable to disturbance by humans—and their dogs, and their ORVs. Any disturbance can flush a plover from its nest, leaving both eggs and chicks (flightless their first four weeks) vulnerable to predators.

Principal plover breeding and wintering sites in Oregon include the Oregon dunes (between Heceta Head and Sutton Creek, between the Umpqua River and Tenmile Creek, and along Coos Bay's North Spit), plus the beach from Bandon to Floras Lake. Now you know what all that fencing at these sites is about. It goes up during nesting season, from mid-March to mid-September. Avoid even the unfenced area between the driftwood line and the foredune at that time, and choose another beach to let your dog run free.

---

the loop trail. The spur leads 0.1 mile uphill and then drops onto open sand dunes. You can see Ziolkouski Beach across the dunes, but no formal trail leads across the sand and through the pine groves on this side of the beach access road.

82 Eel Lake

RATING	DIFFICULTY	ROUND-TRIP	TERRAIN
★★	3	6 miles	Rolling

Features: Lake, forest, wildlife, adjacent to campground; **Contact:** William M. Tugman State Park, *www.oregonstateparks.org* or 800/551-6949

The vision is to eventually have a hiking trail completely encircling freshwater Eel Lake, the centerpiece of Tugman State Park, between Reedsport and

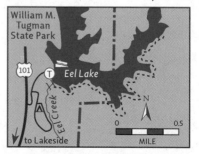

Eel Lake

North Bend. At this writing about 3 miles have been completed, with a little more roughed out. The trail follows the forested hillside above the lake, screening hikers from birds that find refuge on the lake in the off-season; I heard, but never saw, a loon on the lake one winter's day, and it's not unusual to see great blue herons and osprey among the tall Douglas firs.

GETTING THERE

Turn east off US 101 at the sign to William M. Tugman State Park, 1 mile north of the town of Lakeside, and follow signs to the large lakeside day-use parking area.

ON THE TRAIL

Cut across the grass to the signed "fish trap" at the lake's outlet. It was built to capture coho salmon to harvest their eggs for the nearby hatchery and was later converted for use with steelhead. Follow an old gravel road to the right a short distance to a substantial wooden footbridge crossing Eel Creek. From here the trail rises gently and rolls through the forest above the south edge of the lake's eastern arm, feeling more and more remote, especially in the quiet of winter. You'll have views of the lake most of the way except where the trail tucks briefly into deep woods. You can walk at least 3 miles until the trail becomes too rough to continue (though it may be longer by the time you visit). Return as you came.

83 John Dellenback Trail

RATING	DIFFICULTY	ROUND-TRIP	TERRAIN
★★★★	5	5 miles	120 feet elevation gain

Features: Extensive open dunes, beach, adjacent to campground; **Contact:** Oregon Dunes National Recreation Area, *www.fs.fed.us/r6 /siuslaw* or 541/271-3611

The most adventurous and challenging of all the marked routes in Oregon Dunes NRA is John Dellenback Trail across Umpqua Dunes to the beach. It begins on a reasonable enough interpretive loop trail, with a spur to campsites at Eel Creek Campground. Then the trail ends and the real adventure begins: crossing the widest swath of open dunes on the Oregon coast, with help from a few widely scattered wooden posts. Hikers need to stay on their toes and do a little common-sense orienteering to get back to where they started. The elevation gain (125 feet) is just the rise from the parking lot to the edge of the open dunes; you could easily quadruple that figure hiking up and down the open dunes. Pick a fair-weather

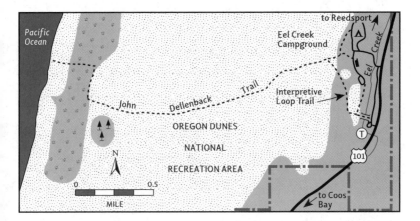

day for this one—preferably a morning before the wind comes up.

GETTING THERE

The trailhead is 8 miles south of Reedsport or 12 miles north of North Bend west off US 101, just south of Eel Creek Campground.

ON THE TRAIL

From the trailhead a long footbridge immediately crosses Eel Creek and leads to a junction, the start of the 1-mile interpretive loop; either

way will lead you through brushy coastal forest, up sandy paths, and around to the start of the dunes hike in 0.5 mile. The right-hand path crosses an Eel Creek campground road before meeting John Dellenback Trail.

Heading west across the open dunes, keep the big tree island on your left. Wooden posts are helpful but not really necessary. When you reach the end of the open sand at the edge of the vegetated deflation plain, not quite 2 miles from the interpretive loop, turn north; in about 0.2 mile, signs will lead you to the start of a

Traversing Umqua Dunes

short trail through the marsh to the beach. Most of the year this trail is very soggy; consider wearing waterproof sandals, because you're going to get wet.

On the return trip, aim toward the blue water tower in the distance, to land in the general vicinity of the interpretive loop, which will lead you back to the trailhead.

84 Bluebill Lake

RATING	DIFFICULTY	LOOP	TERRAIN
★	1	1.25 miles	Flat to rolling

Features: Wetland/lake, extensive boardwalk, adjacent to campground; **Contact:** Oregon Dunes National Recreation Area, www.fs.fed.us/r6/siuslaw or 541/271-3611

Bluebill Lake is a tranquil spot, especially at the end of the day when the frog chorus is tuned up. This forty-acre "lake" is actually dry most of the year but serves as wetland habitat in winter. The trail that circumnavigates it makes a short, pleasant stroll.

GETTING THERE
Just north of McCullough Bridge (north of North Bend), turn west off US 101 at the sign to Horsfall Beach. After crossing the bay and three sets of railroad tracks, veer left onto Trans Pacific Lane, then immediately right onto Horsfall Beach Road. The trailhead is just east of the entrance to Bluebill Campground (2.5 miles from US 101).

ON THE TRAIL
A couple of minutes after you start down the trail you'll reach a split, signaling the start of the loop. Heading counterclockwise,

follow the level trail as it travels through shrubby pine woods at the edge of the lake, though you could also walk up the grassy, dry lakebed itself most of the year. At the far end of the lake a multilevel boardwalk zigzags east to connect with the return trail, a rolling path through the forest back to the start of the loop.

85 North Spit

RATING	DIFFICULTY	ROUND-TRIP	TERRAIN
★★	3	4.2 miles	Nearly flat (beach and soft sand road)

Features: Beach, wildlife, shipwreck site; **Contact:** Bureau of Land Management, Coos Bay, www.blm.gov/or or 541/756-0100

About a mile north of the mouth of Coos Bay lie the scorched and rusting remains of the New Carissa, a 660-foot wood chip freighter that ran aground here on Feb. 4, 1999. After it was set afire in an attempt to burn off the fuel oil, the ship broke in two. The bow was eventually towed offshore and scuttled at sea, but the scorched and rusting stern remained in the surfline for years. It is still there at this writing, though state officials planned to have it removed in 2008. With or without a shipwreck, the North Spit can be an appealing destination for a beach walk, with good bird-watching potential along the way.

GETTING THERE
Just north of McCullough Bridge (north of North Bend), turn west off US 101 at the sign to Horsfall Beach. After crossing the bay and three sets of railroad tracks, veer left onto Trans Pacific Lane and continue past a boat

Opposite: Boardwalk at Bluebill Lake

launch to parking for the North Spit, on your right (4.5 miles from US 101).

ON THE TRAIL

The road and beach are open to four-wheel-drive vehicles except during plover nesting season (March 15 to September 15), so hikers need to keep an eye out for the occasional truck. Start hiking on the sand road, watching for birds in the wetlands on either side of the road. At 0.9 mile the road veers sharply south. You could continue on the sand road to the shipwreck, but the beach is easier to walk on, so climb over the foredune and

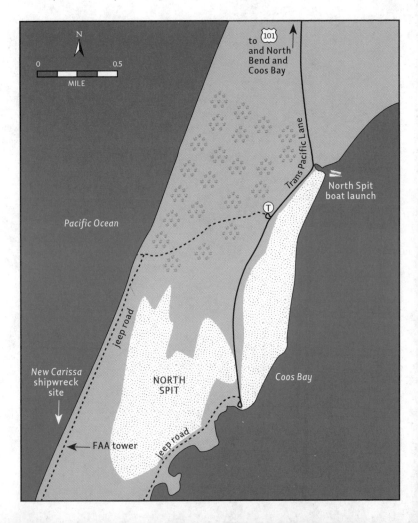

Wreck of the New Carissa

continue south, now on hard beach sand, 1.2 miles to the site of the *New Carissa*, just northwest of a collection of antennas in the foredune. You can continue down to the tip of the spit except during snowy plover nesting season (March 15 to September 15). Return as you came.

86 South Slough

From interpretive center to Sloughside Pilings:

RATING	DIFFICULTY	ROUND-TRIP	TERRAIN
★★★★	3	3 miles	320 feet elevation gain

From Hidden Creek trailhead to Sloughside Pilings:

RATING	DIFFICULTY	ROUND-TRIP	TERRAIN
★★★★	3	2.5 miles	180 feet elevation gain

Big Cedar Trail:

RATING	DIFFICULTY	ROUND-TRIP	TERRAIN
★★★★	1	0.5 mile	Slight ascent

Features: Estuary, creek, forest, wildlife, marsh viewing platform, insectivorous plants; **Contact:** South Slough National Estuarine Research Reserve, *www.oregon.gov/dsl/ssnerr* or 541/888-5558

South Slough is a finger of Coos Bay stretching south from Charleston. Considered by scientists to be a relatively complete estuarine system, it was the country's first federally designated national estuarine research reserve. A small interpretive center near the entrance to the reserve presents the complex interactions of estuarine ecology in terms kids can relate to. Loop trails lead down to the edge of the salt marsh and out onto old dikes that are slowly being reclaimed by the tides, offering many options for hikes of varying lengths. The

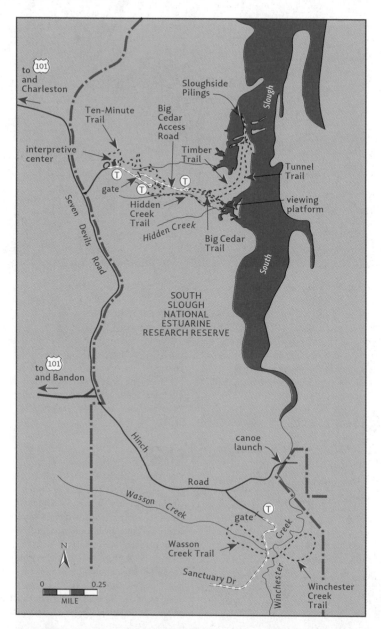

centerpiece of the trail system is Hidden Creek Trail, leading through a variety of eco-systems ranging from Douglas fir forest to skunk cabbage bog. Big Cedar Trail allows disabled visitors to drive down nearly to slough level, park, and proceed on a compacted-gravel trail and boardwalk to reach the mostly level trails at the water's edge; pick up a key to the gate at the interpretive center (call ahead to check hours: 541/888-5558).

GETTING THERE

From US 101 in North Bend or Coos Bay, follow signs west and south about 8 miles southwest to Charleston. Turn left at the sign to South Slough and follow Seven Devils Road south 4.3 miles to the signed entrance to the research reserve, on the left.

ON THE TRAIL

Here are three suggestions for short hikes at South Slough:

From interpretive center to Sloughside Pilings: Begin hiking at the interpretive center on the Ten-Minute (loop) Trail, but leave the loop and follow the trail down the hill. At 0.4 mile the trail reaches gravel Big Cedar Access Road; follow the road down 0.1 mile to the Big Cedar trailhead. Take the left-hand trail (Timber Trail) and follow it 0.5 mile to Sloughside Pilings. Alternately, instead of taking the Timber Trail, take the right-hand trail (Big Cedar Trail); in 0.25 mile you'll reach an elaborate two-level viewing platform overlooking the salt marsh. From here you can follow the Tunnel Trail through dense forest and past another overlook to Sloughside Pilings (0.5 mile). Once you're at the pilings, study guides from the interpretive center can help you spot insectivorous sundew plants here. Spur trails lead along the marsh and onto old dikes. Return as you came or, if you went out on the Tunnel Trail, return via the Timber Trail.

From Hidden Creek trailhead to Sloughside Pilings: Begin at the lower (Hidden Creek) trailhead, accessible by car 0.2 mile below the interpretive center at the end of a gravel spur road. Hidden Creek Trail crosses and recrosses Hidden Creek as it drops down to sea level. A long wooden boardwalk leads through a skunk cabbage bog, odorous and bright yellow in March and April. The route skirts a corner of the salt marsh and then makes a brief zigzag ascent to the viewing platform at the salt marsh. To reach Sloughside Pilings, follow the Tunnel Trail 0.5 mile. Return as you came.

Big Cedar Trail: This is a gently descending route on gravel path and curving wooden boardwalk 0.25 mile to the marshside viewing

Old pilings and crumbling dike at South Slough

platform. From here, those on foot or in a wheelchair can bear right onto the boardwalk through the bog, or left toward the Sloughside Pilings. Return as you came.

In addition to hiking trails, South Slough also offers opportunities for canoeing and kayaking; with tricky tides and dramatic shifts in water level, first-timers are wise to go with a guide from the reserve's interpretive center. Call the reserve to request a copy of the *South Slough Canoe Guide*, with valuable route information as well as interpretive tidbits.

87 Wasson–Winchester Creeks

RATING	DIFFICULTY	LOOP	TERRAIN
★★	2	1.75 miles	Flat

Features: Wetlands, creeks, forest, old farmstead; **Contact:** South Slough National Estuarine Research Reserve, www.oregon.gov/dsl/ssnerr or 541/888-5558

South of the main trail system at South Slough National Estuarine Research Reserve are two shorter trails: Wasson Creek (0.75 mile) and Winchester Creek (0.5 mile). They're just as intriguing, and well worth combining into a 1.75-mile loop hike. The boggy ground around the creeks can harbor mosquitoes all summer long; bring repellent.

GETTING THERE

From US 101 in North Bend or Coos Bay, follow signs about 8 miles west and south to Charleston. Turn left at the sign to South Slough and follow Seven Devils Road south, passing the research reserve entrance at 4.3 miles, and continuing another mile to Hinch Road. Turn left on Hinch and follow it to a junction, bear right onto Sanctuary Drive, and continue 0.2 mile to where a gate blocks the road at a trailhead parking area.

ON THE TRAIL

A trail leads around the gate at the trailhead, cuts through a blackberry thicket, and heads back to the road; follow it down the hill 0.2 mile to where Wasson Creek Trail begins across an old boardwalk on the right. The creek flows quietly alongside the trail, veering away into the meadow around which the trail loops. The trail crosses the creek on another boardwalk and heads up slightly into the Sitka spruce forest. As it drops down to the meadow again, walk quietly and listen for beavers; there are at least a dozen dams arrayed along the creek. The trail ends in 0.75 mile on Sanctuary Drive, 100 yards beyond where it began.

Cross the road and walk about 50 yards farther to reach Winchester Creek Trail. It crosses the creek on an old plank bridge. Just past a grove of Sitka spruce (with one massive tree), the loop begins. Walking clockwise, you'll pass an old boathouse used by the Fredrickson family, whose circa-1905 farmhouse can be seen above the creek on the rise. The trail continues in a circle through the open marsh, which is sometimes completely submerged during winter high tides. Little boardwalks carry you over particularly wet spots. Continue to the end of the loop and back out to Sanctuary Drive, and return as you came.

88 Cape Arago Shoreline

RATING	DIFFICULTY	ONE-WAY	TERRAIN
★★★	3	3.5 miles	Flat, with slight inclines

Features: Outstanding shoreline vistas, forest, formal gardens, hidden beach, wildlife, adjacent to campground; **Contact:** Sunset Bay State Park, www.oregonstateparks.org or 800/551-6949

 Cape Arago Shoreline Trail is a section of the Oregon Coast

Trail between Sunset Bay and Cape Arago State Parks that makes an appealing and varied day hike; if possible, arrange a car shuttle for this one-way walk. Along with visits to a spectacular formal garden, and superb wildlife-watching opportunities, it offers glimpses of sculpted sandstone rocks and reefs offshore that aren't visible except by walking the trail.

GETTING THERE

From US 101 at Coos Bay or North Bend, follow signs about 8 miles west and south to Charleston. Continue south on Cape Arago Highway about 3 miles to Sunset Bay State Park. For shuttle parking, continue about 3 more miles, past Shore Acres State Park, to Cape Arago State Park.

ON THE TRAIL

Look for a trail post near the rest rooms at the south end of the Sunset Bay State Park parking area. *(Note: The route can be muddy in places.)*

Cross Big Creek, ascend the headland, and bear right around a big mowed meadow (Norton Gulch Group Camp), then continue south along the bluff. At 0.6 mile the trail leads back to Cape Arago Highway, follows it south a short distance, and resumes at a stile over the guardrail. It continues through woods some

BEACH GRASS

It seemed like a great idea at the time: Plant aggresive European beach grass at the mouth of Coos Bay, and you'll stabilize the movement of sand, making it easier to keep the river channel open to boat traffic. It worked—better than anyone in 1910 dreamed. Today you'll see this introduced species along almost the entire coast, far beyond its original planting sites.

The result? Dramatic changes in the dune landscape over the last century. Open dunes have shrunk; the forest has grown. At this rate, the Forest Service estimates that the active, open dunes of the Oregon coast will have disappeared in another century.

European beach grass is distinguished by clumps of tall, narrow, slightly curled yellow-green leaves. Its fast-growing, underground stems go both deep and broad. Once established, blowing sand piles up around the plant, creating a mound—and the plant grows up with it. Up rises the foredune, creating a virtual seawall along much of the coast, as tall as thirty feet in places. The foredune intercepts blowing sand, "starving" the active dunes inland and creating a freshwater depression behind itself. The active dunes creep east, flatten, and eventually turn to forest. In one century, European beach grass has made changes to the coastal landscape that otherwise would have taken thousands of years and a major climate change.

It's not the only plant that serves to stabilize dunes, certainly. Before its introduction, the job went primarily to native American dune grass, distinguished by flatter, blue-gray leaves twice the width of the European grass. You'll still find it growing in broad swaths on the north coast, or elsewhere mixed with the invader.

distance from the shoreline; at a junction, veer north and west out to the bluff, where you get views of the lighthouse to the north and rocks to the south (or continue south for a shortcut to Shore Acres through the forest).

Approaching Shore Acres State Park at about 1.8 miles, you may either detour east and enter the formal gardens (exiting through the open gate at the back of the gar-

dens, where you can pick up the trail again) or follow a trail winding to the west of the gardens. (In either case, keep to the paved paths in the vicinity of the gardens.) The botanical gardens were originally part of the estate of Louis J. Simpson, a lumber baron who had a summer home built here in 1906. Among the plantings are many exotic species; at the far end of the garden is a large lily

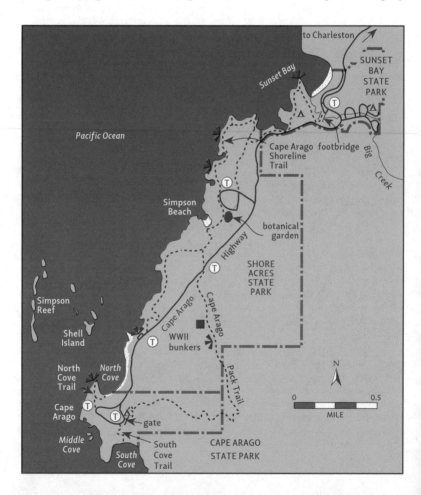

Sunset Bay

pond. The long growing season here makes a visit interesting any time of year, even in mid-winter; at Christmastime the local Friends of Shore Acres group holds an open house and decorates the gardens with about a quarter-million tiny lights.

Continuing past the gardens, the trail leads down to intimate Simpson Beach, into woods, and then back up onto a bluff. At the trail junction about 0.2 mile past Simpson Beach, bear right. (A left turn leads a short distance to the highway just south of the Cape Arago Pack Trail trailhead.) The trail leads toward the shore, then veers back to Cape Arago Highway briefly at 3.3 miles, resumes as trail, and ends at the highway viewpoint 0.5 mile north of the highway's end at Cape Arago. From here you can get the best views of Shell Island, where—with binoculars—you can see sea lions, harbor seals, or elephant seals, depend-

ing upon the time of year. If you return as you came, it's a 7-mile round-trip walk.

89 Cape Arago Pack Trail

RATING	DIFFICULTY	ONE-WAY	TERRAIN
★★	3	2.25 miles	400 feet elevation gain

Features: Forested headland, ocean vistas, historical site, wildlife, adjacent to campground; **Contact:** Cape Arago State Park, *www.oregon stateparks.org* or 800/551-6949

Meandering through old-growth forest east of Cape Arago, the pack trail follows an old wagon road that once led down to Whiskey Run Beach and Bandon. It was revived during World War II as an access route to hidden

HARBOR SEALS AND ELEPHANT SEALS

See that dark piece of driftwood bobbing just inside the waves—or is it a bird? Look again. Could be a harbor seal, popping up to have a look around, then diving back under to fish or flee. They're most numerous around river mouths, but you'll find them off stretches of open beach as well, year-round.

Like their close relations the sea lions, harbor seals spend much of their life in water, and haul out on rocks, reefs, and sandbars, often in large numbers. They're smaller than California sea lions, however. The biggest distinction: True seals' hind limbs point permanently backward; they're sleek in the water but wriggle awkwardly on land. Sea lions can rotate their rear flippers to walk on all four limbs.

The big news on Oregon's coast is the arrival of elephant seals at Shell Island, a quarter mile off Cape Arago. Once hunted nearly to extinction, the animals began moving north from California as their population expanded, first observed at Cape Arago in 1968. Early breeding attempts failed after winter storms washed newborn pups off the tiny island, and still do some years. But in 1997 the first surviving Shell Island pups took to the sea. There's no mistaking elephant seals. They're huge—twenty times the size of a harbor seal, twice as big as a one-ton Steller sea lion—and the male's nose resembles a short, fat elephant's trunk.

If you happen upon a baby seal on the beach in the spring, leave it alone and keep your distance. Seal pups may be left for hours, even overnight, while the mother hunts for food. Chances that it's been abandoned or hurt are slim, and it's much better off without your "help."

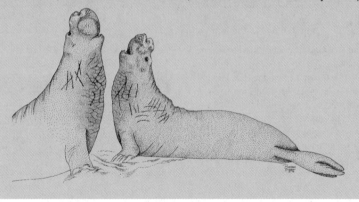

mountainside bunkers. More recently a portion of the road was revived for use by hikers.

GETTING THERE

From US 101 in North Bend or Coos Bay, follow signs about 8 miles west and south to Charles-ton. Continue south on Cape Arago Highway for 5 miles to a small (three-car) pullout about 0.5 mile south of Shore Acres.

ON THE TRAIL

The trail begins on the east side of the highway. It climbs steeply through a dense thicket of salal and huckleberry for 0.3 mile to the old cement bunkers. Continue another 0.3 mile to a picnic table and a view of Simpson Reef. At about 1 mile bear right at a junction, dropping down off the ridge and into an airy forest. The trail crosses a small creek, ascends the opposite hillside for 0.2 mile, then levels off and begins a steady descent down an old roadbed to end at a gravel road leading to primitive Cape Arago Group Camp. Follow the road 0.1 mile down to the Cape Arago State Park parking loop; take a shuttle vehicle back or return as you came (4.5 miles round trip).

90 Cape Arago Coves

North Cove Trail:

RATING	DIFFICULTY	ROUND-TRIP	TERRAIN
★★	1	0.4 mile	120 feet elevation gain

South Cove Trail:

RATING	DIFFICULTY	ROUND-TRIP	TERRAIN
★★	1	0.4 mile	140 feet elevation gain

Features: Pocket beaches, wildlife, tide pools, adjacent to campground; **Contact:** Cape Arago State Park, *www.oregonstateparks.org* or 800/551-6949; **Closed:** March 1–July 1

The coves on the north and south sides of Cape Arago offer good opportunities year-round for watching coastal wildlife, from the tiny residents of tide pools to huge elephant seals. So good, in fact, that the trail to the north cove closes in spring to avoid disturbing the marine mammals that breed here. If you do see a seal pup on the beach, don't touch it; despite appearances, it's probably not abandoned. Its mother is probably fishing nearby.

GETTING THERE

From US 101 in Coos Bay or North Bend, follow signs about 8 miles west and south to Charleston. Continue south on Cape Arago Highway for 6 miles, to where the highway ends at a parking loop in Cape Arago State Park.

ON THE TRAIL

North Cove Trail: Entering the parking loop, watch for the trail marker on the north side. It leads past scattered picnic tables to a junction; go straight for an ocean view, or right to drop down to a large, sandy cove with extensive tide pools at low tide and good wildlife-watching almost any time of year. The trail closes in spring to minimize disturbance to breeding seals; watch (with binoculars) from the Shell Island viewpoint instead. Return as you came.

South Cove Trail: Smaller coves scallop Cape Arago's south and west shores. Park at the far end of the parking loop at Cape Arago State Park and then walk along the road, turning south at the large signboard indicating beach access. The trail winds down to a sandy beach; walk west and north to reach tide pools in both South Cove and, with a climb around the point, Middle Cove.

OREGON COAST TRAIL, SOUTH-CENTRAL COAST

Distance: About 45 miles to Charleston, with boat shuttles at Umpqua River and Coos Bay

From the Siuslaw River Bridge in Florence, follow US 101 0.6 mile south to South Jetty Road; take it west and get back onto the beach at the first beach parking area. The beach extends uninterrupted for a little more than 22 miles from the Siuslaw to the Umpqua, with a few river and creek mouth crossings that can be waded in summer. Trails across the dunes provide access to US 101 in several spots, but it's not always easy to tell exactly where you are. Drinking water is available by detouring 0.75 to 1 mile inland to Waxmyrtle Campground (Hike 70), Carter Lake Campground (Hike 75), and Oregon Dunes Day Use Area (Hike 76), or 1.75 miles to Tahkenitch Campground (Hike 78). Another option is to filter water from Threemile Lake, 0.5 mile inland (Hike 79).

As you approach the Umpqua River, pre-arranging a boat ferry across to the town of Winchester Bay is ideal. Otherwise, turn inland 3.5 miles south of Tahkenitch Creek where you see a wide trail leading off the beach to the end of gravel Sparrow Park Road. Follow it east 4 miles to US 101 and follow the highway south through Gardiner and Reedsport to Winchester Bay. Follow Salmon Harbor Drive west and south as it curves through Windy Cove County Park until you see a collection of high-mounted navigational markers. Head west into the dunes along the south side of

the south jetty to the Coast Guard lookout at the beach, and then turn south. It's 7 miles to Tenmile Creek, and another 8 to Horsfall Beach Access, identifiable by footprints on the foredune. A sand road also leads up and over the dunes and to the parking area. With a boat shuttle across the mouth of Coos Bay to Charleston, you could hike another 7 miles along the dunes (potentially noisy with ORVs, but not as noisy as US 101). Otherwise walk out Horsfall Beach Road to US 101 and then south over McCullough Bridge to North Bend; follow road signs 8 miles to Charleston.

The most significant missing link in the Oregon Coast Trail is that between Cape Arago and Sacchi Beach, north of Seven Devils. From Charleston you may follow Cape Arago Highway to Sunset Bay State Park, where you can return to the OCT to Cape Arago (Hike 88). But to continue south, hikers must return to Charleston.

Walking the beach at the Oregon Dunes

the south coast

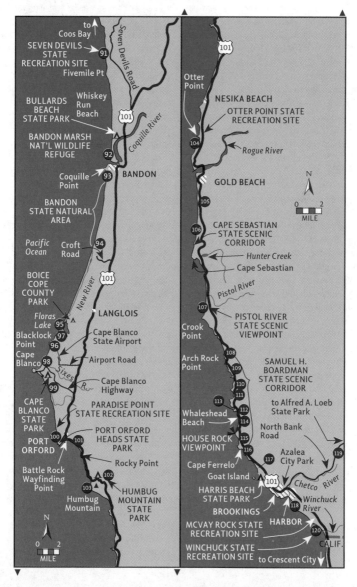

to
Coos Bay
SEVEN DEVILS
STATE
RECREATION SITE
Fivemile Pt
91
Seven Devils Road

BULLARDS
BEACH
STATE PARK
Whiskey
Run
Beach

101

Coquille River

BANDON MARSH
NAT'L WILDLIFE
REFUGE
92
BANDON
93
Coquille
Point

BANDON
STATE NATURAL
AREA

Pacific
Ocean
Croft
Road
94

101
New River

BOICE
COPE
COUNTY
PARK
LANGLOIS
Floras
Lake
95
Cape Blanco
State Airport
Blacklock
Point
97
96
Airport Road
Cape
Blanco
98
Sixes R.
99
Cape Blanco
Highway
CAPE
BLANCO
STATE
PARK
PARADISE POINT
STATE RECREATION SITE
PORT ORFORD
HEADS STATE
PARK
PORT
ORFORD
100
101
Rocky Point
Battle Rock
Wayfinding
Point
102
HUMBUG
MOUNTAIN
STATE
PARK
103
Humbug
Mountain

N
0   2
MILE

101

Otter
Point
NESIKA BEACH
OTTER POINT STATE
RECREATION SITE
104
Rogue River

GOLD BEACH
105
CAPE SEBASTIAN
STATE SCENIC
CORRIDOR
106
Hunter Creek
Cape Sebastian

Pistol River
107
PISTOL RIVER
STATE SCENIC
VIEWPOINT
Crook
Point
108
Arch Rock
Point
109
SAMUEL H.
BOARDMAN
STATE SCENIC
CORRIDOR
110
111
113
to Alfred A. Loeb
State Park
112
Whaleshead
Beach
114
North Bank
Road
HOUSE ROCK
VIEWPOINT
115
116
Cape Ferrelo
117
Azalea
City Park
119
Goat Island
101
Chetco River
HARRIS BEACH
STATE PARK
BROOKINGS
118
Winchuck
River
MCVAY ROCK STATE
RECREATION SITE
HARBOR
120
WINCHUCK STATE
RECREATION SITE
to Crescent City
CALIF.

N
0   2
MILE

MAROONED

"It's like a beach in the tropics," was how a friend described Secret Beach, a pocket of sand in Boardman State Scenic Corridor I'd never gotten around to visiting. But I know the Oregon coast, and this I couldn't quite buy. "Like a beach on the Gulf of Alaska," I could believe: gray days and grayer, brooding mists swirling among somber Sitka spruce, waves assaulting the headland so loudly that conversation stops. But the tropics? I knew better.

The trail, in fact, wasn't too different from some Hawaiian trails I've skidded down: steep and muddy. I clambered over the last rock onto the beach, took one look, and instantly understood. No palm trees, certainly; no exotic fish swimming in blue, clear water. But there was something about it. Maybe it was the creek free-falling onto boulders, gurgling its last few feet into the Pacific. Maybe it was the late-afternoon sun captured in the rock-walled cove, the warmth and stillness. Maybe it was the intimacy of such a little beach.

I wasn't alone. As I arrived, another three or four hikers were dashing between waves to round the rock to the south. I couldn't help but follow, giddy and careless, drenching my shoes in the process. Around that rock I glimpsed them again, rounding the next rock into the next cove. I started to follow, curious just how far south a person could walk on this little beach. But there I stopped, and then I turned around. It's not often you find yourself marooned on a tropical island in Oregon, a million miles from home and only a quarter mile from your car. The solitude, I knew, was another part of the tropical-beach illusion. It would not be me who took that away from them.

The south coast begins at the Coquille River, geologically speaking. Here the Coast Range gives way to the far more ancient Klamath Mountains. You'll see the difference in the sand, in the multicolored tumble of rocks on the beach, in the imposing headlands. Far from urban centers, the south coast is the least developed section of the Oregon coast. From Bandon to Port Orford the highway winds past cranberry bogs and emerald fields of grass scattered with browsing sheep, a mile or more from the shore; with relatively few beach access points, there's plenty of remote beach and headland walking.

South of Port Orford, the highway runs closer to the shore—close enough for sometimes spectacular highway vistas and easy access to beaches. Inland a short distance Siskiyou National Forest begins, and within it three wilderness areas: Grassy Knob, Wild Rogue, and Kalmiopsis. For information on hiking here, contact the Gold Beach or Chetco Ranger Districts. South of Pistol River, a network of contiguous short, scenic trails runs through Samuel H. Boardman State Scenic Corridor, a skinny park stretching more than ten miles along the shoreline. Use the trails for a long one-way hike or short jaunts to dramatic views you can't get from the car window; the main day-use area is Whaleshead Beach, where you'll find beach access, rest rooms, and picnic tables. Much of the coastline in the Brookings area is inaccessible due to the rocky geography and private land ownership, but there are several appealing beach access points, not all apparent from US 101 but easy to reach via Hikes 116, 118, and 120.

Interpretive centers. They are nothing on the scale of the interpretive centers on the central coast, but these two are worth a stop if you're in the area. The Ellen Warring Learning Center at New River is open at least on weekends and has natural history displays on the main floor. The circa-1898 Hughes House at Cape Blanco State Park has been restored and period furnished; visit to get a sense of what life on a coastal farm was like at the turn of the century.

Wildlife-watching. Look for seabirds at Coquille Point in Bandon (the first mainland addition to Oregon Islands National Wildlife

Refuge), Cape Blanco, Cape Sebastian, Crook Point, throughout the Boardman scenic corridor, and Harris Beach. Bird-watching can be very good at Bandon Marsh, with unusual shorebirds frequently appearing between the river's mouth and the marsh upstream. Try the river frontage in Bullards Beach State Park or the refuge viewpoint between the river and highway; to get there, turn west off US 101 south of the Coquille River Bridge (just south of milepost 260) onto Riverside Drive and continue 0.5 mile to the wooden boardwalk and platform on the west side of the road.

Good whale-watching sites include high vantage points at Coquille Point in Bandon, Cape Blanco State Park, Battle Rock Wayfinding Point in Port Orford, Cape Sebastian State Scenic Corridor, and numerous points in the Boardman State Scenic Corridor. Coquille Point, Cape Sebastian, and Crook Point are also good points for viewing seals and sea lions.

Tidepooling. (See Respectful Tidepooling, p. 31.) The south coast has a number of intertidal areas to explore at low tide. Try Fivemile Point, north of Whiskey Run Beach; Coquille Point (accessible via stairs); Cape Blanco; Port Orford (at the boat basin); Rocky Point (3 miles south of Port Orford); a small tide-pool area at the north base of Humbug Mountain, accessible via the state park campground; Lone Ranch Beach in the Boardman State Scenic Corridor; and a rocky intertidal area 0.75 mile north of the beach access on the north side of the Winchuck River.

Off-road cycling. Families may enjoy the short network of paved trails at Bullards Beach State Park; bikes are allowed on hiking trails as well, but most are too sandy to appeal. Look for a free pamphlet, *Biking at Bullards*, with ideas for bike trips in the area (mostly on low-traffic roads). Bikes are allowed to Muddy Lake at New River (Hike 94). All the trails at Blacklock Point (Hikes 95 and 96) are open to mountain bikes, for those who like it wet and wild. The former roadbed on Hike 102 north of Humbug Mountain makes a pleasant, though short, forest ride.

Camping/hostels. Bullards Beach State Park sits on the north shore of the Coquille River, stretching from the 1896 lighthouse at the river's mouth north to the base of the jagged hills called the Seven Devils; the 200-site campground is about in the middle, with paved paths leading to beach access and a horse camp with equestrian trails. Sea Star Hostel, in Bandon's "Old Town," offers inexpensive bunk-bed lodging as well as private rooms. On Floras Lake south of Langlois, Boice Cope County Park is a magnet for sailboarders, with consistently high winds but no real waves or current. The campground isn't much aesthetically, but the sailboarders who gather here create a convivial community. Ask at the adjacent bed and breakfast about lessons and gear rental.

Cape Blanco State Park occupies much of the nearly 2000-acre former Hughes family ranch; it's a windswept promontory, site of the westernmost lighthouse in the forty-eight contiguous states, though the campground is nestled in a grove of trees (no reservations). The campground at Humbug Mountain State Park is in a lush draw at the base of the mountain's north face; a short trail leads under US 101 to a small sandy beach and tide pools (no reservations). Up the Rogue River a few miles from Gold Beach are several primitive Forest Service campgrounds. In the Brookings area, camp at one of several private campgrounds or at Harris Beach State Park, on the northern fringe of town. For more options, drive up the Chetco River on North Bank Road 8 miles to Alfred A. Loeb State Park, with quiet camping (no reservations) a short walk from the world's northernmost redwood trees. Continue up the road to find more primitive riverside campsites.

For reservations at state park campgrounds, call 800/452-5687.

Travelers' tips. Bandon has a thriving "Old

Town" along the river with interesting restaurants and shops; look for motels in town and to the south along Bandon Beach Loop. Blink and you'll miss Port Orford; instead, tarry a bit to enjoy this remote south coast town, with its old lifeboat station north of town and its unusual dry-dock marina, where cranes lift the fishing boats in and out of the water at high tide. Gold Beach is the gateway to the Rogue River; jet-powered tour boats depart several times a day, carrying visitors as much as 104 miles up the wild Rogue canyon. Motels are clustered at the river's mouth and along the highway. Brookings and adjacent Harbor comprise a busy commercial hub on the south coast; you'll find plenty of restaurants and lodging options as well as stores to supply your trip.

Recommended hikes. The beach and bluffs south of Floras Lake (Hike 95) are dramatic; even more dramatic are Blacklock Point (Hike 96) and Cape Blanco's north shore (Hike 98). Pair a visit to Port Orford Heads Lifeboat Station Museum with a short hike to stunning views (Hike 100). Humbug Mountain (Hike 103) is a must, for the forest as well as the summit view. The beach walk to Crook Point (Hike 107) is a beauty, as are the pocket beaches at Secret Beach (Hike 110) and China Creek (Hike 111) and the dunes at Indian Sands (Hike 113). McVay Beach is a find (Hike 120).

91 Seven Devils–Whisky Run Beach

RATING	DIFFICULTY	ONE-WAY	TERRAIN
★	1	1.75 miles	Flat

Features: Beach, solitude, OCT; **Contact:** Seven Devils State Recreation Site, *www.oregonstateparks.org* or 800/551-6949

*"Thicketty and timbered, and some very bad ravines to cross." So wrote a member of a 1928 ex-*pedition of the rough hills south of Cape Arago known as the Seven Devils. It's fair to say it's worse going now, with spiny gorse covering the hillsides as far as the eye can see. There is still no hiking trail through the Seven Devils, but the beach at their base is remote and scenic.*

GETTING THERE

From US 101, either follow signs from Coos Bay west and south to Charleston and head south on rugged Seven Devils Road, following signs to Seven Devils State Recreation Site, or turn off US 101 at one of two signed junctions a few miles north of the Coquille River at Bandon. Either route will lead to a four-way junction of Seven Devils Road, West Humphreys Road, and Whisky Run Road. Follow signs 1 to 2 miles to either Seven Devils State Recreation Site or Whisky Run Beach.

ON THE TRAIL

Merchants Beach lies off Seven Devils State Recreation Site; 1.75 miles south is Whisky Run Beach Access, with Fivemile Point between. A brief gold rush in the 1850s brought miners hungry to glean gold flecks from Whisky Run's black sand beach. A big storm in 1954 apparently washed worthless sand over the gold flecks, though a little gold panning is still reportedly carried on in Whisky Run Creek. Walk the beach north or south, one way (with shuttle) or round trip; or go farther in either direction, if you like.

92 Coquille Lighthouse

RATING	DIFFICULTY	ROUND-TRIP	TERRAIN
★	2	3–3.5 miles	Flat

Features: Ocean and river beach, lighthouse, adjacent to campground; **Contact:** Bullards Beach State Park, *www.oregonstateparks.org* or 800/551-6949

You can drive to Co-quille Lighthouse; it's at the end of the spit in Bullards Beach State Park. Alternatively, walk there via ocean beach or, at low tide, river beach, or on a track through the dunes alongside the road. The light that shines from forty-foot Coquille River Lighthouse isn't visible from sea, but it warms the hearts of those gazing at it from across the river (especially during the holidays, when the lighthouse tower is itself illuminated by tiny lights). Built and lit in 1896, it was decommissioned in 1939. By the early 1970s, neglect and vandalism had made it an eyesore; it was restored in the late seventies and, at the urging of local residents, relit with a solar-powered ornamental light in 1991. It's open daily during daylight hours.

GETTING THERE

Bullards Beach State Park campground is 2 miles north of Bandon off US 101; follow the park road to the campground or, 1 mile farther, the beach access parking area.

ON THE TRAIL

Walk from the campground, if you're camping; otherwise, start at the beach access parking area. Follow the trail over the foredune and head south. At the north jetty, climb back over the dune to the lighthouse. Choose your return route according to tide, weather, and

GORSE

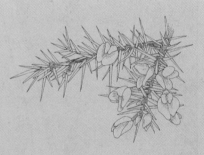

An otherwise mild-mannered wildflower book calls it "a wicked thing," and anyone who encounters this plant would no doubt agree. From a distance gorse looks like Scotch broom, with its small green leaves and bright yellow blossoms that bloom from February to July. But get close and you'll see its signature needle-sharp thorns. And broom's invasive habits are far outpaced by those of gorse, which is quickly taking over roadsides and whole hillsides on Oregon's south coast in particular.

Gorse (Ulex europaeus) is believed to have been brought over from England in the late nineteenth century; it was first noted in a Bandon garden in 1894. In its native Great Britain, gorse was used as a hedge to corral livestock. Apparently it isn't a problem in England because of insects that feed on it and keep its spread in check. In Oregon, however, it has crowded out more than 50,000 acres of native vegetation. Once introduced into Coos County, it spread like wildfire—literally. Natural oils in gorse make it extremely flammable in dry weather, helping to fuel, for example, a fire that consumed Bandon in 1936.

For decades the plant's spread was limited mostly to Coos and Curry Counties on the south coast. But recent years have seen its range extending north, south, and east, causing state agriculture officials to step up control and eradication efforts. Burning seems only to stimulate more growth. Herbicides aren't very effective. Most recently, and most promising, agriculture officials are attempting to kill or control the spread of gorse with tiny spider mites—imported from England and Spain—that feed on the plant's foliage.

your mood: as you came on the ocean beach, around the spit and back on the river beach (spring through fall, at low tide, when the river's low enough), or alongside the road on the horse trail (consisting of tire ruts through the sand). If you return via the river, there's no formal trail back to the road; use your best judgment in deciding when to cut back across

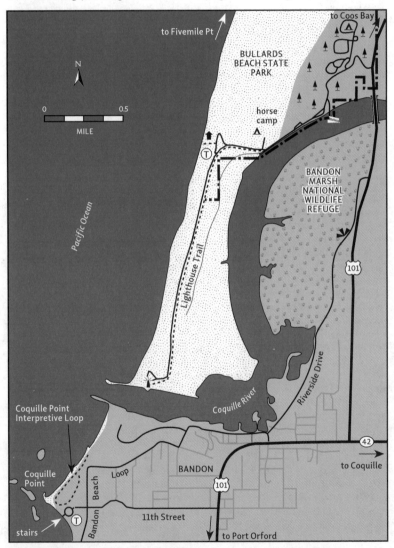

Coquille Lighthouse

the dunes. You can't get lost, as eventually you'll hit the park road. A footbridge leads across a substantial slough draining the dunes just north of the park road; follow it out to the road, and walk along the roadside 0.2 mile to the beach access parking area.

93 Coquille Point

RATING	DIFFICULTY	LOOP	TERRAIN
★	1	1.25 miles (with possible beach)	Flat, with short steep incline

Features: Outstanding shoreline vistas, onshore rocks, beach, wildlife; **Contact:** Oregon Islands National Wildlife Refuge, *www.fws.gov /oregoncoast/oregonislands* or 541/867-4550

Just south of the Coquille River in Bandon is Coquille Point, a wonderful vantage point from which to ob- *serve seabirds on offshore rocks. Looping asphalt trails have been developed atop the cliff; trails lead down the point to the north and south, allowing you to take a loop walk.*

GETTING THERE
From US 101 at the top of the hill just south of Bandon's Old Town, take 11th Street west to where it ends at a parking area on the point.

ON THE TRAIL
A paved path leads from the parking area to a 0.5-mile interpretive loop with viewpoints and informative signs. At the north end of the loop you can take a spur trail that becomes a rutted path as it heads down the point to the beach. The south jetty is about 0.25 mile up the beach to the north. Otherwise, follow the beach south and around the point, cutting through a notch in the rocks. About 0.25 mile past the point, look for stairs leading back up the cliff to the parking area

Coquille Point

If you're interested in a longer beach walk, keep heading south, 0.5 mile to the beach access at the Face Rock viewpoint (passable at low tide), to Devils Kitchen (1.5 miles more), or to a second beach access in Bandon State Natural Area (another 0.6 mile)—or, for that matter, all the way to Floras Lake, some 15 sandy miles south of Coquille Point.

94 New River

RATING	DIFFICULTY	ROUND-TRIP	TERRAIN
**	2	1–2.1 miles	Flat to slight incline

Features: Forest, dunes, wildlife, solitude; **Contact:** Bureau of Land Management, Coos Bay, www.blm.gov/or or 541/756-0100

How new is New River? More than a century, according to local lore. The flood of 1890, they say, created a new northbound channel for Floras Lake. Today New River runs about nine miles north from Floras Lake, parallel to and just inland from the Pacific, before it turns to meet the ocean. Wild chinook salmon run up the river, and as many as 40,000 Aleutian Canada geese use the river every spring to rest and forage before heading out over the ocean toward nesting sites on the Aleutian Islands, stopping again in November on their southward migration.

Wildlife protection is the first priority here; at this writing, nearly 6000 acres of adjacent land here are being considered for designation as a national wildlife refuge through conservation easements. Consequently, the trail system veers hikers away from critical goose habitat, for example, and the last 0.5 mile of road as well as the dunes across the river are closed March 15 to September 15 to minimize disturbance to nesting snowy plovers. Instead, trails lead through dense coastal forest of pine and

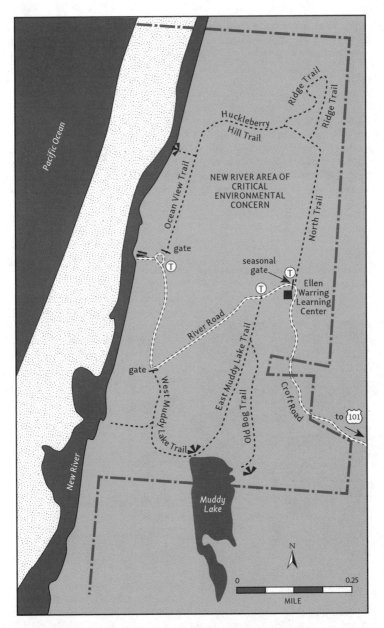

madrone, salal, manzanita, rhododendron, and chinquapin, into hidden meadows, past ocean vistas, and to a quiet lake.

GETTING THERE

Just south of milepost 283 on US 101 (about 8 miles south of Bandon or 5 miles north of Langlois), turn west on Croft Road. Drive 1.5 miles and bear right at the split in the road, following signs to New River Area of Critical Environmental Concern and the parking area outside Ellen Warring Learning Center. Park here or, if the gate is open, 0.5 mile farther down the road, at the canoe and kayak launch at road's end. There's also room for about three cars at the East Muddy Lake trailhead.

ON THE TRAIL

To hike the entire loop from the learning center parking area, head north on North Trail, lined closely with manzanita, for 0.3 mile. Just after the

Old farming equipment, New River

moss-carpeted trail curves left and starts to rise, turn right at the junction with the Ridge Trail. It follows a sandy ridge, then turns sharply left and returns to the main trail at 0.6 mile. Go right to continue up what's now called Huckleberry Hill Trail another 0.2 mile until it veers south and becomes Ocean View Trail. Continue walking south on Ocean View Trail, passing spurs leading to views of the river and ocean, to the boat launch, 1.1 miles from where you started. From here, walk south 0.2 mile on gravel River Road. When the road makes a sharp curve left, hikers may continue straight (through a gate) onto West Muddy Lake Trail (an old road). It leads 0.3 mile to a view of Muddy Lake. The trail continues as a narrower footpath, swinging east and north and becoming East Muddy Lake Trail. At 2 miles it meets River Road; turn right and continue 0.2 mile back to the learning center.

Examine the map for other hiking options. For a short out-and-back hike from the learning center, walk 0.1 mile down River Road, turn left onto East Muddy Lake Trail; walk 0.1 mile more, then take another left on Old Bog Trail; enjoy the view of distant hills and a look at an old cranberry bog at the trail's end (0.5 mile). Return as you came.

95 Floras Lake Beach

To beach:

RATING	DIFFICULTY	ROUND-TRIP	TERRAIN
★★	1	0.8 mile	Flat

To South Beach and Blacklock Point trailhead:

RATING	DIFFICULTY	ROUND-TRIP	TERRAIN
★★	2	2 miles	Slight incline

Features: Lake, dunes, beach, solitude, adjacent to campground; **Contact:** Floras Lake State Natural Area, 800/551-6949

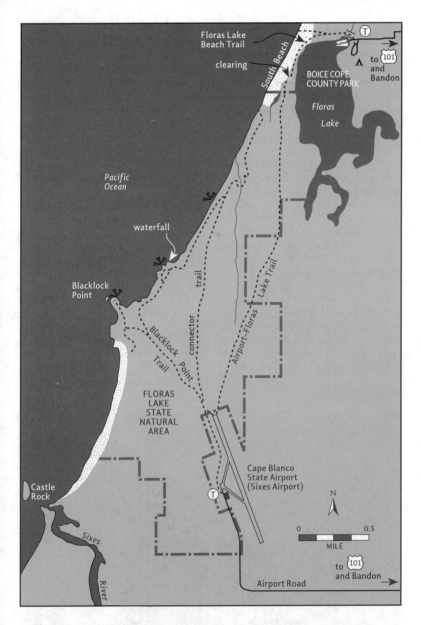

Take a walk from Floras
Lake across the dunes to
one of the more remote beaches on the en-
tire Oregon coast. It's nearly thirteen miles
to the next beach access to the north; if you
walk this way, you're unlikely to meet an-
other soul. Keep your dog on leash during
plover nesting season.

GETTING THERE

From US 101 just south of Langlois (about 14
miles south of Bandon), turn west at the sign to
Boice Cope County Park and follow signs about
3 miles; park in the park's boat launch area.

ON THE TRAIL

The route to the beach may vary, depending
upon measures taken to protect the snowy
plover during nesting season.

The trail to the beach begins at the north
end of Floras Lake. Cross the lake's outlet (the
start of New River) on a footbridge, and follow
the path west along the lakeshore; it can be very
wet much of the year. Signs direct you west to
the beach or south to South Beach and the bluff.
The shortest way to the beach is to head west.

Blacklock Point Trail

Little trail markers help point the way around
the lake. At about 0.5 mile there's a break in the
foredune; detour west here to reach the beach.

To reach South Beach from Floras Lake,
begin walking west, as if you were walking
to the beach, but veer south, following signs
along the lakeshore, to where the trail starts
heading southeast up a bluff at 0.8 mile. Walk
0.1 mile to some boulders and a junction with
the trail to Blacklock Point (see Hikes 96 and
97). Bear right and go another 0.1 mile to the
secluded beach. Return as you came.

96 Blacklock Point

To the point:

RATING	DIFFICULTY	ROUND-TRIP	TERRAIN
★★★★	3	3.5 miles	100 feet elevation gain

To the beach (south):

RATING	DIFFICULTY	ROUND-TRIP	TERRAIN
★★★★	3	3.5 miles	200 feet elevation gain

To the waterfall (north):

RATING	DIFFICULTY	ROUND-TRIP	TERRAIN
★★★★	3	3.75 miles	Slight ascent

To Floras Lake and South Beach on Oregon Coast Trail:

RATING	DIFFICULTY	ONE-WAY	TERRAIN
★★★★	4	4.5 miles	200 feet elevation loss

Features: Outstanding shoreline vistas, forest, waterfall, beach, solitude, OCT; **Contact:** Floras Lake State Natural Area, 800/551-6949

One local resident characterizes Blacklock Point as "the land of the lost" or "the Land of Oz." Even if you don't get lost, the place has that kind of feel to it—like you might encounter winged monkeys or fighting trees. Officially designated Floras Lake State Natural Area, Blacklock Point has never been developed, and though it now has a network of trails, they wind rather confusingly through a dense mix of shore pine and salal. Trail signs help, as does the map in this book.

What's the appeal? Well, one reason is that you're unlikely to encounter another hiker, and the whole area has a mysterious, remote, wild feel. (The airport is occasionally used by private pilots; the only time you're likely to meet a crowd is July Fourth weekend, when there are car races at Cape Blanco State Airport.) The main trailhead is at the airport, but the trail system is accessible from beaches to the north or south as part of the Oregon Coast Trail route; consider a one-day or longer backpacking trip between Floras Lake and Cape Blanco. These trails are open to mountain biking as well as hiking.

GETTING THERE

From US 101 north of Cape Blanco State Park, turn west at the sign to Cape Blanco State Airport (also called Sixes Airport), across the highway from Pacific High School, and continue 3 miles to the gravel parking area at the end of the road.

ON THE TRAIL

Before setting out, be aware that some of the trails at Blacklock Point are old roads with massive potholes. Detours with little boardwalks keep you out of the water in many places. Still, waterproof sandals are a good choice of footwear here most of the year.

The trail starts directly across the road from the parking area. Follow the main trail as it parallels the runway, offering occasional glimpses of it on the right. Just past a spur leading back to the end of the runway at 0.75 mile (see Hike 97), there's another trail junction; go left. (A right turn leads onto a 1-mile connector trail linking with the Oregon Coast Trail). Continue another 0.5 mile to where the trail meets the Oregon Coast Trail. From here you have a few options:

To the point: Bear left at this junction. In another 0.25 mile there's another junction; bear right to reach the point. The trail drops a bit and then rises gently, becoming a narrower footpath. Nearing the tip of the point, the dense shore pine forest gives way to an airier Sitka spruce forest. Pass through a clearing in the spruce, suitable for camping, and continue west to the open, grassy end of the point at 1.75 miles. Return as you came.

To the beach (south): Bear left at this junction, continue 0.25 mile to another junction, and go straight. The trail makes a slow loop to the east and south, and then switchbacks the final stretch to the beach, emerging about 30 yards north of a babbling tannin-colored creek heaped with driftwood. The mouth of the Sixes River is about 1 mile to the south down the beach. Return as you came (or scramble up the steep south face of Blacklock Point and follow the trail back out to the airport).

To the waterfall (north): Bear right at this junction. Continue north not quite 0.5 mile to an opening to the west; follow it out to the bluffs and around to the north, where a creek winds out of the pine woods and pours into a hole in the sandstone, spills out, drops onto a rockpile, and ends on the beach just north of the point here. When the wind is strong, the modest cataract sprays back up! The bluffs here are beautiful, dramatically sculpted by storms, but be careful walking at the edge of the sometimes-undercut cliffs.

Return to the Oregon Coast Trail and continue north not quite 1 mile more to another bluff-top viewpoint and an even better look back to the falls. In about 0.1 mile you'll reach a junction with the connector trail; return on it (heading south) for a 3.75-mile loop.

To Floras Lake on the Oregon Coast Trail (north): Follow the directions to the waterfall, above, until you reach the junction with the connector trail. The trail veers inland and down to a cool creek bottom, then heads back up with switchbacks and stairs. About 1 mile north of the connector trail junction, a short spur trail leads left to a secluded beach. Keep going straight. You'll reach the junction with the Airport–Floras Lake Trail (Hike 97) in 0.3 mile more and, in another 0.3 mile, another junction at a line of boulders. Go left 0.1 mile to South Beach, or straight 0.1 mile to the end of the trail at a viewpoint overlooking Floras Lake. Return as you came (9 miles round trip), or via the connector trail (7.2), or via the Airport–Floras Lake Trail (8.2 miles).

97 Airport–Floras Lake Trail

RATING	DIFFICULTY	ONE-WAY	TERRAIN
★	3	3 miles	200 feet elevation loss

Heading north from the end of Airport–Floras Lake Trail

Features: Headland traverse, dense coastal forest, solitude, OCT; **Contact:** Floras Lake State Natural Area, 800/551-6949

This is the most direct route between Floras Lake and Blacklock Point by foot. Otherwise it doesn't have much to recommend it: no views, just dense forest slowly descending south toward the beach.

GETTING THERE

From US 101 north of Cape Blanco State Park, turn west at the sign to Cape Blanco State Airport (also called Sixes Airport), across the highway from Pacific High School, and continue 3 miles to the gravel parking area at the end of the road.

ON THE TRAIL

The trail starts directly across the road. Follow the signed trail 0.75 mile and turn right on an unmarked spur trail that leads 0.1 mile to the end of the airport runway (or just walk up the runway; it's hard asphalt, but it's dry).

Walk northeast across the end of the runway and pick up the old road leading north. The trail winds slightly as it descends gradually through the forest, eventually dropping onto a red sandstone mound 2.25 miles from the end of the airport. To reach Floras Lake (Hike 95), follow signs north around the lake.

98 Cape Blanco North Shore

To beach:

RATING	DIFFICULTY	ROUND-TRIP	TERRAIN
★★★★	1	0.5 mile	200 feet elevation gain

To Sixes River:

RATING	DIFFICULTY	ROUND-TRIP	TERRAIN
★★★	3	2.5 miles	200 feet elevation gain

Pasture loop:

RATING	DIFFICULTY	ROUND-TRIP	TERRAIN
★★★	3	3.5 miles	200 feet elevation gain

River loop:

RATING	DIFFICULTY	ROUND-TRIP	TERRAIN
★★★	3	3.5 miles	200 feet elevation gain

Features: Outstanding shoreline vistas, onshore rocks, lighthouse, wildflowers, river, historical site, adjacent to campground, OCT; **Contact:** Cape Blanco State Park, *www.oregonstateparks .org* or 800/551-6949

In contrast to the dense vegetation covering all but the very tip of Blacklock Point, Cape Blanco is bare and windswept. The park occupies much of the nearly 2000-acre former Hughes family ranch, which began as an eighty-acre parcel of land purchased by Irish immigrant Patrick Hughes in 1860. In 1870, Cape Blanco Lighthouse went into operation on the point— the oldest operating lighthouse on the Oregon coast, the westernmost light in the forty-eight contiguous states, and, at an elevation of 245 feet, the highest in Oregon as well. Its nearly seven-foot-tall Fresnel lens is still in use and is visible twenty-six miles at sea. It is open for tours weekends in summer.

Cape Blanco offers dramatic hiking. The north shore between the lighthouse and the Sixes River is a natural choice with its panorama of craggy rocks strewn offshore and tide pools at the cape's tip.

GETTING THERE

From US 101 4 miles north of Port Orford, take Cape Blanco Highway west 4.25 miles to a turn-off to Hughes House and the riverside trailhead

SEA STARS

Peek under any big rock at low tide and chances are good that you'll find a sea star—or starfish, a more common but less accurate name. Sea stars are members of a large family that includes sand dollars and sea urchins. Look closely and you'll spot the resemblance: a radial symmetry that usually divides the circular-shaped animal into five parts.

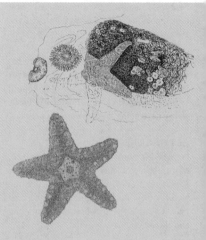

Most common in Oregon is the hard-textured, eight- to twelve-inch common sea star (*Piaster ochraceus*), found in orange, brown, and dark purple. They're commonly seen, partly because, like sea anemones and mussels, many live in the midtide zone, which is uncovered by the sea twice every day, regardless of how low the tide is. Like most sea stars, *Piaster ochraceus*'s five rays cover an army of tiny tube feet with powerful suckers at their tips, enabling them to cling tightly to rocks or to pry open the barnacles, mussels, limpets, and other shellfish they eat. Once the feet start prying, the sea star's mobile stomach goes into action, sometimes extruding from the star's center to spread itself over its prey or slip into a crack in the shell to begin digesting on the spot.

During low tide, sea stars hang out under ledges and in crevices, digesting their food or waiting for the incoming tide. As the tide rises they follow it, grabbing an armful of mussels, snails, or barnacles and "dashing" back under the tide to eat and avoid drying up.

Other kinds of sea stars inhabit Oregon's intertidal zone, including the twenty-four-rayed star, also known as the sunflower star, measuring as much as three feet across and seen only on an extra-low tide.

and picnic area. Park here or continue another 1.25 miles to a gravel parking lot near the tip of the cape, where the Oregon Coast Trail crosses the park road (lighthouse trailhead).

ON THE TRAIL

To beach: From the lighthouse trailhead, follow the Oregon Coast Trail north and down the bank 0.25 mile to the beach; a short distance farther north are the tide pools. Return as you came.

To Sixes River: From the beach below and north of the lighthouse trailhead, walk east and north 1.25 miles to the river and return as you came. Or consider one of the following loop options.

Pasture loop: About 0.2 mile south of the Sixes River, watch for a mowed trail leading east off the beach, onto the foredune and through a pasture. There may be no sign of it from the beach; simply drop over the dune before you reach the river, and cross the pasture until you either run into the path or hit a trail marker post beyond a rise in the pasture. At the post, head southwest up the hill, following the mowed path, which then leads steeply into the woods. (Alternatively, bear left toward the riverside trailhead below Hughes House in 0.3 mile.) Immediately look for a trail marker on the right and follow the trail through the forest and up to the edge of a large field. Follow the field around and down another mowed path to an apparent junction; bear left (or turn right for a view over the beach) and then left again at

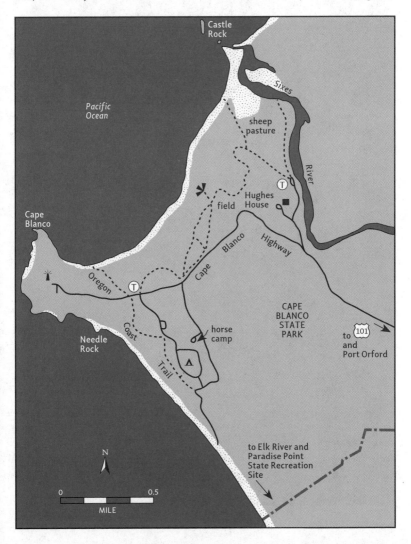

Hughes House at Cape Blanco

another junction just steps away. Continue about 0.5 mile along a mowed path and into a Sitka spruce grove. Spurs lead off here and there, but you can't really get lost, as the park road is nearby. When the trail meets the road, follow the road back west to the lighthouse trailhead, or take a spur trail through the woods, along the bluff, and back to the road a short distance from the lighthouse trailhead.

River loop: A simpler loop from the lighthouse trailhead involves walking the beach to the mouth of the Sixes, then following the river's edge, on sand for about 0.5 mile and then on a footpath off the river, to the riverside trailhead. To loop back, walk up the road, detouring to visit the 1898 Hughes House. Continue back to your vehicle on the road, picking up the pasture loop trail, if desired, when it approaches the road. Leave a shuttle vehicle at the riverside trailhead for a 2-mile one-way walk.

99 Cape Blanco South Shore

Northbound:

RATING	DIFFICULTY	ROUND-TRIP	TERRAIN
★★	2	2 miles	Flat

South to Elk River:

RATING	DIFFICULTY	ROUND-TRIP	TERRAIN
★★	2	2.6 miles	Flat

South to Port Orford:

RATING	DIFFICULTY	ONE-WAY	TERRAIN
★★	4	5.8 miles	Flat

Features: Beach, river, adjacent to campground, OCT; **Contact:** Cape Blanco State Park, *www.oregonstateparks.org* or 800/551-6949

Beach south of Cape Blanco

Most of the hiking trails at Cape Blanco State Park are on the north side of the cape, but the shoreline south of the lighthouse offers plenty of beach to walk, from the tip of the cape to the mouth of the Elk River. Long-distance hikers can wade the river in late summer.

GETTING THERE

From US 101 4 miles north of Port Orford, take Cape Blanco Highway west 5.5 miles to the campground road; follow it south to its end at the south beach access. There is a signed turnoff for Paradise Point State Recreation Site just north of Port Orford, 1 mile west of US 101.

ON THE TRAIL

Start your walk at the south beach access, or follow the Oregon Coast Trail south from the top of the cape (see driving directions, Hike 98). The beach stretches 1 mile north to the base of the cape; return as you came.

Alternately, walk 1.3 miles south from the south beach access to the mouth of the Elk River; return as you came.

Elk River may be crossed with caution at low water in midsummer; some Oregon Coast Trail hikers wade it. If you do, it's another 4.5 miles south one way to Paradise Point State Recreation Site, a virtually unmarked park that consists simply of a parking area on a terrace above the beach. The beach continues another 0.5 mile south before it's stopped by Port Orford Heads.

100 Port Orford Heads

RATING	DIFFICULTY	ROUND-TRIP	TERRAIN
★★★★★	2	0.6–1.2 miles	Slight incline

Features: Headland, outstanding shoreline vistas, wildflowers, historical site; **Contact:** Port Orford Heads State Park, www.oregon stateparks.org or 800/551-6949

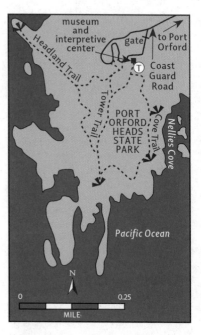

The buildings at Port Orford Heads State Park were originally built for the Port Orford Lifeboat Station, whose staff of "surfmen"—eventually numbering more than a hundred—kept watch over forty miles of coastline from Cape Blanco to Cape Sebastian, from 1934 to 1970. The station was decommissioned after more sophisticated search-and-rescue methods made it obsolete. Walk the short trails, lined in spring with blooms of wild purple iris, to dazzling viewpoints and you'll understand why this was such a valuable lookout site.

GETTING THERE

From the town of Port Orford on US 101, follow signs to Port Orford Heads State Park and park at the small parking area at the top of the head, west of the old barracks and tennis court.

View south from tower site, Port Orford Heads

ON THE TRAIL

The former crew quarters now houses the Port Orford Lifeboat Station Museum and Interpretive Center, open Thursdays through Mondays, April through October. The station's legendary thirty-six-foot unsinkable motor lifeboat is on display outside. An interconnected network of short trails begins here.

Bear left to take the Cove Trail past a view-point where you can see remnants of the 500-step staircase that once led down 280 feet to Nellie's Cove, where the lifeboat was launched from a boathouse (burned down in 1970). After 0.4 mile the trail reaches another viewpoint at the site of the station's observation tower (removed in 1970). Return to your starting point by following the 0.3-mile Tower Trail north up the hill.

Or, for a longer walk, take the Tower Trail

a short distance, bear left on a link trail, then left again on the Headland Trail, which leads to the park's westernmost viewpoint. Returning, follow the Headland Trail a scant 0.2 mile, and bear left to walk another 0.2 mile back to the parking area.

101 Battle Rock

RATING	DIFFICULTY	ROUND-TRIP	TERRAIN
★	2	Up to 5 miles	Flat

Features: Beach, historical site, close to town;
Contact: Port Orford Chamber of Commerce, www.discoverportorford.com or 541/332-8055

 *The highway hugs the shoreline south of Port Orford, but it's high above the beach—out of sight and sound for beach walkers on this long stretch of sand. Enjoy an out-and-back walk south of historic Battle Rock.*

GETTING THERE
Battle Rock Wayfinding Point is at the south edge of Port Orford, off US 101.

ON THE TRAIL
Battle Rock, accessible only at low tide, was the site of a bloody confrontation between arriving settlers and the indigenous residents in June 1851. Gold had just been discovered

Battle Rock, with Humbug Mountain in the distance

in the hills of southern Oregon, and the place was crawling with miners. As the story goes, a party of white men was recruited to establish a trade station at Port Orford. Arriving by steamer, they and their provisions were dropped off on the big rock at the shoreline. It's uncertain who fired first, but a battle ensued, lasting several days. A number of Native Americans were killed. Eventually the settlers managed to slip away, fleeing north to a settlement on the Umpqua River.

At medium or low tide, you can walk south from Battle Rock Wayfinding Point clear to where the beach runs out at the bouldery base of Rocky Point, 2.5 miles south of Port Orford. Return as you came.

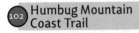

102 Humbug Mountain Coast Trail

North section:

RATING	DIFFICULTY	ONE-WAY	TERRAIN
★	3	2.6 miles	200 feet elevation gain

South section:

RATING	DIFFICULTY	ONE-WAY	TERRAIN
★★	2	1.2 miles	180 feet elevation gain

Features: Forest, adjacent to campground, OCT; **Contact:** Humbug Mountain State Park, *www.oregonstateparks.org* or 800/551-6949

The main function of this trail is to get long-distance hikers off US 101. Campground campers or US 101 travelers might particularly consider the southern section for a short, pleasant, out-and-back forest day hike.

GETTING THERE

To hike the north section of this trail: take US 101 south about 3.5 miles from Port Orford, and then turn onto a road leading east off the highway, just past the sign signaling the northern boundary of Humbug Mountain State Park. Follow this road as it curves right; at the split in the road bear right and park at the gate. To hike the south section, park at either the Humbug Mountain State Park campground (about 6 miles south of Port Orford on US 101) or the picnic area (another mile south).

ON THE TRAIL

With limited parking at the north end of this trail, day hikers are advised to start at either the Humbug Mountain State Park campground or the picnic area, about 6 miles south of Port Orford off US 101.

North section: Walk around the gate and follow the old road leading south. Formerly the route of the coast highway, this long-abandoned road climbs gently for about 1.5 miles, then starts descending. Vegetation growing on the asphalt can make it slippery when wet. At 2.3 miles the trail crosses Dry Run Creek on a wide footbridge before reaching the state park campground road near the registration booth at 2.6 miles.

South section: Continuing south from the campground, the trail quickly crosses a creek, crosses a road, and begins switchbacking up a steep hillside. It tops a ridge at about 0.5 mile, and then begins a gradual descent. Reaching Brush Creek, it follows the creekbank (opposite the highway) until it crosses a side creek on a footbridge and ducks under US 101 to the park's picnic area, 1.2 miles from the campground trailhead. To reach the picnic area's parking lot, continue along the trail until it crosses Brush Creek on a footbridge.

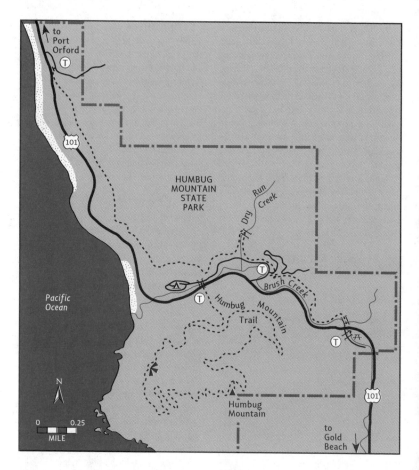

103 Humbug Mountain

RATING	DIFFICULTY	ROUND-TRIP	TERRAIN
★★★★★	5	5–6 miles	1730 feet elevation gain

Features: Forested headland, outstanding shoreline vistas, wildflowers, adjacent to campground; **Contact:** Humbug Mountain State Park, *www.oregonstateparks.org* or 800/551-6949

In spring, wildflowers brighten the trailside and the creeks are raucous. In autumn, fallen bay leaves crunch underfoot, sending their spicy fragrance into the air. There's no season—save, perhaps, during a winter sou'wester—when the hike up Humbug Mountain isn't appealing. But don't expect good whale-watching from the top (as one pair of hikers we encountered did); you'll be much too high to see any detail *in the ocean vista spread below you from the 1750-foot summit meadow.*

GETTING THERE

Look for the trailhead parking area on the south side of US 101 about 6 miles south of Port Orford, just 0.3 mile west of the entrance to the Humbug Mountain State Park campground.

ON THE TRAIL

For campers, an access trail from the campground leads across Brush Creek and under the highway to the trailhead parking area. The trail immediately crosses a small creek and begins climbing through an airy forest of Douglas fir, rhododendrons, and bay trees; it continues up at a moderately steep grade. Just past a 1-mile marker, the trail splits. Bear left and it's another 2 miles to the summit; bear right and it's 1.5 miles to the same point.

The 1.5-mile route reopened in 1993, twenty-five years after it was closed following a major blowdown of trees during the Northwest's infamous Columbus Day Storm; enjoy the views of the ocean and Port Orford on this stretch of trail. Just short of the summit, the two approaches meet; follow the spur trail a few paces to the summit, where you can drink in the view to the south from a small, grassy clearing. Return as you came, or take the other trail to complete the loop.

104 Otter Point

To beach:

RATING	DIFFICULTY	ROUND-TRIP	TERRAIN
★	2	1 mile	Steep incline

To Rogue River:

RATING	DIFFICULTY	ONE-WAY	TERRAIN
★	3	2.6 miles	Steep incline; flat beach

Features: Beach, solitude, OCT; **Contact:** Otter Point State Recreation Site, *www.oregon stateparks.org* or 800/551-6949

North of the Rogue River's north jetty lies a fairly wild stretch of beach, Bailey Beach, bounded on the north by Otter Point. It's accessible from Otter Point State Recreation Site or from beach access at the north jetty (follow signs from US 101 just north of the river bridge). Start at Otter Point for a more remote walk.

GETTING THERE

About 2.5 miles south of Nesika Beach on US 101, look for a sign to the Old Coast Road to the west; take it 0.2 mile south to a 0.2-mile gravel road leading to Otter Point and a parking lot.

Humbug Mountain Trail

Otter Point

ON THE TRAIL

At the south end of the parking lot, go through a break in the pole fence and veer left at the Oregon Coast Trail post (otherwise you'll be on a haphazard network of trails leading out onto the point). Follow a tunnel of salal and evergreen huckleberry, level at first, then slip-sliding 60 feet down the hillside. Stairs made of old tires complete the trip down the hill; cross a creek on a wooden bridge to reach Bailey Beach. Return as you came.

To continue to the Rogue, walk south along the beach. The beach makes a slow curve to end at the north jetty in a little over 2 miles. To leave a shuttle car for a one-way hike, follow signs off US 101 to the north jetty, just north of the Rogue River Bridge.

105 Buena Vista Beach

RATING	DIFFICULTY	ROUND-TRIP	TERRAIN
★	4	6.5 miles	Flat

Features: Beach, solitude; **Contact:** Gold Beach Visitor Center, www.goldbeach.org or 800/525-2334

Dunes on the south coast

At Hunter Creek, US 101 begins its slow ascent of Cape Sebastian. Far below the highway the beach stretches out, wide and remote, inviting to beach walkers with a love of solitude.

GETTING THERE
Park at the wayside just south of the mouth of Hunter Creek, about 1 mile south of Gold Beach on US 101.

ON THE TRAIL
From Hunter Creek, you can walk the beach south for 3.25 miles until it ends at the base of Cape Sebastian. There are a few houses on the hillside above, but not many. There are no major creek crossings. Savor the solitude. Return as you came.

106 Cape Sebastian

RATING	DIFFICULTY	ROUND-TRIP	TERRAIN
★★★★	4	5 miles	920 feet elevation gain

Features: Headland, outstanding shoreline vistas, ancient forest, beach, OCT; **Contact:** Cape Sebastian State Scenic Corridor, www.oregonstateparks.org or 800/551-6949

It's nearly a 1000-foot elevation gain if you ascend Cape Sebastian on an up-and-back hike, and you'll not find a more scenic aerobic workout. For a less strenuous hike, consider leaving a shuttle vehicle at the trail's south end; that way, it's just 200 feet up and 720 feet

Cape Sebastian

down as you slowly descend this towering forested cape, as many locals do. The beach at the cape's base can be a good spot to escape the wind on an otherwise warm day.

GETTING THERE

The north access is at the south viewpoint at Cape Sebastian, 5 miles south of Gold Beach off US 101. The south access is 1.7

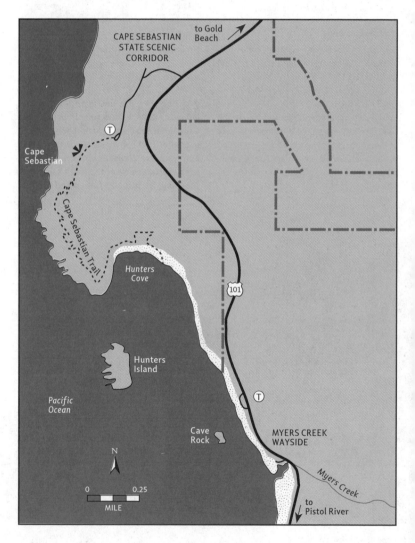

SITKA SPRUCE

In many ways Sitka spruce (*Picea sitchensis*) is the definitive Oregon coastal conifer, car- peting steep seaward cliffs or mingling with Douglas fir and hemlock in airy stands of old-growth forest. Its range is the fog belt along the entire northern Pacific coast from Alaska to northern California, where the world's tallest tree—the coast redwood—takes over. It can be found as far as 100 miles up the Columbia River, but south of the Columbia it is found only within two or three miles of the coast.

Typically, Sitka spruce grow up to 180 feet tall and eight to twelve feet in diam- eter; the largest are 400 to 700 years old. What is said to be the world's tallest Sitka spruce commands a wayside near Seaside, a few miles inland from US 101 on US 26; it measures 16.5 feet in diameter and 216 feet tall at the point where the top has broken off. At Cape Meares State Scenic Viewpoint near Tillamook, short hikes lead to the unusually Big Spruce and to the Octopus Tree, a large spruce whose lack of a single central trunk led to its name.

Sitka spruce was logged heavily during World War I; its comparatively high strength and resiliency and low weight made it ideal for building airplanes. (The largest airplane ever built of wood— Howard Hughes's "Spruce Goose," on display in McMinnville, Oregon—was made of Sitka spruce.) Coastal natives wove its long, sinewy roots into baskets, rain hats, and ropes for whal- ing, used its pitch to caulk whaling canoes, and brewed its inner bark into a tea to soothe sore throats.

miles south of the entrance to Cape Sebas- tian State Scenic Corridor, just north of Myers Creek Wayside.

ON THE TRAIL

From the parking lot at the south viewpoint, follow the asphalt path west as it drops and then ascends past fragrant ceanothus, heads into a grove of trees, and ends at a view- point at the tip of the cape. The trail then heads south, switchbacking down the cape through a Sitka spruce forest. At about 1.5 miles it emerges from the forest onto a rock bench above the bedrock at the base of the cape, curving west with the contour of the mountain before ending abruptly (thanks to an eroded hillside) at the beach. Follow the beach to the wayside.

Approaching from the south, park at the highway pullout. As you walk north up the beach, cross several small creeks, pass the big stratified rock face, cross another little creek, and walk onto the boulders where the beach runs out. The trail is a little tricky to spot. Look up to catch a remnant of trail; it may require a bit of a scramble to get up to it. From here, follow the trail description above, in reverse.

107 Crook Point

RATING	DIFFICULTY	ROUND-TRIP	TERRAIN
★★	2	2.5 miles	Flat

Features: Beach, wildlife, solitude; **Contact:** Oregon Islands National Wildlife Refuge, *www.fws .gov/oregoncoast/oregonislands* or 541/867-4550

South of the Pistol River is a sweet stretch of beach ending with a bang at Crook Point, a grassy headland ringed with huge onshore and offshore rocks. They're all part of Oregon Islands National Wildlife Refuge. The rocks and islands are off-limits, but you can watch seals, sea lions, and nesting seabirds from the mainland; bring binoculars for best views.

GETTING THERE
About 4 miles south of Cape Sebastian, pull off US 101 at Pistol River State Scenic Viewpoint, just south of the river's mouth.

ON THE TRAIL
Either wade the lagoon draining to the river, or walk around the east side of the 0.5-mile-long lagoon. Continue south on the beach another 0.75 mile to where Sand Creek spills

Mouth of Pistol River

onto the beach under a tangle of driftwood, while waves bash the rocks offshore. Return as you came.

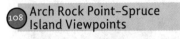

108 Arch Rock Point–Spruce Island Viewpoints

RATING	DIFFICULTY	ONE-WAY	TERRAIN
★★	1	0.3 mile	Rolling

Features: Outstanding shoreline vistas, forest, OCT; **Contact:** Samuel H. Boardman State Scenic Corridor, *www.oregonstateparks.org* or 800/551-6949

The trails of Samuel H. Boardman State Scenic Corridor are not very long, but they get you quickly to some remote and spectacularly scenic spots on the rugged south coast. String them together and you can easily have a full day of not-too-strenuous walking with great views of forested cliffs, arch rocks and islands, and pocket beaches.

GETTING THERE

Boardman State Scenic Corridor begins about 4 miles north of Brookings and stretches north more than 10 miles. The trail system's northern end begins at Arch Rock Point Picnic Area (distinct from and south of Arch Rock Viewpoint), off US 101 about 0.7 mile south of the sign for the park's northern boundary.

ON THE TRAIL

A short paved loop trail leads to a view of the rocks. A separate trail leads south from the south end of the parking area (near the highway); look for the wooden OCT post. It loops west and south along the shoreline and returns to US 101 at Spruce Island Viewpoint. This section of Oregon Coast Trail doesn't offer boffo views like other trail stretches in

Shore pines on the ridge in Boardman State Scenic Corridor

the Boardman corridor, but it's a welcome off-highway link for long-distance hikers.

109 Spruce Island Viewpoint– Natural Bridges Cove

RATING	DIFFICULTY	ROUND-TRIP	TERRAIN
★★★★	3	1.75–2 miles	100 feet elevation gain

Features: Outstanding shoreline vistas, forest, hidden beach, OCT; **Contact:** Samuel H. Boardman State Scenic Corridor, *www.oregon stateparks.org* or 800/551-6949

Get a look at flatiron-shaped Spruce Island, visit hidden Secret Beach, listen to the swish and boom of the waves pounding Deer Point, and peer into Thunder Rock Cove, all in less than 2 miles. (For a quicker route to Secret Beach, see Hike 110.)

GETTING THERE

Boardman State Scenic Corridor begins about 4 miles north of Brookings and stretches north more than 10 miles. This trail stretch begins at the south end of the Spruce Island

Viewpoint parking area, west off US 101 about 1 mile south of the sign for the park's northern boundary.

ON THE TRAIL

Entering the woods, the trail climbs quickly, then veers west and begins to descend through a ghostly spruce forest, veering south to a dramatic viewpoint. It continues no more than a spruce's width from the cliff's edge, rounding a steep-walled cove. At about 0.5 mile it switchbacks up almost to the highway, runs alongside it for a short stretch, then veers west and descends to, at 0.75 mile, a junction with the trail to Secret Beach, perhaps 25 feet below. Continuing south, cross the creek on a wooden footbridge. The trail rolls up, then down, leveling off along the bluff above the south end of Secret Beach. At about 1.5 miles a spur trail leads out to dramatic views of offshore rocks and arches and Thunder Rock Cove. The trail rises quickly to emerge at the north end of the Thunder Rock Cove trailhead parking area.

To continue south, return to the trail at the south end of the parking area. The trail drops gently, then climbs steeply to a spur trail leading up a knoll with a great ocean view. The

North Island Viewpoint

main trail reaches the Natural Bridges Cove trailhead a minute later, 0.25 mile from the Thunder Rock Cove trailhead.

110 Secret Beach

RATING	DIFFICULTY	ROUND-TRIP	TERRAIN
★★★★	2	0.4 miles	100 feet elevation gain

Features: Hidden beach, onshore rocks, forest; **Contact:** Samuel H. Boardman State Scenic Corridor, www.oregonstateparks.org or 800/551-6949

Secret Beach feels like a little piece of tropical paradise wedged into a niche on the southern Oregon coast, with hidden coves and a waterfall spilling onto the sand. This is a tiny beach, not suited to crowds. A visit at low tide allows you to sneak down the coast as far as the rocks allow—which isn't very far.

GETTING THERE
Boardman State Scenic Corridor begins about 4 miles north of Brookings and stretches north more than 10 miles. Look for the small trailhead turnout with room for about four cars at Secret Beach off US 101 between Spruce Island Viewpoint and Thunder Rock Cove access.

ON THE TRAIL
The trail down to Secret Beach from the highway is slick, rocky, and rutted, dropping steeply 0.2 mile alongside musical Miner Creek and crossing the Oregon Coast Trail just above the beach. The creek drops its last ten feet or so in a waterfall onto boulders before streaming into the sea. Linger in this magical spot, or continue a short distance south around the rocks to find a private cove. Return as you came.

Secret Beach

Natural Bridges Cove–North Island Viewpoint (China Beach)

111

RATING	DIFFICULTY	ONE-WAY	TERRAIN
★★★★	3	2.6 miles	400 feet elevation gain

Features: Hidden beach, outstanding shoreline vistas, forest, OCT; **Contact:** Samuel H. Boardman State Scenic Corridor, *www.oregonstateparks.org* or 800/551-6949

A combination of asphalt path and wooden platform leads quickly from the highway trailhead to a lovely view of the deep green cove framed by sandstone arches. Take a quick peek, or continue on the trail for a longer hike to China Beach. Plan to be on the beach at medium to low tide, to round a point necessary for completing the hike. (For a quicker route to China Beach, hike north from North Island Viewpoint or south from the unmarked highway turnout just north of Spruce Creek.)

COASTAL BIRD REFUGES

More than a million seabirds nest on some 1400 islands, reefs, and rocks off Oregon's shore. And virtually all of those rocks are under protection as national wildlife refuges, off-limits to all but the birds, harbor seals, sea lions, and elephant seals that use the rocks for breeding or resting.

The first federally protected bird refuge established on the Oregon coast, at Three Arch Rocks, was signed into law by President Theodore Roosevelt in 1907. Then, as now, it was the site of Oregon's largest seabird colonies: about 220,000 common murres nest on ledges throughout the rocks, and 2000 to 4000 tufted puffins—a "megacolony," as a state wildlife biologist put it—nest on the easternmost rock.

In 1935, Goat Island—west of present-day Harris Beach State Park on the south coast— became the first piece of what would become Oregon Islands National Wildlife Refuge, which today stretches from Tillamook Head to the California border. The refuge's total area is only 762 acres, but those acres provide key nesting habitat for thirteen species of marine birds. The first mainland addition to the refuge—Coquille Point—was made in 1991 specifically to provide a vantage point for viewing offshore rocks. The old-growth forest on the seaward cliffs at Cape Meares became a wildlife refuge in 1938, with the aim of protecting bald eagles, marbled murrelets, and other coastal species.

With offshore islands well protected, coastal wetlands have become the main target for coastal bird habitat protection. In 1983, Bandon Marsh was added to the federal refuge system; in 1991, the US Fish and Wildlife Service made the first acquisitions to create refuges at Siletz and Nestucca Bays as well.

North Island Viewpoint, Boardman State Scenic Corridor

GETTING THERE

Boardman State Scenic Corridor begins about 4 miles north of Brookings and stretches north more than 10 miles. Look for the sign to Natural Bridges Cove between Thunder Rock Cove access and North Island Viewpoint (a highway turnout on US 101 0.2 mile north of the Thomas Creek bridge).

ON THE TRAIL

Past the boardwalk at Natural Bridges Cove, the trail resumes as forest path, leading out through the woods and back to US 101 at about 0.4 mile. Walk just inside the guardrail to where the trail resumes under the highway, crossing Horse Prairie Creek and leading out along the shoreline. The trail takes you back to a highway turnout just north of Spruce Creek at about 1.2 miles. Walk south inside the guardrail 0.2 mile to where the trail resumes, dropping down to China Beach at 1.5 miles. Unless it's high tide, you should be able to round the rocky point just to the south, which leads you to China Beach, stretching south nearly 0.75 mile. When you're ready to continue, look for the trail leading off the beach on the south side of China Creek (0.4 mile south of Spruce Creek). It quickly ascends for 0.5 mile, then levels off, rolling through the woods the last 0.2 mile to a trail junction. A left turn leads quickly to US 101 at North Island Viewpoint. (To continue a long-distance hike, continue on the main trail through the woods 0.2 mile to, and across, the bridge.)

112 Thomas Creek–Whaleshead Beach

RATING	DIFFICULTY	ONE-WAY	TERRAIN
★★★★	3	2.5 miles	250 feet elevation gain

Features: Outstanding shoreline vistas, dunes, forest, beach, OCT; **Contact:** Samuel H. Boardman State Scenic Corridor, *www.oregonstate parks.org* or 800/551-6949

This longer hike (by Boardman State Scenic Corridor standards) takes you through the stunning Indian Sands area and along another interesting stretch of rocky, island-strewn coastline. For a shorter round trip to Indian Sands (and a description of the area), see Hike 113.

GETTING THERE

Boardman State Scenic Corridor begins about 4 miles north of Brookings and stretches north more than 10 miles. Pull off US 101 at the large parking area at the south end of Thomas Creek Bridge, about 0.75 mile north of the Indian Sands trailhead.

ON THE TRAIL

Begin at the large parking area at the south end of Thomas Creek Bridge, about 0.75 mile north of the Indian Sands trailhead. The trail leads down a draw, into a forest, and across a hillside; then it returns to US 101 after 0.5 mile. Follow the trail just below the highway guardrail a short distance and continue as it heads west to a broad view northward, then descends along the contour of a steep draw, climbs over a saddle, and leads onto the dunes at Indian Sands. Posts indicate the trail's route south through the open sand;

spur trails lead east to the main Indian Sands trailhead.

Continue south to where a path resumes. It enters the woods, crosses a couple of creeks, and then leads out to the highway. Walk along the shoulder for about 40 yards and pick up the trail again. It leads into a Sitka spruce forest, climbing a bit to a viewpoint, and drops down to a parking area at the junction of the Whaleshead Beach access road and US 101.

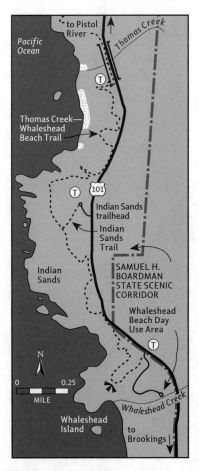

113 Indian Sands

RATING	DIFFICULTY	ROUND-TRIP	TERRAIN
★★★	1	0.4 mile	120 feet elevation gain

Features: Outstanding shoreline vistas, forest, wildlife; **Contact:** Samuel H. Boardman State Scenic Corridor, www.oregonstateparks.org or 800/551-6949

A visit to Indian Sands is unforgettable. Alongside broad, open sand dunes, wind and water have carved ocher sandstone cliffs into fantastic shapes. The color of the rock is particularly striking late in the afternoon. Feral goats roam the area; if you're lucky you may spot some.

GETTING THERE
Boardman State Scenic Corridor begins about 4 miles north of Brookings and stretches north more than 10 miles. The large Indian Sand trailhead parking area is on the west side of US 101 just south of milepost 348, about 12 miles north of Brookings.

ON THE TRAIL
The trail drops quickly through dense coastal forest. Approaching the forest's edge, take either of the spur trails that appear to lead toward the sand, mentally marking your route for your return. The trail ends at Indian Sands. Explore the dunes, wander north or south a bit on the Oregon Coast Trail, and return as you came.

Indian Sands

GRAY WHALES

Of two dozen or so types of cetaceans commonly found in the waters off Oregon, the gray whale is the most visible. Some 15,000 to 20,000 gray whales pass through Oregon waters twice each year from December through May en route between arctic and subtropical waters—at 6000 miles, the longest migration of any mammal. More recently, an estimated 200 gray whales have begun spending their entire summer and fall off the Oregon coast. These resident whales tend to stay closer to shore and are thus easier to spot.

As for the migrants, spring numbers tend to peak around mid-March; cows with their calves start arriving from May through early June. In winter, pregnant females lead the way, reaching the Oregon coast in mid-December; the number of passing whales builds to a peak of about thirty per hour in late December and early January.

The most common way to spot a whale is by observing it blow, exhaling water and vapor out its blowhole. Watch also for sounding (exposing tail flukes as it dives deep), spy-hopping (raising its head partially out of the water), and breaching (surging out of the ocean, then falling back with a huge splash).

Check under the Wildlife-watching heading in each section of this book for the best whale-watching sites. Every year for the week between Christmas and New Year, and again during spring vacation week in March, trained volunteers station themselves at nearly thirty vantage points—from Ilwaco, north of the Columbia, to Harris Beach at Brookings—daily from 10:00 AM to 1:00 PM to help visitors spot migrating whales. Just look for a "Whale Watching Spoken Here" sign.

114 Whaleshead Beach–House Rock Viewpoint

RATING	DIFFICULTY	ONE-WAY	TERRAIN
★★★	3	3 miles	480 feet elevation gain

Features: Beach, outstanding shoreline vistas, forest, OCT; **Contact:** Samuel H. Boardman State Scenic Corridor, *www.oregonstate parks.org* or 800/551-6949

Whaleshead Beach is the longest and most easily accessible beach in the Boardman scenic corridor, and the day-use area here has rest rooms and picnic tables. The beach stretches nearly 1.5 miles south, ending at the foot of Sand Hill. Make a short loop hike near the day-use area, walk the beach out and back for a 3-mile round trip, or at Sand Hill continue south up a section of the Oregon Coast Trail.

GETTING THERE

Boardman State Scenic Corridor begins about 4 miles north of Brookings and stretches north more than 10 miles. Whaleshead Beach Day Use Area is on the west side of US 101 about 7 miles north of Brookings.

ON THE TRAIL

From the day-use parking area, follow the short trail to the beach and head south. About 0.25 mile down the beach you'll see a trail leading off the beach and up to Whaleshead Viewpoint; to make a short loop hike, follow this trail to the viewpoint, then backtrack briefly on US 101 and down the park access road to complete the loop. Otherwise, bypass the viewpoint trail and continue south on the beach a total of 1.5 miles to where the beach runs out at the foot of Sand Hill.

To continue to House Rock Viewpoint, look for a trail leading up brushy Sand Hill.

About 0.5 mile from the beach the trail comes within 20 feet of US 101 before veering away and switchbacking down another 0.25 mile. It then begins a gentle ascent through a dense forest of salal and Sitka spruce to end 1.5 miles from the beach (3 miles from the Whaleshead Beach Day Use

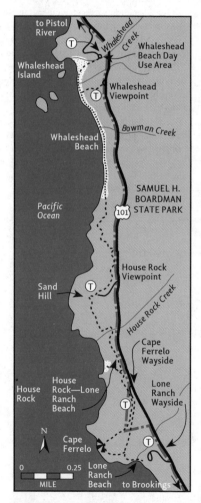

Whaleshead Beach

Area) in the northwest corner of the House Rock Viewpoint parking area (off US 101 between Whaleshead Beach and Cape Ferrelo, about 5 miles north of Brookings).

115 House Rock Viewpoint– Cape Ferrelo

RATING	DIFFICULTY	ONE-WAY	TERRAIN
**	2	1.5 miles	440 feet elevation loss

Features: Outstanding shoreline vistas, hidden beach, OCT; **Contact:** Samuel H. Boardman State Scenic Corridor, *www.oregonstateparks. org* or 800/551-6949

This section of the Oregon Coast Trail leads through deep forest to grassy, windy Cape Ferrelo.

GETTING THERE
Boardman State Scenic Corridor begins about 4 miles north of Brookings and stretches north more than 10 miles. The House Rock Viewpoint parking area is off US 101 about 5 miles north of Brookings. Cape Ferrelo Wayside is about 4 miles north of Brookings.

ON THE TRAIL
Look for an Oregon Coast Trail post off the parking area's southwest corner. The trail heads south, mostly descending through the woods, to emerge at about 1 mile onto open grassy slopes approaching Cape Ferrelo. At 1.3 miles a spur leads west to a tiny beach. Continue on the main trail to the parking area at the Cape Ferrelo Viewpoint. Return as you came for a 3-mile round trip, or park a shuttle car here for a one-way hike.

116 Cape Ferrelo–Lone Ranch Beach

RATING	DIFFICULTY	ONE-WAY	TERRAIN
**	1	1 mile	290 feet elevation loss

Features: Outstanding shoreline vistas, beach, tide pools, OCT; **Contact:** Samuel H. Boardman State Scenic Corridor, *www.oregonstateparks .org* or 800/551-6949

Cape Ferrelo isn't the tallest cape on the coast, but it offers some outstanding views. A walk south from the cape on the Oregon Coast Trail leads to Lone Ranch Wayside, the southernmost day-use area in Samuel H. Boardman State Scenic Corridor. At low tide, scattered rocks form tide pools at Lone Ranch Beach.

Iris

GETTING THERE

Cape Ferrelo Viewpoint is about 4 miles north of Brookings off US 101, near the southern end of Boardman State Scenic Corridor. Lone Ranch Beach parking area is about 0.5 mile farther south on US 101.

ON THE TRAIL

From the parking lot at Cape Ferrelo, follow Oregon Coast Trail posts south and west 0.5 mile through the grassy hillside to the viewpoint at the tip of the cape. Here the trail turns south and begins descending. Watch carefully for a sharp (possibly unmarked) right turn in the trail; take it and follow the trail to its terminus at the north end of Lone Ranch Beach (or, at the junction, continue straight to swing back to the parking area at Cape Ferrelo). From the end of the trail, it's a short walk along the beach and up the bluff to the Lone Ranch Beach parking area.

117 Harris Beach

Beach walk:

RATING	DIFFICULTY	LOOP	TERRAIN
★★	1	1 mile	Slight incline

Butte hike:

RATING	DIFFICULTY	ROUND-TRIP	TERRAIN
★	1	0.4 mile	200 feet elevation gain

Features: Beach, outstanding shoreline vistas, tide pools, wildlife, adjacent to campground; **Contact:** Harris Beach State Park, *www.oregonstateparks.org* or 800/551-6949

Unlike the long, wide beaches characteristic of the north coast, the shoreline at Harris Beach State Park consists of a series of coves defined by rocky outcrops, with spirelike sea stacks just offshore. It's a small park, offering short hikes to some dramatic spots.

GETTING THERE

Just north of Brookings, turn off US 101 at the sign to Harris Beach State Park. Park at the viewpoint on the park entrance road.

ON THE TRAIL

From here, South Beach Trail leads 0.2 mile down to the beach. At high tide the surf here can put on a dramatic show; at low tide, see how far you can walk (or scramble, at the beach's rocky end) north or south, or investigate the tide pools at the north end of South Beach. Return as you came.

For a 1-mile loop, walk north on the beach 0.3 mile from South Beach Trail and climb back up the hill on Rock Beach Trail, which hits the park entrance road at the junction with the campground road. You can also drive to the main 0.5-mile-long beach, just off the day-use parking area; except perhaps at high tide, it's possible to round the point to the south and continue walking on South Beach 0.75 mile or more.

It's a quick 0.2-mile walk to the viewpoint at the top of Harris Butte, the park's high point; the trailhead is off the main park road just past the campground entrance. Looking west you can see Goat Island, half a mile offshore. This was the first of Oregon's offshore islands to be included in Oregon Islands National Wildlife Refuge; puffins,

Driftwood-and-kelp sculpture on Harris Beach

auklets, murres, gulls, guillemots, storm petrels, and cormorants are among the seabirds nesting on the island. Return as you came.

118 Chetco Point

RATING	DIFFICULTY	ROUND-TRIP	TERRAIN
★★	1	0.5 mile	Level, rough trail

Features: Hidden beaches, outstanding shoreline vistas, close to town; **Contact:** City of Brookings, www.brookings.or.us or 541/469-1100

Smack in the middle of Brookings is a long, rocky peninsula with hidden beaches on either side.

GETTING THERE
In Brookings, turn off US 101 on tiny Wharf Street (just south of the traffic light at Center Street, about 0.5 mile north of the Chetco River bridge) and follow it west past a fenced housing development, a playing field, and the city water-treatment plant. Park at the road's end.

ON THE TRAIL
Follow an informal path out onto the neck of the point. Scramble down one of the trails leading to pocket beaches to the north and south, or continue to the trail's end at a lovely little beach with an excellent view south to the California coast. Return as you came.

119 Redwood Nature Trail

RATING	DIFFICULTY	ROUND-TRIP	TERRAIN
★★★	2	1–2.5 miles	370 feet elevation gain

Features: Redwood forest, creek, river, adjacent to campground; **Contact:** Alfred A. Loeb State Park, www.oregonstateparks.org or 800/551-6949

Drive up the Chetco River a few miles for a treat: a hike in a lush forest of redwood, Douglas fir, and tanoak. These are the northernmost redwoods in the world. While not quite as impressive as those growing in the heart of the redwood zone farther south, there are some big trees on this loop, some as old as 800 years.

GETTING THERE
In Brookings, just north of the Chetco River bridge on US 101, turn east onto North Bank Road. Go 8.4 miles up the road to a trailhead on the left, where the 1-mile loop hike begins. Riverview Trail starts in the picnic area at Alfred A. Loeb State Park, 0.6 mile west of the trailhead.

ON THE TRAIL
Pick up an interpretive pamphlet, if available, at the station by the rest room just up the trail. Shortly the trail reaches a junction; turn left to hike clockwise, following the order of numbered posts, which correspond with explanations in the trail pamphlet. The brochure focuses mostly on natural history but weaves in some human history as well; one post marks an old log-cage bear trap built years ago and long abandoned. For the first 0.5 mile, Douglas firs predominate along the trail as it ascends steadily. After crossing a footbridge over a creek, you'll start seeing big redwoods and lots of rhododendrons. The trail peaks at about 0.75 mile. Cross another creek, then start switchbacking down through the forest to recross the creek and meet the start of the loop.

Extend the hike by parking at the Loeb State Park picnic area and picking up the 0.75-mile Riverview Trail on the left side of the park entrance road. The trail mostly rolls along, in and out of leafy ravines, threading a narrow corridor between the Chetco River and the road. With wide gravel

Redwood Nature Trail

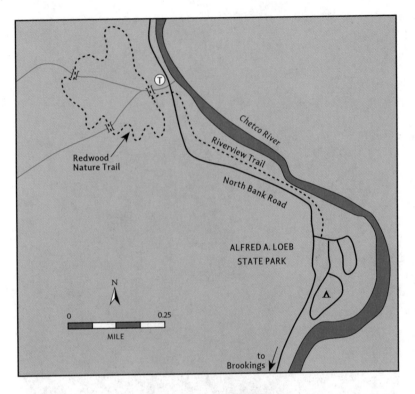

bars and a lazy current, the river is inviting in summer and easy to access from the trail, especially toward either end. It ends across the road from Redwood Nature Trail. After walking the loop nature trail, return the way you came.

120 McVay Beach

RATING	DIFFICULTY	ROUND-TRIP	TERRAIN
★★	2	3 miles	Flat

Features: Beach, river, onshore rocks, colorful stones, tide pools, OCT; **Contact:** McVay Rock State Recreation Site, *www.oregonstateparks .org* or 800/551-6949

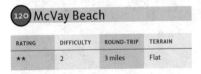 *South of the craggy coastline at Brookings/Harbor lies an inviting stretch of sand known mostly to locals. McVay Rock State Recreation Site sits among the lily fields north of the Winchuck River. A big grass field invites kite flying, Frisbee tossing, or playing with the family dog; to the west lies the beach and, just offshore, a collection of rock monoliths. Houses are scattered along the shore; it's not a remote beach. But it's lovely, and long—the longest beach in Oregon south of Pistol River.*

GETTING THERE

About 1.5 miles south of the Chetco River bridge on US 101, turn west on Pedrioli Drive, go 0.7

mile, turn south on Ocean View Drive, and continue 1.1 miles south to the park entrance road. (From the south, turn west off US 101 onto Ocean View Drive about 0.5 mile north of the Winchuck River and drive 1.1 miles to the park.) A gravel road leads a short distance alongside the boulder-studded field to a parking area by the beach. For a one-way hike, leave a shuttle car at Winchuck State Recreation Site off US 101 about 0.5 mile north of the California state line.

ON THE TRAIL

A trail leads from the parking area down to the sand. The beach stretches north about 1 mile, and south 1.5 miles to the Winchuck River and beyond into California. Along the beach walk to the Winchuck River are expansive tide pools and rocky points, some with natural arches and caves, and piles of Klamath Mountain stone in gray and green and ocher and white, smoothed by the intertidal tumbler. At the river, return as you came. Or leave a shuttle car at Winchuck State Recreation Site, on the river's north bank, for a one-way hike; walk the river's edge east to the parking area, or if the tide is too high, follow an informal trail east 0.25 mile from the beach through the shrubby forest and dunes.

OREGON COAST TRAIL, SOUTH COAST

Distance: About 105 miles to Lone Ranch Wayside; 10 miles more to California border

From Charleston, follow lonely Seven Devils Road south about 13.5 miles (the last one-third or so is gravel), then head west where the sign indicates Seven Devils State Recreation Site. There are no services whatsoever on this road.

From Seven Devils take the beach south, carefully rounding Fivemile Point at low tide. Follow the beach 5 miles to Bullards Beach State Park; if you hit the Coquille River, you've gone 1.5 miles too far (unless you can hitch a boat ride across the river's mouth to the Ban-

McVay Beach

don boat basin). Take the park road out to US 101 and follow it into Bandon's Old Town, following First Street around the bay as it turns into Jetty Road and leads you to the south jetty. Walk the beach south some 16 miles, past New River and Floras Lake (you'll have to climb the foredune to see them). There are freshwater and other amenities at Boice Cope County Park on the east side of Floras Lake. About 0.2 mile before reaching a red sandstone bluff just south of Floras Lake, cut over the foredune to find a trail heading up through an opening in the salal and shore pines, heading southeast. Take it 0.5 mile to a junction; from here, the quickest way out to US 101 is on the Airport–Floras Lake Trail (Hike 97), to the left. Otherwise, through-hikers continuing south and planning to ford the Sixes River should bear right on the trail following the bluff for a more direct and scenic route to Blacklock Point (Hike 96). Ford the Sixes River with care at low water (summer).

A 0.25-mile trail leads up from the beach near the tip of Cape Blanco. Go east 0.1 mile to where the trail resumes across the road as a mowed path, then a forest trail. Pass the campground and continue on the south beach access road to the beach. Follow the beach south 5.5 miles, taking care fording Elk Creek. About 1.5 miles north of the bluffs at Port Orford Heads, leave the beach on a little trail at Paradise Point State Recreation Site and follow the road out to US 101. Return to the beach at Battle Rock in Port Orford, and walk down the beach 2.5 miles to Rocky Point, distinguished by the boulders at its base. If, at low tide, you can scramble around the point, continue down the beach another 0.3 mile and watch for a path heading up the brushy hillside; it leads to a gravel road leading to US 101. Follow the highway shoulder 0.2 mile to pick up Hike 101 around Humbug Mountain. (If the tide is high, look for a path leading off the beach and up to US 101 just 0.9 mile south of Battle Rock, and walk the highway shoulder 1.8 mile.) Past Humbug, return to the highway for several miles; about 0.5 mile after crossing Euchre Creek, a little trail leads off the highway over dunes to beach. Leave the beach at Nesika Beach and follow Nesika Beach Road to US 101. Cross the highway and immediately turn south on the old coast highway, parallel to the current highway. Keep to the old road as it crosses US 101; in 0.2 mile turn right into Otter Point State Recreation Site (Hike 104). At the north jetty, walk out to US 101 and over the Rogue River bridge, then take the first right (Harbor Way) and right again on South Jetty Road; follow it out past an RV park to the beach.

In 2 miles leave the beach on a trail on the north side of Hunter Creek to follow the highway up Cape Sebastian; take Hike 106 down the cape's south side and stay on the beach to Pistol River. (*Note: The state parks department plans to build a trail and primitive hikers' camp on Cape Sebastian's north side; it was not completed when this book went to press.*) Return to the highway to cross the river and get to the trail system at Samuel H. Boardman State Scenic Corridor. Follow Hikes 108, 109, 111, 112, 114, 115, and 116.

The Oregon Coast Trail essentially ends at Lone Ranch Wayside. Beyond this point a combination of headlands and private land currently steers the official OCT route onto US 101 through Brookings and to the California border just south of the Winchuck River. To end with a beach walk at the border, however, follow Hike 120; wade the Winchuck River (shallow enough to cross safely in summer) or walk out to US 101 and cross the highway bridge on foot. The California state line is about 0.5 mile south of the Winchuck River by road or beach.

The first public beach access in California is at Pelican State Beach, 0.3 mile south of the Winchuck River off US 101.

Visitor Information

Oregon Coast Visitors Association: 541/574-2679 or 888/628-2101, *www.visittheoregon coast.com*

NORTH COAST
Astoria/Warrenton Area Chamber of Commerce: 503/325-6311 or 800/875-6807, *www.oldoregon.com*

Seaside Chamber of Commerce and Visitors' Bureau: 503/738-3097 or 888/306-2326, *www.seasideor.com*

Cannon Beach Chamber of Commerce: 503/436-2623, *www.cannonbeach.org*

Nehalem Bay Area Chamber of Commerce: 877/368-5100, *www.nehalembaychamber.com*

Garibaldi Chamber of Commerce: 503/322-0301, *www.garibaldioregon.com*

Rockaway Beach Chamber of Commerce: 503/355-8108, *www.rockawaybeach.net*

NORTH-CENTRAL COAST
Tillamook Chamber of Commerce: 503/842-7525, *www.tillamookchamber.org*

Pacific City-Nestucca Valley Chamber of Commerce: 503/965-6161 or 888/549-2632, *www.pacificcity.net*

Lincoln City Visitors & Convention Bureau: 541/994-8378 or 800/452-2151, *www.oregon coast.org*

Depoe Bay Chamber of Commerce: 541/765-2889, *www.depoebaychamber.org*

CENTRAL COAST
Central Oregon Coast Association: 541/265-2064 or 800/767-2064, *www.coastvisitor.com*

Greater Newport Chamber of Commerce: 541/265-8801 or 800/262-7844, *www.new portchamber.org*

Waldport Chamber of Commerce and Visitors Center: 541/563-2133

Yachats Chamber of Commerce: 541/547-3530 or 800/929-0477, *www.yachats.org*

Florence Area Chamber of Commerce: 541/997-3128, *www.florencechamber.com*

SOUTH-CENTRAL COAST
Bay Area Chamber of Commerce: 541/269-0215 or 800/824-8486, *www.oregonsbay areachamber.com*

Reedsport/Winchester Bay Chamber of Commerce: 541/271-3495 or 800/247-2155, *www.reedsportcc.org*

SOUTH COAST
Bandon Chamber of Commerce: 541/347-9616, *www.bandon.com*

Gold Beach Visitor Center: 541/247-7526 or 800/525-2334, *www.goldbeach.org*

Port Orford Chamber of Commerce: 541/332-8055, *www.discoverportorford.com*

Brookings-Harbor Chamber of Commerce: 541/469-3181 or 800/535-9469, *www.brook ingsor.com*

Index

About the Author

Bonnie Henderson grew up in Portland, Oregon, and spent most family vacations hiking and backpacking in the wilderness areas of the Northwest. During college she began guiding whitewater raft trips and leading teenagers on wilderness backpacking trips in the Rocky, Cascade, and Olympic Mountains and later taught cross-country skiing at Mount St. Helens. With a master's degree in journalism, she has worked as a newspaper reporter and editor, and a magazine editor and writer, and is a regular contributor to *Sunset*. She is also the author of *Best Hikes with Kids: Oregon*. She lives in Eugene. Contact her through her website, *www.bonniehenderson writes.com*.

THE MOUNTAINEERS, founded in 1906, is a nonprofit outdoor activity and conservation club, whose mission is "to explore, study, preserve, and enjoy the natural beauty of the outdoors...." Based in Seattle, Washington, the club is now the third-largest such organization in the United States, with seven branches throughout Washington State.

The Mountaineers sponsors both classes and year-round outdoor activities in the Pacific Northwest, which include hiking, mountain climbing, ski-touring, snowshoeing, bicycling, camping, kayaking, nature study, sailing, and adventure travel. The club's conservation division supports environmental causes through educational activities, sponsoring legislation, and presenting informational programs.

All club activities are led by skilled, experienced instructors, who are dedicated to promoting safe and responsible enjoyment and preservation of the outdoors.

If you would like to participate in these organized outdoor activities or the club's programs, consider a membership in The Mountaineers. For information and an application, write or call The Mountaineers, Club Headquarters, 300 Third Avenue West, Seattle, WA 98119; 206-284-6310. You can also visit the club's website at www.mountaineers.org or contact The Mountaineers via email at clubmail@mountaineers.org.

The Mountaineers Books, an active, nonprofit publishing program of the club, produces guidebooks, instructional texts, historical works, natural history guides, and works on environmental conservation. All books produced by The Mountaineers Books fulfill the club's mission.

Send or call for our catalog of more than 500 outdoor titles:

The Mountaineers Books
1001 SW Klickitat Way, Suite 201
Seattle, WA 98134
800-553-4453
mbooks@mountaineersbooks.org
www.mountaineersbooks.org

OTHER TITLES YOU MIGHT ENJOY FROM THE MOUNTAINEERS BOOKS

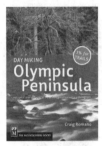

Day Hiking: Olympic Peninsula
Craig Romano
More great day hikes up the coast in one of the National Park Service's crown jewels

Best Hikes with Kids: Oregon
Bonnie Henderson
Big fun for little feet—discover the best hikes for kids

Best Hikes with Dogs: Oregon
Ellen Bishop
Where to hike with Fido—all trails recommended as dog safe and dog fun!

100 Classic Hikes in Oregon
Douglas Lorain
A lush, all-color guide to simply the best hikes in Oregon

Tent and Car Camper's Handbook: Advice for Families & First-Timers
Buck Tilton, Kristin Hostetter
The lowdown on car and tent camping—no experience necessary

The Don't Die Out There Deck
Christopher Van Tilburg, M.D.
A playing card deck that puts survival tips in the palm of your hand

---